Complete Guide to Orchids

Meredith® Books

Des Moines, Iowa

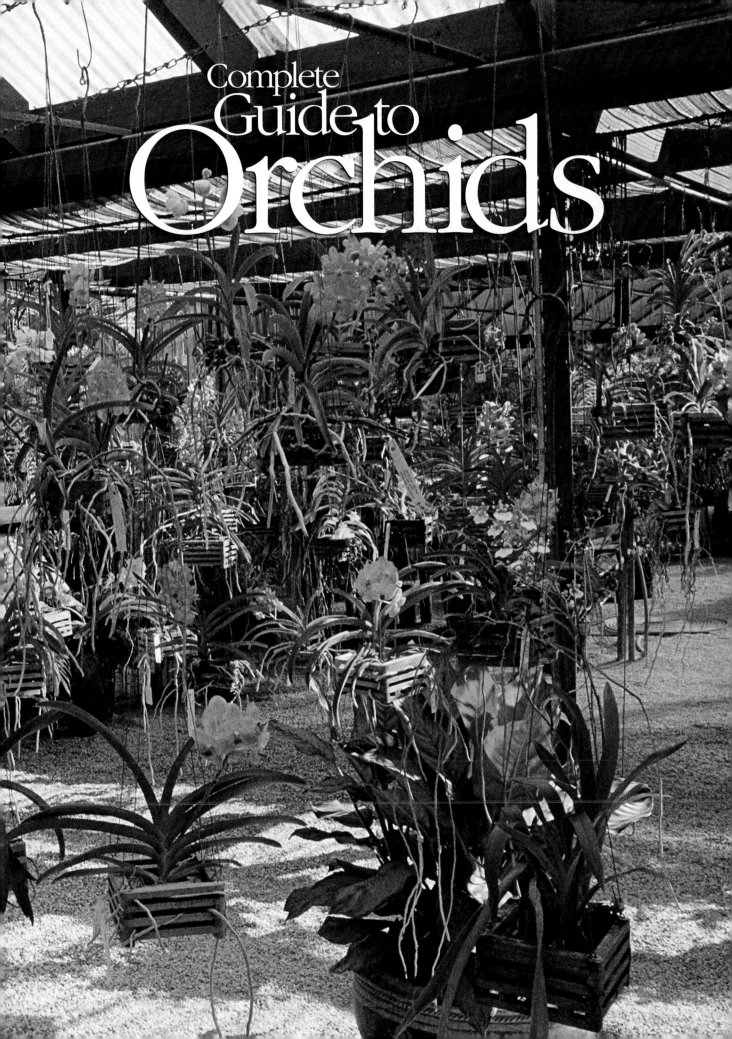

Complete
Guide to
Orchids

Growing and Caring for Orchids 60

Orchid Troubleshooting 84

Orchids A–Z 96

Appendix

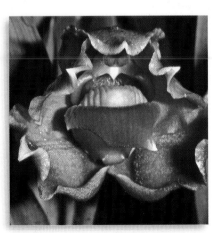

The Story of Orchids

A cymbidium hybrid

Cirrhopetalum **Elizabeth Ann 'Buckleberry', AM-FCC/AOS**

Earliest References

The history of orchidmania abounds with the breath-stopping exploits of intrepid jungle explorers, controversial theories argued over by botanists, and sensational stories that rival the wild-eyed reports of modern-day sightings of alien visitors. Since orchids were first documented and cultivated—in the Orient, Europe, the Americas, and elsewhere—their exotic flowers have piqued the curiosity of those with a passion—and the funds—for the eccentric and bizarre. Orchids inspire extreme devotion because of their complexity, beauty, and profusion. In fact, caught up in the frenzy of acquisition for these mysterious plants, enthusiasts are soon lost in what many describe as orchiddelerium. Having started with one plant, they soon find that they can't stop with just one. Purchasing that "just one" becomes "just a few more." Soon there are a multitude of orchids, and the open expanse of lawn in the backyard earmarked for the addition of a swimming pool is given over to plans for a state-of-the-art greenhouse. Once infected, an orchidaholic is a goner—but happy to be a member of this acclaimed club.

The fragrance and allure of native orchids, especially cymbidiums, have captured the attention and imagination of writers, artists, and philosophers for millennia. In China, Confucius (551–479 BC) spoke of an orchid, which he called *lan,* as the "King of the Fragrant Plants." *The Materia Medica of the Mythical Emperor,* dating from the Han dynasty, included *Dendrobium (shih hu)* and *Bletilla (pai chi),* while *Treatise on Orchids of Chin Chang,* published in 1233, discussed 22 orchids. Inspired by their voluptuous curves and vivid colors, artists captured the plants' beauty and grace as in Cheng Sze-shiao's 1306 portrait of *Cymbidium goeringii.*

Japanese orchid lovers

In ancient Japan, cymbidiums and the wind orchid, *Neofinetia falcata (fuuran),* were equally prized. Much like today's business people who can't leave home without their credit cards, feudal lords and Samurai warriors would take their orchids with them when they traveled. Seeking variations on a theme, growers combed the known habitats for plants showing slight differences. They

Herbalist Nicholas Culpeper wrote about orchids in the 17th century.

then cosseted and coddled their rare specimens until they had created a new variation, such as *Dendrobium moniliforme (sekkoku),* which, after centuries of cultivation, diversified into more than 100 forms. Besides growing and painting orchids, the Japanese also wrote about their experiences. In 1728, Jo-an Matsouka authored a book illustrated with many beautiful woodblocks. It offered four rules for growing cymbidiums: In spring, do not put them outdoors; in summer, do not expose them to too much sun; in autumn, do not keep them too dry; in winter, do not keep them too wet. This advice distills the knowledge from the host of tomes in the botanical sections of today's libraries and bookstores.

Herbals

The Greek philosopher Theophrastus (370-285 B.C.), in his manuscript *Enquiry into Plants,* was the first to use the term *orchis* to describe orchid plants. The word refers to the testiculate tubers of some Mediterranean terrestrial orchids. *Orchis* became both the name of a genus and the root of the name for the orchid family (Orchidaceae). Pliny, a Roman naturalist, wrote more about orchids in his *Natural History.* Orchids' presumed medicinal properties earned them recognition in the 15th, 16th, and 17th centuries. According to Nicholas Culpeper, 17th-century herbalist, apothecary, and astrologer, "They are hot and moist in operation, under the dominion of Dame Venus, and provoke lust exceedingly, which, they say, the dried and withered roots do restrain." Though early European herbalists described and illustrated orchids because of their supposed medicinal properties, only about a dozen kinds of orchids were known to Europe by 1561.

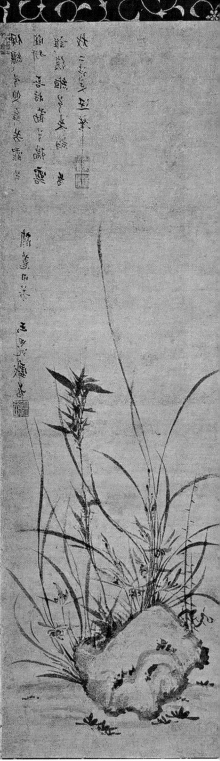

This Japanese scroll of orchids is from the 15th century Muromachi period.

Western Cultivation

The first tropical orchid to reach England, *Bletia purpurea,* arrived in 1731, when a dried specimen was shipped from New Providence, Bahamas, to Peter Collinson, a Quaker cloth merchant. Collinson thought the shriveled tubers showed some life, so he passed them along to a gardening friend. Much to the grower's surprise, the plant put forth a flower in 1732. In 1737, two species of *Cypripedium,* the dainty, pouched lady's-slipper orchid, arrived. Later came *Calopogon tuberosus, Encyclia fragrans, Cymbidium ensifolium,* and the nun's orchid, *Phaius tankervilleae.* By 1794, the Royal Botanic Gardens in Kew was growing 15 epiphytic orchids. By 1813 the number had blossomed to 60, including some brought from the West Indies by Captain William Bligh of the HMS Bounty. Around 1812 a nursery in England called Messrs. C. Loddiges & Sons began cultivating orchids at its greenhouse, and the commercial production of orchids began. Only the privileged few could afford such an expensive hobby, but the way was paved for stores that today can offer orchids at prices to tempt even the most frugal gardeners.

Cypripedium, or lady's-slipper orchid

Encyclia fragrans

First orchid hybrid

While species continued to hold a fascination for collectors, the possibility of crossing two orchids to create a hybrid intrigued John Dominy, who worked for James Vietch & Sons, a prestigious English orchid nursery. Ignoring a warning that he "would drive botanists mad," he crossed two species of *Calanthe* and produced *Calanthe* Dominii *(furcata × masuca)* in 1854 and then saw it flower in 1856 as the first orchid hybrid. Flushed by this success, he experimented with hybridizing cattleyas and other orchids, eventually making more than 20 crosses. Others followed. As more and more hybrids were developed, lists were compiled to document the new arrivals. Shortly thereafter, Frederick K. Sander began a register of orchid hybrids, *Sander's List of Orchid Hybrids,* that was continued by his descendants until 1961, when it was taken over by the Royal Horticultural Society.

The orchid business

In England, the true fascination with orchids started in 1821 with the well-publicized blooming of the spectacular lavender *Cattleya labiata,* the forerunner of today's corsage orchid. The demand for these exotic and beautiful flowers was so great that orchids became big business almost overnight. Wealthy collectors and commercial nurserymen commissioned professional explorers to gather plants from equatorial regions around the world. Thousands of plants were collected and sent to Europe where, because of the huge demand, they sold for exorbitant prices, especially at auctions in Liverpool and London, where a particularly rare specimen might fetch a thousand pounds or more.

Orchid survival

The plant explorers endured many hardships—dangerous sea voyages, wild animals, thieves, and exotic diseases—but the orchids and the trees that bore them suffered far worse. To attain their prizes, ruthless hunters chopped down centuries-old trees, stripped the flowers from the fallen branches, and packed the plants into crates. The crates were then hauled overland to the nearest seaport, where they often sat for days or weeks before being stacked into the dark, dank holds of ships. Once aboard, the orchids had to undergo long voyages to England or France.

Not surprisingly, few of the plants survived these voyages. Those that lived long enough to reach the greenhouses of collectors were subjected to the most trying of growing conditions. Before the mid-1800s, most orchid growers shared the misconception that their plants had been gathered from steamy jungles. When the plants arrived, growers put the orchids in stove houses—sweltering greenhouses heated to unbearable temperatures by coal- or wood-burning stoves that required someone to keep them stoked at all hours. The owners thought that this duplicated the natural conditions. No ventilation was provided for fear the steam and heat would escape. Against such odds, even the toughest orchids had hardly a chance, certainly not those from higher altitudes that were adapted to relatively cool nights. John Lindley, the father of orchid taxonomy, made recommendations to change orchid-growing methods. Sir Joseph Paxton was the first to put these new ideas into

effect—providing sunlight, cooler temperatures, and good air circulation.

As proof of their enduring nature, enough orchids survived and bloomed to fuel the Victorian demand for more plants. For more than 100 years, orchid hobbyists and their suppliers spent fortunes sponsoring explorers in search of new species they could name after themselves, their friends, and their families. The less affluent were also fascinated by orchids. Lured by the imaginative stories of writers such as H.G. Wells, who portrayed orchids as sinister plants with a thirst for human blood, crowds flocked to orchid shows to gape and marvel at these exotic immigrants.

By 1844, *Epidendrum macrochilum roseum* was available to gardeners. Today it is known as *Encyclia cordigera* var. *rosea*.

Orchids in American Commerce

Above:
Albert C. Burrage was a founding member in 1921 of the American Orchid Society. Its first meeting was held at the Massachusetts Horticultural Society headquarters in Boston, above right.

Greta Garbo in *Wild Orchids* (1929)

Orchid growing took longer to catch on in the United States, although a few nurseries could supply wealthy customers with plants after the mid-1800s. By the turn of the 20th century, several of these purveyors had earned solid reputations, among them Butterworth's, Armacost & Royston, Lager & Hurrell, and the Fennell Orchid Company—all nurseries that cashed in on their popular new crops.

Thomas Young Nurseries in Bound Brook, New Jersey, was established in 1905 as a cut-flower nursery. With his two small greenhouses, Young continued to supply his clients for more than two decades. When he sold his nursery in 1929, the same year Greta Garbo starred in the silent film *Wild Orchids,* it brought in a record selling price that allowed Young to retire.

Burrage and the American Orchid Society

Albert C. Burrage, a lawyer from Boston, greatly influenced the rise in popularity of orchids in the United States. Having amassed his own impressive collections of orchid plants and literature, Burrage was among the founding members of the American Orchid Society (AOS), which was established April 7, 1921. Serving as the Society's first president (1921–1929), Burrage was joined by Oakes and Blanche Ames, America's first couple of orchidology. Oakes was a distinguished orchid botanist

at Harvard University who studied and wrote extensively about the plants. His wife, Blanche, was a superb illustrator, recording the plants' details in pen and ink and watercolor.

Hirose of Hawaii

As orchid growing came into its own on the mainland, big changes were unfolding in the Hawaiian Islands, where orchids were introduced in the 1860s. Orchid propagation had taken a quantum leap forward in 1922, when Lewis Knudson of Cornell University in Ithaca, New York, shared his discovery that orchid seed could be sown on an artificial growing medium under sterile conditions. His innovation made it possible for orchids to be grown on a massive scale. By the 1930s, the economic potential of orchids became evident. The Hawaiian Islands proved fertile for a booming orchid nursery industry. Among the pioneers was Y. Hirose, who raised orchid species, made his own hybrids, and flew his crop from Hilo on the Big Island of Hawaii to the mainland. More good fortune befell Hawaii when *Vanda* Miss Joaquim (*hookeriana* × *teres*) arrived from the Singapore Botanic Gardens and subsequently developed into a cash crop, providing flowers for leis and export.

W. W. Goodale Moir's efforts with miniature equitant oncidiums and intergeneric *Oncidium* and *Laelia* hybrids

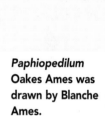

America's first couple of orchidology, Blanche and Oakes Ames.

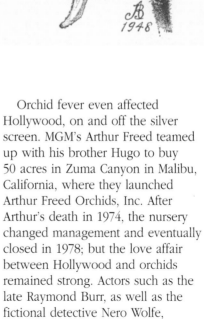

PAPHIOPEDILUM
Oakes Ames

AB
1948

influenced future generations. Roy Fukumura's passion for developing new phalaenopsis (moth orchids) and vandas led to *Ascocenda* Yip Sum Wah (*Vanda* Pukele × *Ascocentrum curvifolium*). *Ascda.* Yip Sum Wah has received more than 100 awards from the American Orchid Society, making it the most highly awarded orchid hybrid.

Post-World War II

After World War II, orchid growing in the United States bloomed, as it shifted from primarily a cut-flower industry to one geared toward supplying plants for hobbyists eager to raise plants in greenhouses and later in the home and under lights. Converts sought out cultural information and, to meet the demand, authors produced popular books, among them Mary Noble's *You Can Grow Orchids* series and Rebecca Northen's *Home Orchid Growing.*

Paphiopedilum **Oakes Ames was drawn by Blanche Ames.**

Orchid fever even affected Hollywood, on and off the silver screen. MGM's Arthur Freed teamed up with his brother Hugo to buy 50 acres in Zuma Canyon in Malibu, California, where they launched Arthur Freed Orchids, Inc. After Arthur's death in 1974, the nursery changed management and eventually closed in 1978; but the love affair between Hollywood and orchids remained strong. Actors such as the late Raymond Burr, as well as the fictional detective Nero Wolfe, collected them.

Ascocenda Yip Sum Wah has won more than 100 awards.

Orchids have become big business, requiring large commercial greenhouses.

Orchids Today

Beginning in 1995, orchids have been included individually in the U.S. Department of Agriculture's Floriculture Crops Summary Report, which documents sales of bedding plants, cut cultivated greens, cut flowers, flowering potted plants, and foliage plants. In 2002, orchids accounted for $106 million in sales, second only to poinsettia and surpassing the ever-popular chrysanthemum. More than 12.7 million orchids were sold that year, with 90 percent of the plants grown in nurseries in California, Florida, and Hawaii.

While commercial growers rush to meet consumer demand, breeders continue to create new hybrids—more than 120,000 are registered with the Royal Horticultural Society. They also continue to study plants in nature in an attempt to unlock the mystery of growing these plants that instill obsession in those seduced by their charm.

Orchid habitat

Orchids are found the world over, in all but the harshest climates of permanent frost and major deserts. While more than 25,000 species have been documented, new ones continue to be discovered every year, leading botanists to suggest that as many as 35,000 species exist. About 220 of these species are native to North America. Europe is home to a slightly greater number—266 species. Australia claims another 900 orchids. However, by far the majority are native to the tropical regions of Central and South America, Africa, Madagascar, Asia, and New Guinea.

While North America is home to relatively few orchid species, North American lady's slipper orchids (*Cypripedium* spp.) are prized by orchid fanciers around the world. Hikers who come upon specimens in the forest are cautioned against picking them. The Endangered Species Act protects cypripediums and other native orchids.

Endangered orchids

Even though the number of orchids removed from the wild has diminished since the Victorian orchid boom, countless species of orchids have become extinct because of the disappearance of much of the planet's pristine wild areas and orchid thieves' flagrantly illegal collecting of rare exotic beauties. Orchids continue to be

5 WAYS TO GET STARTED WITH ORCHIDS

- Attend orchid shows and plant sales.
- Visit greenhouses and nurseries.
- Join a local orchid society.
- Read *Orchids,* the magazine of the American Orchid Society.
- Talk to other growers.

collected and smuggled from their native lands into countries where there are customers who will pay a high price for an unusual specimen.

Purchasing only plants known to have been propagated by legitimate orchid growers will discourage the gathering of wild orchids and their exploitation. Avoid advertisements offering orchids described with the words "wild collected."

The latest discoveries

New orchids continue to be discovered, especially in countries previously off limits. In China and Vietnam, plant explorers such as Leonid Averyanov seek out new slipper orchids and dendrobiums. In Peru, a sensational orchid trumpeted as the greatest orchid find in decades was discovered in 2002. Called *Phragmipedium kovachii,*

If Susan Orlean's book *The Orchid Thief* made the ghost orchid, *Dendrophylax* (syn. *Polyrrhiza*) *lindenii,* a celebrity, the movie *Adaptation* made this epiphytic orchid a star.

Discovered in 1844 in Cuba by Jean Jules Linden, this leafless orchid was later found elsewhere, including in the Bahamas and, in Florida, Everglades National Park, Big Cypress National Preserve, and the Fakahatchee Strand.

The ghost orchid consists of only a stem and pencil-thick roots that cling to the bark of bald cypress, pop ash, and pond apple trees. When it comes into flower, its 3- to 5-inch-tall white flowers appear to float in the air as they dangle from the host trees. Each blossom of this summer-flowering orchid bears a long spur, inside which is nectar, suggesting this species is pollinated by the giant sphinx moth. When out of flower, the plant is easily camouflaged because of its lack of leaves (the roots carry out photosynthesis and absorb water and nutrients).

Dendrophylax (Polyrrhiza) lindenii

The ghost orchid is endangered, making it illegal to collect it from the wild. Although seed-grown plants are available, the ghost orchid is like any star—best admired from a distance.

its spectacular 8-inch-wide purple to pink flowers are certain to inspire hybridizers much the way the discovery of *hragmipedium besseae* did when it was found in 1981. The introduction of *Phrag. besseae* to the horticultural trade spurred hybridizing in this genus of New World slipper orchids. As with other introductions of orchids from the wild, permits are necessary for plants to legally enter the United States. Using only a few plants, or seed capsules, new introductions can be made without destroying natural populations.

Today professional hybridizers may pay thousands of dollars for an irresistible trendsetter. Orchid societies meet regularly around the world to trade plants and tips. Their dazzling shows of artfully composed landscapes filled with stunning hybrids surely exceed the wildest dreams of the Victorians.

The acclaimed
Phragmipedium kovachii

Orchid Botany

Orchids have caught the attention of botanists for centuries, luring scientists with their fantastic shapes, odd colorations, and diverse fragrances. Mesmerized by these unworldly plants, early botanists who sought to classify them studied plant structure, leaves, flowers, pollen, and reproductive structures. Dissecting flowers to examine them in detail and later combining herbarium studies with fieldwork—studying pollination mechanisms or distribution patterns—researchers sought to bring order to the orchid family *(Orchidaceae)*. They continue to do so today. Orchid taxonomists have expanded their information base to include genetic relationships revealed by analyzing plant DNA to determine which orchids share common ancestors. While the techniques for understanding orchid biology and studying orchid classification have been refined and expanded, the basic structure of an orchid remains the same.

Monopodial orchids grow mainly upward.

Types of Orchids

Despite the vastness of the family, orchids have two basic growth patterns: monopodial and sympodial. While different genera of orchids are crossed with one another to create new entities, seemingly with greater abandon than in any other plant family, monopodials are crossed only with monopodials and sympodials only with sympodials; the two types are never interbred.

Knowing whether an orchid is monopodial or sympodial also offers a clue as to how best to propagate the plant.

Monopodial

A monopodial orchid grows predominantly upward. It has a main stem, which produces new leaves at its tip, and it flowers from buds at the juncture of recently matured leaves and the stem. The word monopodial (Latin for "single foot") describes the single-stem growth habit. *Vanda* and *Phalaenopsis* are examples of common monopodial orchids. Other monopodial genera include *Aerides, Angraecum, Ascocenda, Ascocentrum, Ascofinetia, Doritaenopsis, Doritis, Kagawara, Neofinetia, Neostylopsis,* and *Trudelia*.

One way to tell the difference between a monopodial and a sympodial orchid is to look around the base where the plant emerges from the growing medium. If it is monopodial, there will be no new shoots or baby plants growing up, only the original stalk. If it is sympodial, one or more new shoots can be seen emerging or in various stages of growth.

In nature, both types may seem to move horizontally or vertically away from the point of origin. In cultivation, most monopodials tend to expand upward while the sympodials move horizontally. The exceptions are the monopodials *Doritis, Phalaenopsis* and crosses involving both—the progeny of which are known as *Doritaenopsis*—that may grow upright for a time but will eventually sprawl across the surface of the growing medium. This

Phalaenopsis **Taisuco Pixerrot, above left, and** *Ascocenda* **Su-Fun Beauty 'Memoria Jane Figiel', above, are both monopodial orchids.**

appearance usually signals the need to rework and repot the plant to remove the oldest roots and the lowest stalk from which the oldest leaves may already have matured and dropped off.

Although monopodial orchids vary in size and potential height, *Arachnis* is typical of the largest. The habit and appearance of *Arachnis* species will vary, depending on whether they are grown in a basket or cradle without staking or grown in a pot and staked upright

In either case, the stalk eventually will be bare some distance upward from the base, with strong, vital air roots all along the way up. At repotting time, the oldest roots and most of the old, bare stalk can be removed, thus bringing the newer, vital parts back down so they begin at or emerge from the growing medium.

If the growing tip of a monopodial orchid is damaged or removed, one or more new shoots may emerge from the main stalk. After a time, strong roots will grow from the base of these stalks into the air. Once they are at least a few inches long, the offshoots can be removed and potted as new plants.

Monopodial orchids lack thickened pseudobulbs to store moisture and sustain them through extended dry seasons. They are better suited to a range between even moisture and slightly dry than to extremes. Avoid allowing the medium to become bone dry. If it is dry for so long that the leaves shrivel, the plant may be unable to assimilate moisture. It will remain shrunken or unnaturally floppy even if properly watered. Sometimes a plant can be salvaged by treating the uppermost leaves and stalk as a cutting, setting them to grow in a fresh medium.

Symifodial

A sympodial orchid grows outward along the surface of the growing medium; its stem, called a rhizome, is often horizontal. New shoots originate from buds on the rhizome and send out their own roots. The flower spikes of sympodial orchids may originate from the base of the plant—usually from the base of a recently matured pseudobulb or from between the leaves at the top.

Sympodial (Latin for "many-footed") describes the spreading growth habit of orchids in this classification. Cattleyas and paphiopedilums are familiar examples of sympodial orchids.

In nature, cattleyas are often seen growing on the rough bark of a tree, with rhizomes and pseudobulbs spreading outward and upward. When potted, the same cattleyas will expand across the surface of the growing medium and unless repotted into a larger container will grow over the edge and down the side of the pot, or may simply dangle in the air.

Paphiopedilums in nature are more likely to occur in pockets of humus. Their movement is less obvious since it is more likely to be side to side with new shoots arising next to the older ones. The result is that a clump of leaves is formed with the

This sympodial orchid demonstrates the classic characteristics, including spreading rhizomes.

oldest at the center and the youngest at the perimeter.

Sympodial orchids include species with pseudobulbs that store moisture to sustain them through periods of drought. Some sympodials lack such moisture reservoirs—paphiopedilums, for example—and are as vulnerable in drought as monopodial orchids. With a few exceptions, sympodial orchids tend to be better adapted to moisture extremes, especially dryness, than the monopodials. However, extreme or prolonged dryness can result in deeply shriveled pseudobulbs and in withered leaves that are unable to take up moisture when they are watered or rained upon.

Besides the ever-popular *Cattleya* and *Paphiopedilum* (slipper orchid) and other frequently cultivated sympodial orchids include *Aspasia, Brassavola, Brassia, Brassocattleya, Brassolaeliocattleya, Cattleytonia, Cochleanthes, Colmanara, Cymbidium, Dendrobium, Encyclia, Laelia, Laeliocattleya, Leptotes, Lycaste, Masdevallia, Miltassia, Miltonidium, Miltonia, Miltoniopsis, Odontioda, Odontocidium, Oncidium, Otaara, Phragmipedium, Potinara, Psychopsis, Yamadara,* and *Zygopetalum.*

Laeliocattleya Rojo is a typical sympodial orchid.

At right *Cattleya skinneri* shows how the rhizome in a sympodial orchid travels horizontally across the surface of the growing medium, rooting as it goes along.

Three Growth Habits

Most orchids can be classified into one or two of three basic categories, according to the conditions under which they or their predecessors have evolved. These include epiphytes (air plants or tree-dwellers), terrestrials (earth plants, plants that grow in soil), and lithophytes (plants with roots that attach themselves to rocks).

Epiphytes

Most tropical orchids are epiphytes that have adapted to living above the ground where the light is more plentiful. When Charles Darwin first saw epiphytic orchids clinging to the branches of their hosts, he thought they were parasites, drawing nourishment from their hosts through tenacious, leechlike roots. This was, of course, a false assumption: True parasites are rare among plants. Two of the better-known examples are mistletoe (*Viscum album*) and a golden yellow, stringlike vine called dodder (*Cuscuta* spp.).

Orchids use the branches of trees only as a place to live. They absorb their nutrients from the decaying organic matter that accumulates around their roots. They photosynthesize sugars from the sunlight streaming through the gaps in the forest's leafy canopy. They damage trees only when they grow too heavy for the branches to bear. Occasionally, massive colonies of orchids, often accompanied by ferns, bromeliads, and epiphytic gesneriads (African violet relatives), crash to the forest's floor.

In adapting to their aerial environment, epiphytic orchids have developed thick roots coated with velamen, a spongy material that allows them to stick to the bark of trees and absorb water rapidly. To survive periods of drought, many species have pseudobulbs, thickened stems that can store both water and food. In other epiphytic species, the leaves themselves are thickened storage organs.

Epiphytic orchids need to dry out between waterings. The time this takes will be brief in warm, sunny weather when plants are in active growth and longer in cool temperatures. Because their pseudobulbs act as storage organs, epiphytes grow well with less frequent fertilizing than terrestrials. Epiphytic orchids tolerate underwatering better than overwatering, but water regularly and avoid extreme dryness. Otherwise the orchid plant may live, almost indefinitely, but it will not bloom and prosper.

Typically orchids in a home greenhouse require watering and fertilizing twice a week in warm weather, once a week or less often in winter. Between waterings in warm, bright weather, leaves and exposed roots benefit from a light misting of water early in the day. Avoid leaving water standing in the centers of plants or in cupped leaves, which can lead to fungus problems.

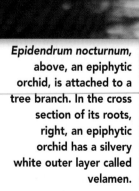

Epidendrum nocturnum, above, an epiphytic orchid, is attached to a tree branch. In the cross section of its roots, right, an epiphytic orchid has a silvery white outer layer called velamen.

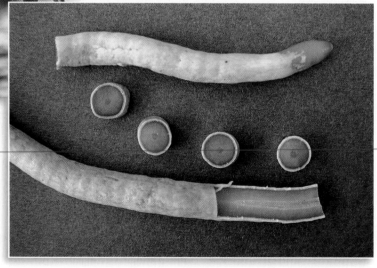

Terrestrial orchids

In the tropics, some orchids live in the humus-rich soil at the edges of streams, in clearings, and in other spots on the ground where dense shade is dappled by patches of sunlight. These orchids are terrestrial—that is, they live on the ground.

Most terrestrial orchids, such as paphiopedilums, are similar to their tree-dwelling relatives. Because they generally live in rich, fluffy humus, their roots resemble those of epiphytes, though roots of terrestrials tend to be more hairy. To further blur the distinction, an epiphyte in its natural state may end up living as a terrestrial if it falls out of a tree onto a sunny spot where there is abundant humus.

Cymbidiums are often classed as semiterrestrial, a term that indicates their adaptability to various growing media. Like paphiopedilums, they need perfect drainage and aeration around the roots. But they also need sufficient humus to maintain a slightly moist environment at all times.

Neither epiphytic nor terrestrial orchids are likely to adapt to the ordinary potting soil used to grow plants such as begonias and geraniums. Soilless mixes that combine peat moss, perlite, or charcoal chips are sometimes combined with bark chips to form a satisfactory growing medium for paphiopedilums and cymbidiums.

Two terrestrials that could never be mistaken for epiphytes are the Australian orchids *Rhizanthella gardneri* and *Cryptanthemis slateri*. These species grow underground, never seeing daylight, even when flowering and setting seed. Little else is known about these oddities.

Lithophytes

Botanical references that discuss the natural habitats of orchids often list an epiphytic species as also lithophytic, growing with its roots attached to rocks or in extremely rocky terrain where there is scant humus. Lithophytes absorb nutrients from the atmosphere, rain, and decaying matter accumulated on the rocks.

Vandas can be lithophytes. They and their relatives such as *Ascocenda,*

A terrestrial orchid, such as this *Spathoglottis plicata*, usually grows in moist humus.

Ascocentrum, and *Trudelia* are sometimes grown in wood-slat baskets filled with chunks of lava rock. Lithophytes need constant humidity. In warm, sunny weather they need the roots and rocks drenched with water daily, with warm air to quickly dry any excess. These orchids grow successfully in South Florida and along the Gulf Coast, where high humidity is common and outdoor temperatures are warm enough to sustain growth most of the year with a brief time indoors during the coldest part of winter.

When an epiphytic orchid, such as *Laelia bradei,* grows on a rock, it is a lithophyte.

Ascocentrum miniatum is now called *Ascocentrum garayi.*

Marvelous Miniatures

Many of today's orchid hobbyists specialize in miniatures, which offer variations on a familiar theme. Miniature orchids have assumed new status as enthusiasts search for plants that take up less space, especially important to growers who are confined to windowsills or who use artificial lights.

Although definitions vary, most miniatures are 6 inches tall or shorter (excluding the flower spike). Some would fit comfortably in a teacup, while others would be at home in a thimble-size container. The smallest orchids are in the genus *Platystele,* which is native to the New World tropics. A flowering plant of *Platystele halbingeriana* or *Platystele jungermannioides* is the size of a thumbnail. To view these and other minute flowers, some growers rely on a hand lens to bring the delightful and often complex flowers into focus.

One advantage miniatures offer is they are easy to move around to find microclimates to their liking. If a plant is sulking, try moving it to a new location, perhaps giving it more light or placing it where it will receive better air circulation. In cultivation, miniatures may require different or more intense care than their larger counterparts. Take the time to learn their specific needs. When cultural conditions allow, group miniatures together to avoid losing them on a greenhouse bench. Tucked between larger containers, miniatures may not receive the water or the care they need to grow and flower. But given the attention they deserve, miniatures become key players in the connoisseur's orchid collection.

In nature, miniature orchids occur in many environments, especially as epiphytes on the trunks and limbs of shrubs and trees. In the New World tropics, miniature orchids are almost always present on calabash trees, which can be host trees for twig epiphytes. Orchid tourists who encounter calabash trees often see a tangle of tiny epiphytes—orchids, bromelaids, and others—clinging to the stiff branches.

Many orchid genera with standard-size plants also include miniatures. For example, *Cattleya luteola,* a small version of the showy corsage orchid, tops its 2-inch leaves with yellow flowers borne two to five to a stem on a petite plant. Phalaenopsis, dendrobiums, and paphiopedilums all include miniatures, each with its own unique beauty. *Ascocentrum ampullaceum* and *Ascocentrum garayi* are miniatures ideally suited to bright light and warm temperatures. No group of orchids offers more miniature choices than the Pleurothallid Alliance, which embraces masdevallias, restrepias, pleurothallis, and lepanthes, among others.

Miniature hybrids abound, especially in the Cattleya Alliance, where the plants are often small in stature but the flowers retain their showy appeal. The influence of *Sophronitis coccinea* has led to new generations of *Cattleya*-like hybrids with dynamic flowers. These provide a springboard to a new world of lilliputian hybrids.

Anatomy of Orchids

The mysterious appeal of orchids is a combination of an unexplainable emotional reaction and a scientific interest in the plant itself. Botanists know that orchid flowers are the most advanced and intricate in the entire plant kingdom. In their evolution, orchids have become specialized, developing complex and effective mechanisms that induce insects and other animals to pollinate their blossoms.

Flower structures

Orchids reproduce with variations on a basic theme of three petals and three sepals. In cattleyas, these parts are easily identified. The two uppermost petals are brightly colored; the highly modified lower petal is a large, ruffled labellum (Latin for "lip"). The sepals stick out between and behind the petals like the points of a three-pointed star.

The labellum is often the largest and most colorful part of an orchid flower. It can take many different forms. In slipper orchids, the labellum forms a slipper-shaped pouch. In many oncidium flowers, it fans out like a skirt, inspiring the common name dancing-lady orchid.

Orchids share this combination of three petals and three sepals with lilies. Orchids, however, are distinguished from other flowers by the column, an intricate structure formed by the fused male and female reproductive parts—the stamen and pistil. Although the stamen and pistil are close together on the column, self-pollination is prevented by a divider called the rostellum. Self-pollination may also be prevented by a variety of other mechanisms, most of which are designed to attach pollen to an insect after it has passed the pistil and is on its way out of the flower.

The column can be the most interesting part of an orchid flower. Some columns look like the faces of humans, insects, or birds; others resemble African masks. They may bear wings or wear what appear to be caps, goggles, or ruffled bonnets. The column of the tiger orchid, *Rossioglossum grande* (also known under an older genus name, *Odontoglossum*), resembles a doll.

Pollination

Orchid pollen, usually massed into clumps called pollinia, is different from the fluffy powder produced by most other insect-pollinated plants.

In cattleyas, an insect (usually a bee) is lured under the column by a supply of nectar or by the flower's enticing fragrance. On its way out, the bee's back becomes coated with a sticky adhesive that catches and attaches one or more of the pollinia.

The pollinia in the genus *Catasetum* are spring-loaded. When a bee bumps the trigger, the pollinia eject from the flower onto the insect's body, where they stick tightly. Triggering the flower with the tip of a pencil held out of the line of fire will cause the pollinia to shoot several feet into the air.

Special behavior

Charles Darwin observed that the nectar produced by the flowers of *Angraecum sesquipedale* (from Madagascar) was held at the bottom of a long, pointed tube, far out of the reach of any insect he had ever seen. Assuming that this nectar attracted pollinators as it does in other flowers, he postulated that *Angraecum* flowers must be pollinated by a "huge moth, with a wonderfully long proboscis" able to tap the nectar. Forty years later, Darwin was proved correct when scientists on Madagascar found the very type of moths he had envisaged.

Parts of an orchid flower.

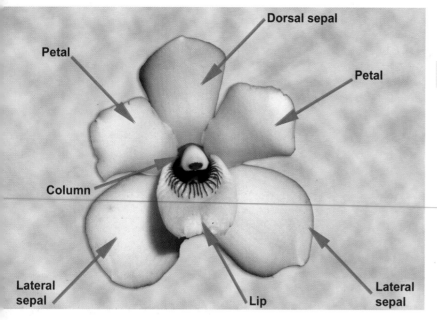

Dorsal sepal

Petal

Petal

Column

Lateral sepal

Lip

Lateral sepal

That was the beginning. As more orchids were studied, botanists were astounded by the variety and sophistication of their colors and structures. They were amazed by the way some orchids mimic the appearance and odors of female insects to inspire the amorous attentions of males—a natural phenomenon, which has been delicately dubbed "pseudocopulation."

Orchids in the genus *Ophrys* seem to have perfected this seductive mimicry, enhancing their uncanny resemblance to female wasps or flies with a fragrance nearly identical to the insects' sex attractant. But when a male insect attempts to mate with one of these flowers, all it gets for its trouble are pollinia to transfer to another flower, where the insect is duped again.

Not all orchid mimicry is seductive. Some oncidiums challenge the territorial instincts of bees by dangling their threatening (to the bees, anyway) flowers at the ends of long, slender stalks, a trick botanists call "pseudoantagonism." When the flowers move in the breeze, the bees attack. After furiously bumping the flowers, the bees come away with wads of pollen stuck to their heads, pollen they will transfer to other flowers in ensuing battles.

In the early morning, *Coryanthes speciosa,* the bucket orchid, produces a delightful fragrance that attracts bees. The part of the flower that produces this fragrance is slippery and positioned above glands that secrete fluid into the "bucket." Because the flower is so slippery, the bee slides into the bucket, wetting its wings and preventing flight.

After frantic struggling, the bee finds a way out through a narrow tunnel at one end of the bucket. It clambers up through this tunnel and emerges with pollinia stuck to its body.

The next day the bee, recovered from its ordeal but still carrying its payload of pollen, becomes overwhelmed by the fragrance of another bucket orchid. This time some of the pollen rubs off while the bee is escaping through the tunnel and thus pollinates the flower.

Some paphiopedilums pander to the appetites of flies with the foul (but faint) fragrances of rotting fruit or meat. Brown, green, and purple petals with fuzzy black warts resembling clusters of flies complete the effect. When a fly lands on the flower to join other flies for a meal, it cannot hold on to the slippery surface and slides off into a large pouch formed by the flower's lower petal. Once in the pouch, the fly can escape only by crawling up a narrow tunnel, rubbing off any pollen it received from other flowers and picking up a new load as it exits.

Floral longevity and abundance

Orchid flowers are borne on inflorescences known as spikes, either singly or in clusters, which may have from 2 to 25 or more flowers. The flowers at the base of a spike will often open before those at the tip. Because the flowers last a long time, many plants dazzle observers by displaying all their flowers for most of the time the plant is in bloom.

Orchid flowers are as durable as they look. The waxy flowers of paphiopedilums last for more than a month, while their spikes can linger for three months.

The spikes of *Phalaenopsis, Oncidium,* and a few other orchids may send out side branches with new buds after the main flowers on the spike have faded. In this way, a plant may remain in bloom for six to eight months. A floriferous *Phalaenopsis* may even have two blooming cycles in one year.

Orchids display their flowers for long periods while waiting for insects to pollinate them. Once fertilized, orchid flowers quickly fade as the plant turns its energy to making seed. Unless an appropriate fly or bee comes along or other pollination methods are used, plants will remain in bloom until the flowers die.

Some oncidiums attract bees by mimicking a swarm of bees, thereby carrying out pollination.

Certain orchids bloom for as long as eight to ten months.

How Orchids Are Named

Orchids are not exactly like other plants. The orchid family is incredibly large, and orchid species interbreed so easily that it is often difficult to tell where one species stops and the next begins. It is the taxonomists' challenge to organize the myriad forms and colors of orchids into discrete categories.

The complexity of these categories is reflected in the fine distinctions made among apparently similar plants and hybrids that have elaborate family trees. However, the basic principles are those followed in the naming of any plant.

Few people can rattle off the various rules and exceptions of orchid naming. For any grower, however, even a general notion of the system will contribute to the enjoyment derived from this remarkably diverse family of plants.

Orchids are named under the same international system that governs the naming of all other plants. To understand how an orchid gets its name, start at the top with the orchid family *(Orchidaceae).* For most plants, the next major category used below family is the genus (or

Brassavola is a genus of New World orchids.

genera if you are speaking of more than one). Because the orchid family is so large, botanists use intermediate categories between the family and genus called subfamily, tribe, and subtribe, categories that can be helpful because they show how the plants in the different genera are related. The genus *Miltonia,* for example, is in the subtribe *Oncidiinae.* This subtribe also includes the genera *Oncidium, Odontoglossum,* and *Brassia,* all of which have similar characteristics and hybridize easily.

The genus name, such as *Miltonia* or *Brassia,* is an essential part of an orchid's identification. To show that it is a genus name, the word is printed in italics, and the first letter is capitalized.

As for most plants, a genus is divided into species, the basic units of classification in both the plant and animal kingdoms. The species name is printed in italics but is not capitalized. The genus *Miltonia,* for example, contains the species *spectabilis.* An easy way to remember how genus and species names are related is to look at the first few letters of both words. Genus is general; species is specific. The plants in a given species are similar, but you will still find differences in flower size, shape, and color, as well as in the leaves, stems, and pseudobulbs.

Sometimes certain plants in a species share a characteristic that makes them different from others in the species, but not quite different enough to justify a new species name. If such a group is found in nature, it is called a variety.

Variety names are often preceded by the abbreviation var. and are printed in italics and not capitalized. *Miltonia spectabilis* var. *moreliana,* for example, has rose rather than white flower petals, but aside from this difference in color it is virtually identical to the white-petaled forms of *Miltonia spectabilis.*

Variety names are used primarily by botanists, who study populations of wild plants. In horticulture—the study of cultivated plants—the term "cultivar" is used more frequently.

Cultivars are plants selected for their desirable features and propagated in ways that perpetuate these features. A cultivar may be selected from a species, a hybrid, or a variety. It may be propagated by division, offshoots, mericloning, or any other asexual method that produces offspring similar to the parent plant.

Cultivar names are printed in roman letters. The first letter is capitalized, and the entire name is enclosed in single quotes. For example, one of the prettiest forms of *Miltonia spectabilis* var. *moreliana* has been widely cultivated and awarded. This clone, named 'Royalty', AM/AOS (see Awards, page 29), is a cultivar of a variety. It takes its place at the bottom of the family tree.

Orchids with more than one name

Unfortunately, not everyone uses the same names for orchids. Over the years, taxonomists have tried and discarded several schemes for organizing orchids along evolutionary lines. The goal—a classification system that shows how plants are related—is worthwhile but becomes difficult to attain when many names must be changed to reflect a new botanical discovery.

To return to the family tree, the name of the cross between *Miltonia spectabilis* and *Miltonia clowesii* is *Miltonia* Bluntii (the word's Latin ending shows that this is an old hybrid, named before the rules prohibited Latinized hybrid names). *Miltonia* Bluntii is a primary hybrid, also known as an interspecific grex—produced when one species is crossed with another species. Primary hybrids are not as common as more complex hybrids produced when a hybrid is crossed with a species or another hybrid. Now that the value of species orchids is becoming widely recognized, primary hybrids are coming back into vogue.

Common names

Common orchid names are as confusing and misleading as the common names of other plants. Although easier to pronounce, the words rarely point directly to a specific plant and are thus of little value. A single common name often applies to several species—species that have nothing else in common. For example, there seems to be at least one spider orchid on every continent, and new ones are probably dubbed every day. It is better to call them all orchids, a very general but at least correct name. Most orchid species do not have common names. The genus name is often used informally as the common name. In this book, for example, when the genus *Cattleya* or *Phalaenopsis* is discussed, the word is treated as a common name, as in "cattleyas are easy to grow" or "phalaenopsis can be confidence builders."

This orchid, a paphiopedilum, is a complex hybrid.

Lycaste brevispatha is a species.

AN ORCHID FAMILY TREE

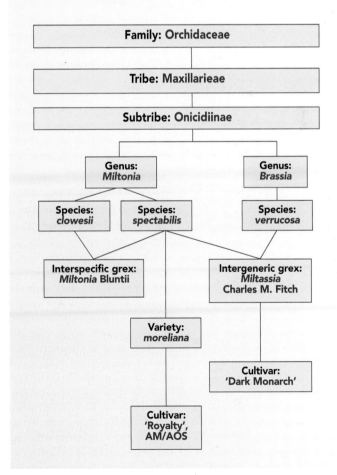

Family: Orchidaceae

Tribe: Maxillarieae

Subtribe: Onicidiinae

Genus: *Miltonia*

Genus: *Brassia*

Species: *clowesii*

Species: *spectabilis*

Species: *verrucosa*

Interspecific grex: *Miltonia* Bluntii

Intergeneric grex: *Miltassia* Charles M. Fitch

Variety: *moreliana*

Cultivar: 'Dark Monarch'

Cultivar: 'Royalty', AM/AOS

Breeding Orchids

Because orchid seed is never sold off the racks the way other flower seed is, the idea of growing orchids from scratch rarely occurs, much less the thought of cross-pollinating and creating new plants. Ever-increasing numbers of amateur orchid growers, however, are dabbling in breeding. Mastering the techniques for starting the infinitesimally small seeds is necessary in order to do this.

Step 1 of breeding is to have in bloom at the same time potential pollen (male) and seed (female) parents that are genetically compatible. Typically, to be compatible, the parents will be of the same genus or at least from the same tribe, if not subtribe.

Often the stronger of the two plants will be selected to play the female role. Take pollen from the flower selected as the male. It will be found in 2 to 12 golden masses on the column, which are called pollinia. Dip tweezers or a sharpened stick under the anther, which holds the pollinia. The pollinia will stick to it. Set this pollen aside while you remove the pollen from the flower of the selected female parent. Now press pollen from the male parent onto the stigma of the female, which is on the underside of the column.

After pollination, the seed capsule (pod) will begin to swell, and five to nine months later the seeds will be ripe. As it matures, watch the seed capsule for splitting as well as yellowing.

Sowing seeds

Orchid seed is sown on nutrient-enriched, sterile agar in a sterilized glass or plastic flask. Purchase materials from orchid suppliers (see Orchid Resources on page 216), or engage the services of an orchid specialist to do the flasking.

A fluorescent-light garden is often the ideal place for starting orchid seed. After four to six months, there will be tiny seedlings (technically "protocorms") in the flask. After 8 to 18 months, they can be separated, graded, and put back into the flasks to grow for about one to two years.

At this point, the seedlings will be ready to transplant about an inch apart into seedling-grade orchid bark in community pots.

A year or so later, transfer them into individual pots. The first flowers occur in two to seven years, with some phalaenopsis and phragmipediums likely to flower in two to three years. Standard cattleyas take as long as seven years.

Hybrids

The orchid's wide-ranging sexual compatibility gives breeders the freedom to produce stunning new orchids by crossing plants that are only remotely related. The offspring of these crosses are called hybrids.

When two orchid species in the same genus are crossed, the resulting hybrid

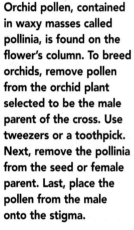

Orchid pollen, contained in waxy masses called pollinia, is found on the flower's column. To breed orchids, remove pollen from the orchid plant selected to be the male parent of the cross. Use tweezers or a toothpick. Next, remove the pollinia from the seed or female parent. Last, place the pollen from the male onto the stigma.

Epidendrum Costa Rica is a primary hybrid.

Brassolaelia Morning Glory is a primary intergeneric.

Burrageara Stefan Isler is a complex intergeneric.

seedlings are given a name. Orchid breeders name their hybrids after family members, spouses, mountains, rivers— almost anything as long as it does not sound like Latin. (In 1959, taxonomists changed the rules to prohibit Latinized hybrid names because it was hard to tell the species from the hybrids.)

To be made official, a hybrid name must be registered with the Royal Horticultural Society (RHS), which lists it in *Sander's List of Orchid Hybrids*. Once a hybrid has an official name, all plants resulting from those parents carry that name, even if subsequent crosses produce different-looking results, which they often do.

Intergeneric hybrids

Orchid breeders have great fun crossing orchids of different genera. This is remarkable genetics; few plants other than orchids can be interbred in this way.

An intergeneric hybrid may be named in one of two ways. In the simplest way, the hybrid name is formed by combining the two genus names, as in *Miltassia* from *Miltonia* and *Brassia*. These names make it easy to remember the parents of the hybrid. The hybrid of *Miltonia spectabilis* and *Brassia verrucosa,* for example, is called *Miltassia* Charles M. Fitch. It has a very popular cultivar, 'Dark Monarch' (see

An Orchid Family Tree, page 25 for more information on orchid names.)

When a bigeneric hybrid (a hybrid of two genera) is crossed with a plant in yet another genus, the three names may be lumped together as was done in naming *Sophrolaeliocattleya,* the cross of *Sophronitis, Laelia,* and *Cattleya.*

When the names of the genera do not flow smoothly together, taxonomists avoid tongue twisters by giving the hybrid an entirely new name ending with *ara.* For example, the hybrid *Cochlioda* × *Miltonia* × *Odontoglossum* was named *Vuylstekeara* to honor C. Vuylsteke, a Belgian orchid breeder. Another delightful hybrid, *Potinara,* results from crossing *Brassavola, Laelia, Cattleya,* and *Sophronitis.*

Orchid Organizations

It was inevitable: Orchid growers were bound to get together to share their ideas, swap divisions and seedlings, discuss how they grow their plants, reveal how they hybridize orchids, and have a good time hanging out with their orchid buddies. Nationwide, there is rarely an evening during the workweek when an orchid society is not holding a meeting.

Wherever there are orchid people with their orchid plants, there are orchid societies: Canada, Mexico, Costa Rica, Ecuador, Brazil, France, Italy, South Africa, Singapore, Japan, Australia, and New Zealand, among others. Although the greatest number of local orchid societies is in the United States, the oldest orchid organization devoted entirely to these plants is the North of England Orchid Society, founded in 1897. Since the American Orchid Society took root in 1921, American orchid organizations have proliferated as new groups form, prosper, and nurture the enthusiasm of a public infatuated with orchids.

Local orchid societies invite neophytes to attend their meetings. In some cases, a beginners' hour introduces the ABCs of orchid culture. (A list of local orchid societies is available at www.aos.org.) Mingling with orchid hobbyists offers an excellent opportunity to learn about regional growing conditions and about the types of orchids your neighbors raise, as well as their growing environments, potting media, fertilizers, and insect controls. Newsletters, an annual show and sale, and sometimes field trips to members' private growing areas are natural extensions that also build relationships.

Joining a local orchid society is the first step toward forming an orchid-meeting habit that leads to orchid groups at the regional, national, and international levels. Several organizations serve the needs of different regions of the United States, such as the Southwest Regional Orchid Growers Association and the Mid-America Orchid Congress. More recently, specialty groups have come into vogue, each one focusing on a particular genus—*Phalaenopsis, Pleurothallis, Oncidium,* and *Cymbidium,* among others. There is one club for orchid stamps, another for orchid pins. These specialty groups publish information and photographs of selected genera, species, and hybrids. Frequently they present lectures at larger orchid assemblies, making it possible to attend the programs of several groups over the course of a weekend. Some groups, such as the International Phalaenopsis Alliance, hold their own national meeting—complete with a show and lectures—as well as regional get-togethers.

Shows

Orchid shows offer a splendid opportunity for immersion in orchids. Held throughout the year, these festivals of flowers are especially plentiful from winter through spring, when many orchids bloom. Varying in size from modest to majestic and staged in venues ranging from bank lobbies to shopping malls to botanical gardens, they show off orchids in landscaped displays and on tables, as well as in flower arrangements and in art. Demonstrations, lectures, and plant sales add up to a memorable experience and ample networking opportunities.

An extensive, regularly updated calendar of orchid shows is posted on www.aos.org. Many newspapers list orchid shows in their calendars of garden events and special events. Botanical gardens that host orchid shows often promote them to the local community.

An orchid show display

Behind the scenes

Attendees see the results of months of planning and hard work by volunteers, who donate their time, energy, and financial resources to arrange publicity, invite vendors, coordinate judging, lay out floor plans, and deal with the other elements that go into producing an orchid show. Orchid show setup often begins three or four days before the show. Trucks with sand and landscape plants arrive, exhibitors enter the hall with their flowering plants, designers orchestrate the creation of displays, custodians hustle, judges and clerks fan out across the showroom floor, and ribbons or trophies are placed. Despite occasional mishaps, the elements come together as the show opens to the public and hosts welcome those eager to see the award-winning orchids and to buy plants.

The presentation of orchids often follows botanical classification and divides the many types of orchids into divisions and classes into which exhibitors can enter their prized specimens. Having brought in their plants and entered them, exhibitors then wait for judging to take place, which for some of the larger shows may be an all-day event. Frequently, there are two types of judging: ribbon judging, where judges evaluate plants on a merit basis, and AOS judging, where judges recognize superior orchids with special awards.

Awards

With so many species, varieties, hybrids, and cultivars, it can be difficult to distinguish outstanding orchids from merely pretty ones. The international awards system codified by the American Orchid Society in 1949 sets the standard.

When evaluating an orchid, judges compare it with all others of the same type that they have seen. To make such comparisons, an orchid judge goes through at least six years of training in the United States—three years as a student judge and three years on probation.

In most cases, orchids are judged solely on the basis of their flowers. Judges consider color, size, shape, and substance

Setting up an orchid display often begins several days before the show opens.

(thickness), as well as the way the flowers are borne on the stems. They also evaluate the sharpness and clarity of any stripes, spots, or other markings on petals.

A 100-point scale is used. To be considered for an award, an orchid must pass an initial screening. If the judges think the orchid has a chance of receiving an award, it is entered in formal judging.

Among the flower awards, the highest and best award is the First Class Certificate (FCC/AOS). For this, the orchid must be awarded 90 points or more. Next is the Award of Merit (AM/AOS), which means the plant must receive between 80 and 89 points. A plant bearing the letters AM/AOS after its name will have exceptionally beautiful flowers. The third flower award is the Highly Commended Certificate (HCC/AOS). An HCC/AOS plant, having received between 75 and 79 points, is also an excellent orchid.

Species orchids may be eligible for two additional awards. The Certificate of Botanical Recognition (CBR/AOS) is awarded to cultivars of species or natural hybrids deemed worthy of recognition for their rarity, novelty, or educational value. The Certificate of Horticultural Merit

Orchid show judges must train for at least six years.

Orchid Organizations

(continued)

An orchid can win one of 10 AOS awards.

(CHM/AOS) is given to well-grown species considered particularly interesting from a horticultural standpoint.

Other awards are determined by assessing the entire plant, not just the flowers. The Certificate of Cultural Merit (CCM/AOS), which includes plants that score 80 to 89 points, and the more elusive Certificate of Cultural Excellence (CCE/AOS), which requires 90 to 100 points, are awarded to the grower of an outstanding specimen plant that has enjoyed perfect growing conditions.

These awards do not require a new hybrid or new species. To have your efforts rewarded with a CCM/AOS is commendable, and to receive a CCE/AOS is a notable achievement.

More resources

Local botanical gardens and county extension service offices often have displays or information tables at orchid shows.

Professional staff and volunteers at a county extension service booth frequently can answer questions about orchids and give directions to other local resources. Many extension service offices provide written materials, ranging from pamphlets to culture sheets to booklets.

Master Gardeners hand out advice, too. They can point growers toward resources for having water tested and ailing orchids analyzed (usually for a small fee).

A display by a local botanical garden at an orchid show may also inspire show visitors to visit the garden, not only at orchid show time but also during other seasons when different orchids are in bloom. Members of these gardens may enjoy free repeat visits and reduced-price orchid classes. Sales at these gardens occasionally offer orchid plants in flower as well as divisions of plants selected from the institution's private collection.

TYPES OF AMERICAN ORCHID SOCIETY AWARDS

The awards here are defined by the American Orchid Society and granted by judges at shows sanctioned by the society or at its judging centers. Similar awards granted by other orchid societies—Japan Orchid Society, Royal Horticultural Society—are indicated by a different set of initials following the award abbreviation. For example, if you see SM/WOC printed after a cultivar name, it means the orchid received a silver medal at a World Orchid Conference. An AM/HOS means the flower was granted an Award of Merit by the Honolulu Orchid Society.

Name	Abbreviation	Definition
Award of Distinction	AD	Awarded to recognize a worthy new trend.
Award of Quality	AQ	Awarded to recognize improved quality in the strain.
Award of Merit	AM	A flower scoring 80 to 89 points on a scale of 100 points.
Certificate of Botanical Recognition	CBR	Awarded to rare and unusual species of educational interest.
Certificate of Cultural Excellence	CCE	This award distinguishes growers of plants that exhibit an extreme degree of skill in cultivation, having received 90 points or more on a scale of 100.
Certificate of Cultural Merit	CCM	Rather than designating an individual flower of high quality, this award recognizes the grower and not the plant. The CCM may be given more than once if a plant continues to thrive and increase in both the size and number of flowers. The plant must score 80 to 89 points.
Certificate of Horticultural Merit	CHM	Awarded to a well-grown and well-flowered species or natural hybrid with characteristics that contribute to the horticultural aspects of orchidology.
First Class Certificate	FCC	The highest flower-quality award, given by AOS judges to flowers scoring 90 or more points on a scale of 100 points.
Highly Commended Certificate	HCC	Granted to a flower scoring 75 to 79 points on a scale of 100 points. The majority of awarded orchids receive this citation.
Judges' Commendation	JC	Given to orchids for distinctive characteristics that the AOS judges, by an affirmative vote of at least 75 percent, feel should be recognized but cannot be scored in customary ways.

Orchid festivals bring together commercial orchid growers, with or without an orchid show. Some festivals take place at a nursery or other public place. Others resemble a home tour—visiting one nursery after the other. These events offer extensive selections and often include growers from other regions who bring in plants new to local growers. Overseas vendors may offer bare-root plants, which provide an opportunity to stock up on plants at lower prices (check to make certain these are from cultivated sources; avoid plants labeled as "wild collected"). Lectures, demonstrations, and extensive sales offerings make festivals increasingly popular with both the general public and orchid aficionados.

BIGGER AND BIGGER: Like the Hollywood musicals of the 1930s and 1940s, some orchid shows have grown into spectacles that dazzle and compete successfully with the best cultural events in town.

Each year, Japan's annual Tokyo Dome Show fills a sports stadium, attracting hundreds of thousands of visitors. In New York, the Greater New York Orchid Society's show and sale at Rockefeller Center spills out onto a tent-covered ice-skating rink. And when the World Orchid Conference meets every three years in a different country, such as Scotland, Singapore, Germany, or Canada, a huge extravaganza unfolds as exhibitors from around the world carry, cart, ship, and mail their prized plants and flowers to compete with the world's top hybridizers and growers.

It's easy to get onto the orchid-show circuit, but it's best to start at home with a local show where regional hobbyists and vendors will help boost a beginner's enthusiasm and confidence with useful advice.

Getting the most out of an orchid show

Attending an orchid show on the first day allows viewing of flowers when they are freshest and vendors' booths are stocked with first-pick plants. If the show offers a preview party—and many do—it may be worthwhile to buy a ticket because the showroom floor is less likely to be crowded and the flowers are at their prime. Preview parties offer the opportunity to mingle with the exhibitors and judges—the backbone of the event—and ask questions.

Many orchid societies hand out a show program with cultural advice and advertisements from growers, as well as acknowledgments for those who put on the show. It's a great place to write down thoughts while strolling through the exhibits or attending a lecture or demonstration.

BUYING AT THE SHOW: Use a digital or one-time-use camera to make a record of orchids to buy later. Write down the plants' names (but avoid walking into displays or removing tags from plants). Attach the camera to a wristband to free hands for scribbling down names and notes (such as plant descriptions or general impressions), as well as for picking up catalogs, brochures, and business cards of exhibitors.

Some experienced and enthusiastic show-goers bring along a wagon, shopping cart, or bags in which to haul home purchases that need protection from cold in winter and excessive heat in the summer.

Before making a purchase, take a brief tour of the shopping area to see what vendors are offering and decide which plants to buy.

Take the time to speak with sellers, asking questions about a plant's flowering season or cultural needs. In particular, ask what elevations the plants come from. There is no point buying an orchid originating from high in the Andes if you'll be growing it at sea level.

Orchid shows are designed to appeal to both the general public and orchid experts.

Buying Orchids

This extensive private orchid collection was sparked by a single gift.

The first orchid for many newcomers may well be a gift. It will probably be in flower or at least in spike, meaning the buds are about to unfurl, hopefully into glorious bloom. An orchid of this size is a better beginning than a seedling or offset that may not attain flowering size for a year or more. Many neophytes begin their orchid collection with a phalaenopsis, which can remain in flower for four to six months at home or even in an office.

Start with only a few plants representing no more than two or three kinds of orchids. Plan for success by selecting from orchids rated for beginners in the list on page 34 and among the individual orchids discussed in the Orchids A-Z listing beginning on page 96.

With more confidence, proceed to the intermediate and advanced categories. Fortunately, the easily grown orchids are most often available from local sources, particularly the chain stores. Orchids frequently encountered in such places include phalaenopsis, oncidiums, cymbidiums, and *Dendrobium phalaenopsis*.

Eventually, take a more sophisticated approach: a specialty grower or one of the many catalog sources. (See Orchid Resources starting on page 216.) The best friends and allies of an orchid grower could be the specialists who devote their lives to cultivating orchids. Avoid any suppliers of unknown reputation, those who offer collections of bare-root plants of dubious origin, and most importantly any orchid described as "collected from the wild."

Building a Quality Collection

After you have purchased a number of orchids in flower and noted which ones grow best, you will find some types hold special appeal. Novelty phalaenopsis, miniature cattleyas, heirloom paphiopedilums, or newly created phragmipedium hybrids can be fascinating.

Or perhaps you want to collect only orchids with yellow flowers or species native to Brazil or those known to grow in cool temperatures.

Whichever direction you choose, take advantage of available resources—read books and articles in orchid periodicals, purchase new seedlings and plants, and watch your own plants grow.

As the plants come into bloom, carefully observe the flowers, noting their color, substance, texture, and quantity. Then edit your collection: Keep plants whose flowers show potential and cull the losers, replacing them with new acquisitions.

Visit nurseries during prime flowering seasons to see masses of a single species or hybrid in flower. Take the time to study the flowers—color, pattern, texture, substance, number per inflorescence, size, and lip shapes. Be alert for variations. That first-bloom seedling that catches your eye could be tomorrow's champion.

At orchid shows, look closely at displays with award-winning plants, noting what types are taking home the certificates and trophies.

Better yet, get involved with an orchid show and ask if you can serve as a clerk. Clerks assist judges by pulling plants for consideration, writing records, and placing ribbons. Often, judges will discuss flowers and plants, giving the clerks a prime opportunity to hear the pros and cons of specific entries. While clerks are not part of the awards discussion, proximity to the judges allows for an insider's education.

To keep abreast of what's hot among the trendsetters, subscribe to *Awards Quarterly,* which chronicles orchids receiving awards from American Orchid Society judges. From the thousands of orchids that appear in orchid shows annually, only about 2,000 receive the nod of an orchid judge.

These volunteer judges evaluate orchids at orchid shows and at regional judging centers. The American Orchid Society has 30 judging centers, including one in Canada, where each month orchid species and hybrids are placed before the judges for their consideration. Plants that receive an award are described in detail and photographed in color. This information is sent to the awards registrar, who processes the data prior to giving it to the editor of *Awards Quarterly,* thereby providing readers with a catalog of excellence in orchids.

Watch for remakes. Often, hybridizers will remake a cross using superior parents. By using improved clones of the parents, they hope to improve the quality of the offspring, perhaps with better texture, substance, flower size, or coloration. Often the offspring will be superior to the hybrids made previously, providing you with an opportunity to improve your collection.

As you hone your skills, consider joining a specialty group where other orchid growers share a similar passion. Trading divisions, seedlings, and plants with fellow members and buying specimens at their specialty auctions are great ways to secure new types that will improve the quality of your collection.

In addition to flowering-size specimens, consider buying a community pot, or compot, a tray of young seedlings, to secure a number of plants at reduced cost. When the seedlings flower, you can pick out the best to keep, then trade the others or donate them to your local society's plant sale table.

Many orchid enthusiasts focus their collection in a specific direction, whether it's a color, a region, or a genus.

Building a Quality Collection
(continued)

ENDANGERED ORCHIDS

The orchid's popularity has had some unfortunate effects. When the Victorians discovered the beauty of these plants, a huge demand was created. At the time, plants had to be collected from the wild.

Orchid sellers sponsored plant hunters on expeditions throughout the world. These plant hunters sent back shipments weighing tons and containing thousands of plants. When one of these botanical conquistadors found a valuable species, he took every plant he could find, wreaking ecological havoc. Moreover, only a small fraction of the plants collected survived. Countless species became extinct. Although the number of orchids removed from the wild by collectors has diminished since the Victorian orchid boom, you still find wild-collected orchids for sale.

Discourage the gathering of wild orchids and their exploitation by purchasing only plants known to have been propagated by legitimate orchid growers, especially those known to be seed grown or propagated artificially. Avoid advertisements offering orchids described with the words "wild collected."

The greatest danger to wild orchids is habitat destruction, which destroys all orchids, not just the prettiest. It is estimated that billions of orchids are destroyed yearly by land-clearing operations. You can help protect orchids in their native habitats by patronizing nurseries that sell artificially propagated orchids.

BEGINNER ORCHIDS

Brassavola
Brassia
Cattleya
Cymbidium
Encyclia
Epidendrum
Oncidium
Paphiopedilum (some)
Phaius
Phalaenopsis
Spathoglottis

Cattleya Pumpernickel 'Stardust'

Masdevallia Angelita

Odontioda Susan Bogdanow 'Aalsmeer'

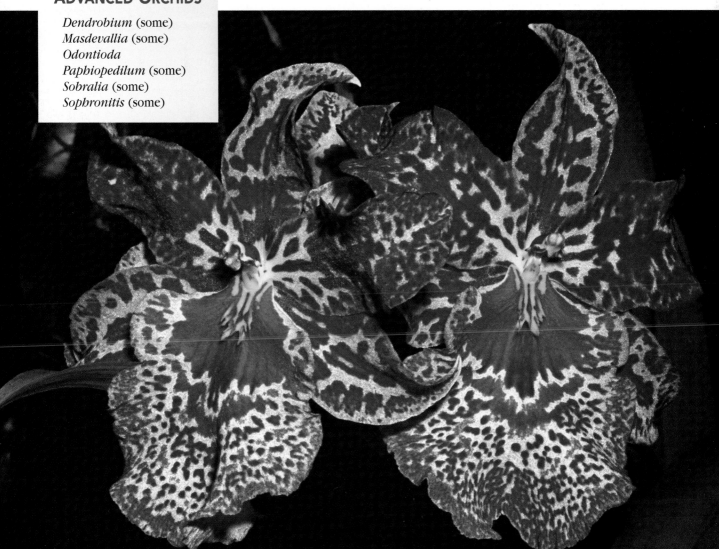

Expanding Your Collection

Bollea violacea

Cochleanthes discolor

Dendrochilum cobbianum

Grammatophyllum scriptum

After stocking up on the standards, it is natural to branch out into less common orchids. Having mastered the ABCs of orchid care, you can buy rarer orchids that will challenge you with new growing requirements, while offering distinctive colors and fragrances.

Among the thousands of species in the orchid family are dozens in cultivation that will pique your curiosity. Obscure orchids, once called "botanicals," are popular among growers. The following selection of 10 orchids—some of them rare, some of them becoming more readily available—is for the hobbyist ready to expand beyond the hybrids sold at nurseries and garden centers. Find more in Orchids A-Z, beginning on page 96.

BOLLEA VIOLACEA: This New World species is gorgeous, even when not in bloom, with fans of broad light green leaves. The waxy flowers appear from the leaf axils in summer, displayed on 4-inch-tall stems against the foliage. The flowers are dark violet purple and have a round shape. The wonderful perfume is a bonus. This species will grow and flower well in shadier conditions, such as those suggested for paphiopedilums and phalaenopsis. Keep the medium evenly moist (do not allow it to dry out completely between waterings) and use a relatively small pot for the plant's size. Native to the Guianas.

COCHLEANTHES DISCOLOR (syn. *Warscewiczella*)**:** The plant habit for this species is similar to *Bollea violacea,* though it is more compact—5 to 7 inches tall—making it amenable to windowsill culture, where its pert fans of soft yellow-green leaves are pretty year-round. The multiple flowers emerge singly from the leaf axils in late winter and are displayed well on upright stems. Perky blooms are slightly tubular with petals, dorsal sepal, and lip going forward, and the lateral sepals swept back. Base color is a soft ivory white

offset by a contrasting blue lip and petal tips. The medicinal fragrance is odd but not displeasing. This species grows well with paphiopedilums and phalaenopsis. Widespread from Costa Rica to Venezuela.

DENDROCHILUM COBBIANUM: Many orchids are almost ugly when not in flower—but not dendrochilums. These Old World orchids are ornamental foliage plants whose leaves create a pleasing backdrop for other orchids and blend beautifully with companion plants. *Dendrochilum cobbianum* is one of the most popular of the chain orchids—so-called for their chains of tiny blooms artfully arranged in two ranks on each arching inflorescence. The inflorescences, or spikes, develop in late winter from new growths. The plants grow prolifically and rapidly into specimens with multiple growths. Some forms are creamy light yellow while others have darker yellow, contrasting lips with a distinctive musky fragrance. This plant is grown under the same conditions as cattleyas, in a proportionately small pot with an evenly moist medium. Native to the Philippines.

GRAMMATOPHYLLUM SCRIPTUM: When mature, this tropical orchid reaches massive proportions—as much as 24 to 30 inches tall and equally wide. The inflorescences may reach more than 4 feet and are densely flowered like a foxtail with waxy 3-inch, extraordinarily long-lasting blooms. The typical form is yellow with distinct brown barring. Also commonly seen is the brilliant, pure yellow var. *flavum.* These plants require bright tropical conditions with 65° F nights and 75° to 80° F days. Growers in South Florida, Hawaii, and other warm regions do well with this fantastic display plant. Keep evenly moist and fertilize regularly to enjoy the flowers, which appear in the summer. Native throughout the South Pacific.

HUNTLEYA BURTII: This fabulous fan orchid grows about 12 to 15 inches tall, making it just a little larger than its relative, *Bollea violacea.* Single large, glossy flowers are borne on 6-inch-long inflorescences, usually several at a time. The 5-inch-wide

Huntleya burtii

flowers are light yellow with darker golden checkerboard reticulation, boldly offset by a white center. Plants are grown in bright conditions on the warm side of intermediate (no lower than 60°F at night and to the low 80s in the day) and kept evenly moist, whether in a pot or on mounts. The long-lived flowers are pleasingly fragrant. Native to Panama.

MAXILLARIA TENUIFOLIA: This orchid looks like a smallish spider plant with slender dark green leaves about 8 inches long. The 2-inch-tall dark red flowers, which contrast with the red-spotted yellow lip, appear in spring and summer, announcing their arrival with a delicious coconut aroma that can be savored from a distance. The species can be cultivated in a pot or wood-slat basket. The spacing of the pseudobulbs on the upright-growing rhizome makes this a good candidate for attaching to a piece of wood or cork where the rhizomes can sprawl about and create a mass of foliage. Native from Mexico to Nicaragua.

PERISTERIA ELATA: Known as the holy ghost or dove orchid, *Peristeria elata* is the national flower of Panama. Mature pecimens are large plants and can grow to more than 48 inches tall, with pseudobulbs as large as a baseball and with broad, palmlike leaves. Thick, upright inflorescences emerge from the new growth in late winter, to flower in early summer with 10 to 20 pristine 1-inch white, cup-shaped flowers whose lip and column resemble a dove. The flowers open sequentially, a few at a time, over a long period. *Peristeria elata* is grown in intermediate to warm temperatures and needs space. Keep it evenly moist and repot carefully to avoid disturbing the roots.

PESCATOREA LEHMANNII: Easy to grow and moderately compact, this fan orchid offers large, long-lasting blooms of bright color. Ranging from solid grape purple to nearly white, flowers are most commonly seen with a white background overlaid with grape-colored stripes. The purple lip is hairy. Choice clones are becoming more available through selective breeding. Two or three fragrant flowers bloom in late winter to early spring, beautifully framed

by the medium green foliage on this 8- to 12-inch-tall plant. It grows like *Bollea violacea* and benefits from being placed in a proportionately small pot to facilitate the frequent waterings this plant enjoys without danger of overwatering. A native of mid-elevation Colombia.

SEDIREA JAPONICA: Probably one of the best orchids for the home grower, this plant is rarely available. *Sedirea* is a true dwarf, with mature plants reaching no more than 10 inches across; it resembles a small phalaenopsis plant. The medium-length lateral inflorescences produce four to six soft green, 2-inch-wide flowers that are lightly barred with rose and have a sweet perfume. This species requires the same culture as a phalaenopsis and produces a bounty of flowers in early spring. Keep the medium evenly moist. This desirable year-round plant is handsome even when not in bloom. Native to Japan.

STENORRHYNCHOS SPECIOSUM: Most people do not consider this a typical orchid, although it conforms closely to the rosette growth habit of many terrestrials. It will grow well with phalaenopsis and is ideal for lower-light levels during winter months, as it is generally deciduous. It needs no care during the winter, not even watering. In spring, new rosettes will appear—often multiples on larger plants—with their attractive, striped foliage. Late in the autumn, a bright red inflorescence will appear from the center of each rosette. *Stenorrhynchos* should be kept moist as growth progresses, with moisture gradually withheld as the growth matures and begins to deteriorate. Repot as dormancy breaks in later winter. Widespread in Central and northern South America and the Caribbean.

Maxillaria tenuifolia

Peristeria elata

Pescatorea lehmannii

Sedirea japonica

Stenorrhynchos speciosum

Shopping for Beginners

Orchids are available from many sources, but most plants are purchased from flower shops, garden centers, big-box retailers, and orchid nurseries. Grocery stores occasionally have flowering phalaenopsis, cattleyas, dendrobiums, and cymbidiums. Plant nurseries and garden centers are good places for the beginner to shop.

The plants at local retailers may have been stressed by the distribution system. The leaves should be firm and unbroken, but slight damage is little cause for worry. Inspect any visible roots; they should be a healthy white with greenish tips. Lift the pot and peek in the holes in the bottom. The potting medium may be slightly decomposed, but you should still be able to make out the individual pieces. Roots visible through the drainage holes may be dark, but they should not be slimy and rotten.

A plant with an inflorescence (flower cluster) that is beginning to mature is ideal. One or two of the lowest flowers will be open, but the rest should still be in bud. Look carefully at the open flowers. Except for slight variations in size and in intensity of colors, the plant will always produce flowers like the ones you are seeing. The main priority, of course, is to select the flowers you like. But you should also consider whether the flowers are good examples of the species or hybrid. This will become more important to you as your collection grows. During selection, resist

An orchid nursery is one of the many places you can buy orchids.

any temptation to touch the orchid flowers. Oils given off by the hands will cause the edges of the orchid flower to turn brown.

Nurseries and plant centers

Begin by visiting nurseries regularly to see what new orchids are in flower and to develop a relationship with sales staff. They will be helpful in answering questions and informing you when new shipments arrive. Many nurseries restock on the same day each week, making regular trips a wise choice for the connoisseur interested in having first crack at the recent arrivals. Some nurseries offer free classes, advice, and Web sites with listings of plants as well as cultural recommendations.

IN THE BAG: Nurseries, garden centers, and big-box stores may have racks laden with orchids packaged in plastic or net bags. These plants, whether in containers or bare-root, range from young plants a few years away from flowering to specimens that could bloom within a year. Often, they represent newer crosses not yet available as flowering specimens at the same nursery. Many of the bags have color pictures attached so you will have an idea of the color, pattern, and form even if you cannot decipher from the name what the plant will look like.

When you get home, remove the plant from the bag and water it thoroughly. Once watered, plants that are potted can be added to your collection.

Bare-root plants can be cleaned (remove damaged leaves and roots with a sterilized single-edge razor blade) and potted up. Place ascocendas and vandas into wood-slat baskets, with or without chunks of horticultural charcoal.

Pot other orchids using a standard potting mix for the particular type of orchid you have purchased. Some bare-root plants also lend themselves to mounting on a piece of wood or cork.

FLORISTS: Many florists stock orchids as flowering plants and even as cut flowers, especially oncidiums, dendrobiums and mokaras. Although the prices for orchid plants in bloom may be higher than those at big-box stores and nurseries, florists offer services such as delivery (sometimes for an extra charge). In addition, florists will

Plants often come wrapped in plastic or net bags.

arrange cut orchid flowers as well as combine flowering orchid plants with bromeliads, ivy, ferns, and other foliage plants to create decorative baskets and other containers. Many florists, of course, still create cymbidium or cattleya corsages for special occasions.

BEWARE OF MIXED MEDIA

If you purchase an orchid—perhaps one in full flower—from an unfamiliar source, check the growing medium to be sure it is all of one type. Sometimes orchids for the mass market are grown cheek-by-jowl in small pots in a nursery where they are copiously watered and fertilized and pushed to reach flowering size. Immediately before distribution to the retailer, they may be transplanted into larger pots with a different medium, such as peat moss or new bark chips, added to fill in around the old growing medium. Water such a plant with care and repot it as soon as flowering finishes.

It is best to order only from catalogs that include complete information on each orchid.

Mail and Web Ordering

There are hundreds of mail-order orchid opportunities. They range from corporations with sprawling greenhouse complexes and sophisticated ordering and shipping operations to avid orchidophiles who sell a few plants to help offset the cost of their hobby. The big nurseries publish glossy color catalogs. Small firms may send out photocopied pages listing only names and prices. The size of the business does not necessarily determine the quality of its plants. Until you become an expert, you will need pictures and descriptions to help you make selections. See Orchid Resources on page 216 for a list of mail-order nurseries that publish informative catalogs and ship high-quality plants.

Many nurseries offer an orchid-of-the-month program, with selections keyed to your level of experience and your growing conditions. This system will help you maintain a high level of interest, excitement in new arrivals on a regular basis, and a steady increase in experience without acquiring too many different orchids all at once. It also helps build a collection with blooms all year.

Deciphering mail-order catalogs

The best orchid catalogs spell everything out: the plant's entire name, its parentage if it is a hybrid, its cultural requirements, stage of growth, plant and pot size, and the price. Other catalogs are more cryptic. In the case of hybrids, the descriptions may tell not what the flowers actually look like but how the breeder expects (or hopes) they will turn out. Purchasing hybrids that have never bloomed before is a game of chance.

Catalog writers use a number of methods for describing plant size. Most commonly, the pot size is listed. To complete the picture, good catalogs will include additional information to indicate what the plants are like in each pot size. "Blooming size" generally means the plant will bloom within a year of purchase, given proper care. For cattleyas and other sympodial orchids, many growers list the number of pseudobulbs. Monopodial orchids are commonly sold by the inch. Phalaenopsis plants, for example, are measured from the tip of one leaf to the tip of the opposite leaf.

If you are a beginner, limit your purchases to mature, blooming-size plants. These usually come in pots 4 inches across or larger. Later, when you have more experience, you can try growing less-expensive immature plants shipped in community pots (shallow trays containing one dozen to three dozen seedlings) or in small, individual containers.

Online ordering

In addition to mail-order sources, orchids are now easily ordered through sites on the Internet. Many orchid nurseries use websites to supplement their printed catalogs, allowing them to make frequent updates to their listings and to offer specials. Another bonus is longer descriptions that allow the grower to share more information about the plants' flowering season, size, and cultural needs. An extensive list of commercial growers is found at www.aos.org, with many of the entries having links to their own websites. Also available online are orchid growing supplies such as greenhouses, light stands and bulbs, containers, media, fertilizers, stakes, and labels. You will also find books, note cards, jewelry, playing cards, shirts, candles, fabrics—anything that would catch the orchid fancier's attention.

Just as you would for a nursery or catalog vendor, make sure the web business you plan to deal with is reputable. Ask other growers if they have bought plants or supplies from the vendor and if they were satisfied with the products and delivery. Avoid special deals that appear to be too good to be true. By e-mailing friends or asking questions on one of the Internet orchid forums, you can rate a nursery's performance and reliability.

Caring for new arrivals

Orchids may be shipped with or without pots, depending on the preference of the customer and the practice of the grower. Many people ask for plants to be shipped bare-root to minimize shipping costs and to allow them to pot the plants in their own growing media and containers. New growers may wish to receive their plants in pots.

When you receive a bare-root plant, inspect the leaves and roots, cutting off any damaged portions with a sharp, sterile knife or razor blade. Always use a sterilized cutting tool when working with orchids to prevent the spread of viruses. If you are using single-edge razor blades, use a new blade for each plant, then discard it. Wearing a fresh set of plastic gloves for each plant you handle is another way to prevent the spread of viruses.

Potted orchids are allowed to dry out before they are packed so they will not rot in the box. When you receive a potted orchid, inspect the leaves and cut off any damaged parts. Then water the plant. If the pot arrives broken, slip the root ball into a new pot. Do not disturb the roots unless they are badly damaged.

Many nurseries are experts at packing orchids, wrapping the pots with sheets of paper or plastic held in place with tape to keep the medium intact. Even greater care is put into wrapping buds and flowers; many growers gently tuck shredded paper about the blooms and then wrap them again to provide extra protection. Unpacking such a shipment can take time.

Finding bargains

If you are looking for bargains, join an orchid society where plants are exchanged in a spirit of appreciation and enjoyment; profit is rarely considered. At these meetings, you may find local growers selling plants at low prices. Society members increase the variety of their collections by trading divisions, seedlings, and keikis (offshoots). Some societies also offer annual auctions where bargains can be found among the higher-priced items.

Orchid shows can also be a good source of plants. Although the exquisite specimens in the display area will not be for sale, most shows have areas where growers sell plants at reasonable prices. Usually, the best bargains are bare-root orchids or recently potted divisions that are fun and exciting to bring home and watch grow.

While everyone loves a bargain, not every bargain is a wise investment. Sometimes growers are inspired to rescue discarded plants or sale plants that are no longer in flower and may have been sitting on a back bench at a nursery. These plants may be so deteriorated that the amount of time necessary to nurture them back to health outweighs any financial savings. When salvaging a plant, remember that it may be infected with a virus or some other ailment. Keep it separated from your main collection until you are sure it is healthy.

Online orchid nurseries can update their listings and frequently offer specials.

Growing Environments
AND GROWING AREAS

That lofty canopy is where most of the epiphytic orchids originate, up in the air where moist breezes blow and there is abundant sunlight. Orchids of one kind or another grow in varying conditions almost all over the world.

The first step in growing orchids is to look closely at the available conditions. How much light is there? What is the temperature range? Consider these factors first, because they are the most difficult and expensive to modify. Humidity and ventilation can be altered more easily. The amount of light, heat, water, and air that orchids require is described in this chapter. Use this information to determine the type of orchid environment you can most readily provide.

Orchid flowers last longest if they are in bright light but protected from sun shining directly on them. A shaded south-facing window is ideal.

In nature, orchids grow primarily in trees as epiphytes or in the ground as terrestrials. Those from the trees tend to make the best houseplants. Because they are epiphytic, their needs for light, water, and humidity are different in some ways from ordinary houseplants. Different, however, isn't necessarily synonymous with difficult.

Orchids' reputation for being finicky stems from a misunderstanding about their origins. The word "jungle" suggests hot, dank, steamy, and even dark conditions. Yet jungle has another meaning in context. Literally, a jungle is an early stage of what eventually becomes a rain forest, a noun coined in 1903 to define a tropical woodland with an annual rainfall of at least 100 inches, marked by lofty broad-leaved evergreen trees forming a continuous canopy.

Move orchids to where you can enjoy them once their flowers have opened.

Light

Like most flowering plants, orchids often grow and bloom best in as much light as they can tolerate without burning. If there are several spots in your home where you might want to grow orchids, the brightest of them is nearly always to be preferred. An unobstructed south-facing window is ideal because it receives bright light for most of the day and will usually capture enough light to carry the plants through the winter. In summer, however, a south-facing window can burn even the most light-demanding species. Some orchids will thrive in east- or west-facing windows. The duration of light is as important as brightness—two hours of searing afternoon sunlight are no substitute for six hours of diffuse radiation. Plants have a limit on how much light energy they need; any extra stresses them.

The direction a window faces gives only a general indication of how much light is available to the plants inside. Many windows are shaded by outdoor plants or roof overhangs. Outdoor light levels vary from region to region. Also, the color and texture of walls and other surfaces inside the window influence the intensity of light in the room. For these reasons, many growers shy away from imprecise

descriptions of exposure and discuss light in terms of a standard measurement, the foot-candle.

Light requirements

Measure the light intensity in your growing area using a camera or with hand shadows (see boxes on pages 45 and 46); then you can choose the kinds of orchids that will grow best for you. The ideal light chart shows the light requirements of some orchids described in this book. Notice that most of them adapt to light intensities in the medium range—1,500 to 3,000 foot-candles. Some species within a genus—or some of their hybrids—may be exceptions. An intergeneric hybrid (a cross of plants in two or more genera) may tolerate a broader range of light intensities

Just the right amount of light is important for orchids. In the left photo, on the left, the plant has received the correct amount of light and has medium-green leaves and is producing many blossoms—both signs of good health. To the right of the same photo, the plant has dark green leaves and no blossoms, two signs that an orchid is not getting enough light. In the photo to the right is the other extreme. This orchid was exposed to too much light and the leaves sunburned.

LIGHT TIPS

Light is a key ingredient in successful orchid growing. Too much light will burn the leaves; too little light—or light at the wrong time—will keep the plants from flowering. By following these basic lighting tips, you can ensure that your plants will receive the illumination they need to grow and bloom.

■ Turn plants occasionally to keep them from becoming lopsided. Avoid turning them when they are in bud; if you do, the flowers may twist at awkward angles to face the sun.

■ Move an underexposed orchid into stronger light gradually over a period of several weeks. Increase

the light intensity by no more than 100 to 200 foot-candles at a time.

■ Remove plants from bright light once their flowers have opened. Bright sunlight can fade colors.

■ Watch new acquisitions closely so they do not burn as they adapt to light exposure that may be stronger than they are accustomed to receiving.

■ If you suspect a plant is receiving too much sun, feel the leaves. If they feel noticeably warmer to the touch than the surrounding air, reduce the light intensity.

■ Keep plants and windows clean. Dust and dirt block valuable sunlight, robbing your indoor garden of sustenance.

■ Some orchids need periods of uninterrupted darkness to flower. Plants may be prevented from flowering by the illumination of a single table lamp.

Light
(continued)

than either parent. Before purchasing an unfamiliar orchid, learn about its light requirements.

If you already have some orchids, the most practical way to see if they are receiving the right amount of light is to look at the plants. When orchids are receiving the correct amount of light, their leaves are light to medium green and pseudobulbs are full and firm. The plants should bloom dependably if other conditions are also right.

When light is inadequate, leaves are unable to manufacture enough food for the plant to grow and flower well. Leaves become elongated, flimsy, and dark green. Pseudobulbs are soft or shriveled. Flowers—if they appear—are undersized, faded, and floppy.

At the other extreme, orchids that get too much light are often scorched. The leaves may develop a yellow or reddish tinge. Also, the excess light causes the plants to dry out. Although the plant may bloom, the flower buds and racemes may be deformed and the edges of the petals browned—a result of water stress.

Direct sun can burn orchids during the brightest hours from late winter to autumn in most regions and year-round in southern areas and at high elevations. Generally, plants with thick, leathery leaves are slow to burn; plants with thin leaves burn more easily. Phalaenopsis leaves, however, which may seem thick and leathery, burn quickly in full sun as do those of paphiopedilums. Cymbidiums, cattleyas, dendrobiums and oncidiums have foliage that will take large doses of sun if gradually conditioned.

Besides intensity of light, there is also the matter of duration, that is, the length of the day. Some orchids bloom as the days grow longer when spring moves toward summer; others are the opposite, blooming as the days shorten when autumn dwindles into early winter. For these, flowering may be prevented by any exposure to light beyond a 12-hour day at the time they are preparing to bloom.

IDEAL LIGHT RANGES IN FOOT-CANDLES

Plant name	Light range in foot-candles								Approximate range
	Low			**Medium**			**High**		
	500	1,000	1,500	2,000	2,500	3,000	3,500	4,000	
Brassavola				▓	▓	▓	▓		2,000–3,500
Brassia				▓	▓	▓			2,000–3,000
Cattleya				▓	▓	▓			2,000–3,000
Cymbidium									
Standard				▓	▓	▓			2,000–3,200
Miniature			▓	▓	▓	▓			1,500–3,000
Dendrobium			▓	▓	▓	▓			1,500–3,200
Epidendrum			▓	▓	▓	▓			1,500–3,200
Laelia				▓	▓	▓			2,000–3,000
Ludisia	▓	▓	▓						500–1,500
Masdevallia	▓	▓	▓	▓	▓				500–2,500
Miltonia	▓	▓	▓	▓	▓				500–2,500
Odontoglossum		▓	▓	▓					1,000–2,000
Oncidium				▓	▓	▓	▓		2,000–3,500
Paphiopedilum				▓	▓				2,000–2,500
Phalaenopsis		▓	▓						1,000–1,500
Phragmipedium					▓	▓	▓		2,500–3,500
Sophronitis			▓	▓	▓				1,500–2,500
Vanda					▓	▓	▓		2,500–3,800

Another consideration is spectrum of color in the light. Orchids use reds and blues, but not greens, which are reflected. Red is critical for flowering. A 50-50 combination of cool-white and warm-white fluorescent tubes provides the essential balance of red and blue rays for healthy plants grown under lights.

The most accurate way to make sure that plants are receiving proper light is to measure the light intensity with a foot-candle light meter. Different meters are available. Some come equipped with a separate sensor to allow you to easily read the dial while measuring the light from different angles. One-piece meters have the sensor built into the top of the unit.

Measuring light in foot-candles

A foot-candle is the amount of light falling on a 1-square-foot surface located 1 foot away from one candle.

Here are some familiar examples:

The light intensity outdoors at noon on a clear summer day in temperate regions may be as high as 10,000 foot-candles; a midday reading on an overcast winter day may be as low as 500 foot-candles.

The light intensity indoors also varies. The direct sunlight entering a window on a clear summer day may be as high as 8,000 foot-candles next to the glass but is usually closer to 4,000 to 5,000 foot-candles. At the same time, the intensity of light in the shade at the side of a very bright window may be only 600 foot-candles.

The brightness of electric lights can be deceiving. A supermarket seems bright, but the light intensity is usually only about 500 foot-candles. Because your pupils adjust so effectively to light, it's difficult to estimate light intensity merely by looking.

The easiest and most accurate way to learn how much light is available to plants is to measure it with a foot-candle light meter. Purchase a meter that can measure light intensities at least as high as 5,000 foot-candles.

Any camera with a built-in light meter will provide fairly accurate readings that can be translated into foot-candles.

Set the film speed at ASA 25 and the shutter speed at 1/60th of a second. Aim the camera at a flat sheet of white matte paper or cardboard, held at the level where the plant's leaves would be. Hold the camera close enough so that all you see when you look through the viewfinder is the paper. Do not block the light with your head, hands, or camera.

Adjust the f-stop (lens opening) until a correct exposure for taking a picture is shown on the light meter in the camera. Use the table to convert the f-stop setting into a foot-candle estimate.

For best results, take the readings at the brightest time of a sunny day, preferably in summer. This will give you an idea of the maximum intensity to which the plants will be exposed and will enable you to avoid scorching them with too much light.

The average light intensity (of long-term importance to growth and flowering) is more difficult to measure accurately, but you can estimate it by taking several readings at different times over a period of several days.

F-STOP	FOOT-CANDLES
f/2.8	200
f/4	370
f/5.6	750
f/8	1,500
f/11	2,800
f/16	5,000

A commonly used meter, made by General Electric, has a filter that clips over the sensor for use at high-light intensities.

You can also estimate light intensity using a photographic meter or a camera with a built-in light meter. Most cameras have light meters that measure light intensity in f-stops. See Measuring Light: Cameras on this page for simple instructions on converting f-stops into foot-candles.

MEASURING LIGHT: HAND SHADOWS

In the same direct way that using your fingers can tell you instantly about moisture conditions in a pot of growing medium, your hand can tell you about the degree of light reaching the leaves of an orchid plant. Position yourself so that you can hold your hand about 1 foot from the plant, between it and the window. If you see no shadow at all, there may not be enough light to grow an orchid, only to enjoy it while in bloom. A possible exception is the jewel orchid,

Ludisia discolor, which is grown primarily for its beautiful leaves and tends to thrive in less light. If you see a faint to moderate shadow, there is probably adequate light for phalaenopsis and paphiopedilums. If you see a sharp shadow, this indicates light sufficiently bright to grow ascocendas, cattleyas, cymbidiums, dendrobiums, epidendrums, encyclias, laelias, oncidiums and many other orchids.

Modifying light

If necessary, you can diffuse midday sunlight, add some shade, or otherwise reduce the intensity of sunlight on your orchids. Easily opened sheer or open-weave curtains may be all you need. Vertical blinds are ideal because they can be adjusted to allow the right amount of light to fall on plants. The moving bars of sunlight shining through the slats of a vertical blind mimic dappled light playing through the leaves of trees. Horizontal blinds are not as efficient in modifying light because the sun tends to strike the plants in the same band, over-exposing some parts while shading the rest.

You may avoid covering the windows with anything if you can move the plants back a few feet;

light intensity decreases rapidly as you move away from the source.

Artificial lights

Some of the finest orchids grow and bloom where there is little or no sunlight. Electric lights will brighten a marginally sunny windowsill, illuminate a bookshelf growing area, or transform a windowless basement into a tropical wonderland. Growing orchids under lights is similar to growing them on a windowsill except that you regulate the amount of light the plant receives by adjusting its distance from the lights and by varying the length of time the lights are on.

In some ways, electric lights are better than sunlight for orchids. Grown in the sun, few plants maintain unblemished leaves; grown under lights, plants can have perfect foliage. The cool glow of the lights cannot burn the leaves, and the plants grow more symmetrically because the light comes from directly overhead. Also, the constant intensity of the lights ensures that the leaves will all be approximately the same size no matter what time of year they are produced.

Orchids can thrive under artificial light.

BEST ORCHIDS FOR GROWING UNDER LIGHTS

Almost any orchid can be grown under lights, but the most successful are compact plants that fit readily under the tubes so that most of their foliage is bathed in bright light. Tall, light-loving plants such as vandas and the tall dendrobiums are hard to fit comfortably under fluorescent lights, although they can be grown under high-intensity lamps, which will provide enough illumination to induce them to flower. Plants such as phalaenopsis that have short foliage and long flower spikes grow well under lights if you train the spikes between and around the fixtures as they are developing. To get started, try any of these orchids in your first light garden:

Cattleya (compact hybrids best)
Dendrobium (compact species such as
    Den. senile and *Den. cuthbertsonii*)
Encyclia cochleata
Encyclia tampensis
Ludisia discolor
Macodes petola
Masdevallia (if conditions are cool enough)
Miltonia (species and hybrids)
Odontoglossum (multigeneric hybrids)
Oncidium (small species and hybrids)
Paphiopedilum (excellent for beginners)
Phalaenopsis (practically foolproof)
Phragmipedium
Sophronitis

Maximize the light intensity for your plants—it's impossible to overexpose them using fluorescent light. Use fixtures with reflectors. Paint the walls and other surfaces in the growing area with flat white paint. To flower well, orchids need to be placed with the tops of the leaves 3 to 6 inches beneath the tubes. Most commercially available plant stands have adjustable shelves. If you build your own light garden, suspend the fixtures over the plants with chains so that you can alter the distance link by link. Place small plants on inverted pots to raise their leaves to a level matching that of the larger, taller specimens.

Finding the right spot

You probably have several places in your home suitable for growing orchids under lights. If your garden is near a window, you may save on lights, as the plants will respond well to the natural light. You can create a growing area without sacrificing needed living space by using a basement, stairwell, or another out-of-the-way place. The concrete floors and walls of most basements will likely be unharmed by humidity or a little water. Some growers line the walls and ceilings of their basement growing areas with plastic to

maintain humidity. If the basement or other space lacks windows, a fan or two will provide the air movement needed by plants.

Lighting types

Fluorescent lights—the tubes used in offices and classrooms—turn electricity into

The bright, indirect light in this window area creates ideal conditions for an orchid collection.

Light
(continued)

When in bloom, orchid plants look especially beautiful placed within the circle of the brightest light cast by a desk or floor lamp. Place the flowers a safe distance from the lightbulb.

light more efficiently than do the incandescent lights used in homes. Full-spectrum bulbs emit light with a spectral distribution approaching that of sunlight. These bulbs give a more natural rendering of plant colors while producing the wavelengths required for growth and flowering. Trade names include Tru-Bloom, Naturescent, Gro-Lux WS, and Vita-Lite. Standard cool-white and warm-white fluorescent lamps are much less expensive and, if used in a 50-50 ratio, provide a satisfactory balance of light for vigorous growth and flowering.

The best fixtures for orchid growing are 48 or 96 inches long and hold four 40-watt or 74-watt bulbs. Aluminum fixtures resist corrosion and conduct heat away from the lighting unit most effectively. A fixture that is the plant's only source of light should hold four bulbs. Two-bulb fixtures will suffice for supplementing natural light, or they can be paired to simulate a four-bulb fixture. Four 40-watt tubes in a 48-inch fixture will adequately light a 2- by 4-foot growing space; four 74-watt tubes in a 96-inch fixture will light a 3- by 8-foot plant bench.

In addition to holding the tubes, the fixture houses a ballast, a transformer that regulates the power. Ballasts vary in quality; the better they are, the less power they use, the less heat they produce, and the longer they last. Electronic ballasts are the coolest and most efficient but also the most expensive.

High-intensity-discharge lighting

The latest innovation in orchid lighting is High-intensity-discharge (HID) grow lights. Their main advantage is brightness—a quartz HID lamp will sustain orchids with light needs too high to be met with fluorescents. Of the two types of HIDs, metal halide (MH) bulbs produce light in the blue spectrum, which is critical to the growth of plant leaves. High pressure sodium (HPS) bulbs generate orange and red light, necessary for budding and flowering. Most growers employ them in combination. These qualities are also found

LIGHTING SYSTEMS: PROS AND CONS

■ Incandescent lightbulbs burn too hot to be placed in proximity to orchid plants. Sockets for one or two may be configured into a fluorescent fixture in which 25- or 40-watt bulbs provide sufficient red-spectrum rays to boost flowering.
■ Any part of the orchid plant that touches an incandescent bulb will burn.
■ Table and floor lamps outfitted with incandescent bulbs can illuminate an orchid plant in bloom provided the flowers are at least 12 to 18 inches from lightbulbs.
■ 75-watt reflector floodlights and spotlights with built-in reflectors can be used in a ceramic socket and placed 3 feet or more from flowering orchids to show them off, adding drama and emphasizing color, shape, form, and texture.

■ The heat given off by incandescent bulbs has a drying effect that can be offset by placing the orchid plants on a pebble humidity tray or by operating a cool-vapor humidifier in the same room.
■ Fluorescent lights are more efficient than incandescents and give off relatively little heat. Keep orchid plant parts from actually touching the tubes, however, or they may be disfigured.
■ The utilitarian appearance of fluorescent fixtures at best can be hidden behind a valance, or they can be used in a room where their appearance does not matter.
■ High-intensity-discharge lights offer maximum brightness.

in Agrosun bulbs, which deliver a combination of blue and red light.

Mount reflectors at least 1 foot from the ceiling to prevent it from getting too hot. Because HID bulbs generate more heat than fluorescent bulbs, place them 2 to 3 feet above orchid plants. They can illuminate tall specimens such as dendrobiums, vandas, and epidendrums that are hard to fit under fluorescent fixtures.

To further reduce heat buildup, some growers incorporate the Hydrofarm Light Track, which features a motorized HID lamp moving back and forth along a 6-foot-long track every 20 minutes. Other modifications on this theme—fixtures with arm extensions that move in a regular pattern—illuminate plants uniformly while helping to avoid overheating the plants.

HID bulbs range from 400 watts to 1,000 watts. One 1,000-watt HPS bulb will generate as much light as 111 incandescent 100-watt bulbs. One 400-watt MH bulb will put out as much light as 20 fluorescent 40-watt tubes. If they are used 12 to 14 hours a day year-round, the HID bulbs weaken and are best replaced every 1½ to 2 years. Often, these bulbs are used by themselves (rather than combining them with fluorescent tubes). Alternatively, an orchid light room might be fitted with only HID bulbs.

Although it was once necessary to hire an electrician to install these fixtures, models are now available that can be put in place by homeowners. Buy the unit, hang it up, and plug it in, and you are ready to grow orchids the HID way.

Adjusting day length

Use a timer with your lights to set the day length for your plants. Some orchids require seasonal variations in day length in order to bloom. For these, you will need to adjust the timer every few months to mimic the seasons, as follows:

High-intensity-discharge lights can transform a room into a light garden.

TIMER SETTINGS BY SEASON

November to January	16 hours/day
February to June	18 hours/day
July to August	16 hours/day
September to October	12 hours/day

This schedule keeps the temperature in the growing area tolerable during the hottest part of the year and brings spring-flowering plants into bloom for winter holidays.

When growing orchids in living areas, remember that some species require nights of uninterrupted darkness for flowering. These light-sensitive species include unifoliate (single-leaved) cattleyas such as *Cattleya labiata, C. mossiae, C. percivaliana,* and *C. trianaei.*

Other orchids sensitive to night lighting include *Bulbophyllum falcatum, Dendrobium phalaenopsis, Oncidium splendidum* and *Phalaenopsis amabilis* A reading lamp left on at night produces enough light to prevent these plants from blooming.

Aside from occasionally wiping the dust off the tubes, all you need to do to keep your lights burning brightly is replace the tubes after they have been in service about a year.

Temperature

A maximum-minimum thermometer takes the guesswork out of measuring the perfect temperature for your orchids.

In nature, the temperature begins to drop when the sun sets and is at its lowest before dawn. Orchids are accustomed to this temperature fluctuation and, in fact, most of them depend on it.

Without a day-night fluctuation of 10° to 15° F, the plants will grow healthy foliage but may refuse to flower. Cool nighttime temperatures allow orchids to store rather than expend the carbohydrates they manufacture during the day—the carbohydrates they need to produce beautiful blossoms.

To make it easier to describe the temperature needs of orchids, orchid growers divide the plants into three temperature categories: warm, intermediate, and cool. Although the exact temperature ranges associated with these terms vary (some growers use wider ranges), the following ranges are most common:

WARM
80° to 90° F day
65° to 70° F night

INTERMEDIATE
70° to 80° F day
55° to 65° F night

COOL
60° to 70° F day
50° to 55° F night

Most orchids grow best in temperatures in the intermediate range. Given adequate humidity and ventilation, many orchids will tolerate higher daytime temperatures than those shown above—as long as they cool off at night. Thus, the night temperature is the most important temperature factor to consider when selecting orchids.

Although some determined hobbyists have used space heaters, infrared lights, and heating cables to create warm spots in their homes for orchids, such efforts are necessary only if you are trying to grow plants that require much warmer temperatures than you can naturally provide. It is more practical to determine what temperatures you have and then select the plants accordingly.

Measuring temperature

Unless you spend a great deal of time at home during the day and get up before dawn each morning, you may find you do not really know the maximum and minimum temperatures in your orchid-growing area.

A special maximum-minimum thermometer can measure these temperatures for you. These special thermometers generally have two sides; one side records the highest temperature, and the other records the lowest. It also displays the current temperature. Mount this thermometer as close to the plants as possible, but take care to keep it out of direct sunlight.

Orchid-supply companies offer maximum-minimum thermometers.

IDEAL NIGHT TEMPERATURE RANGES

Plant name	Cool	Intermediate	Warm
	50°–55° F	55°–65° F	65°–70° F
Brassavola	▬▬▬▬▬▬▬▬▬▬▬▬		
Brassia	▬▬▬▬▬▬▬▬		
Cattleya		▬▬▬	
Cymbidium			
Standard	▬▬		
Miniature	▬▬▬▬▬		
Dendrobium	▬▬▬▬▬▬▬▬▬		
Epidendrum	▬▬▬▬▬▬▬▬▬▬▬▬		
Laelia		▬▬▬▬▬▬▬	
Ludisia	▬▬▬▬▬▬▬▬▬▬▬▬		
Masdevallia	▬▬▬▬▬		
Miltonia	▬▬▬▬▬		
Odontoglossum	▬▬		
Oncidium	▬▬▬▬▬▬		
Paphiopedilum	▬▬▬▬▬▬		
Phalaenopsis		▬▬▬▬▬▬	
Phragmipedium	▬▬▬▬▬		
Sophronitis	▬▬▬▬▬		
Vanda	▬▬▬▬▬▬▬▬▬		

ADDING BOTTOM HEAT

Sometimes the only suitable lighting situation for orchids will be a place where temperatures are too cold in winter.

You may have an east-facing window with ideal light for phalaenopsis, but the room may be too chilly to suit them. A simple solution involves building a wood flat sized to fit the top of your plant table and about 5 inches deep.

Line the flat with heavy plastic to prevent leaks. Pour about 3 inches of potting soil into the flat and level the surface. Place a soil-heating cable over the soil, cover it with another inch or so of soil, and then top it off with a layer of gravel.

Place the orchid pots on the gravel and turn on the heating cable. Gentle bottom heat will help keep the orchids healthy even though air temperatures may be cooler than ideal.

Especially in older homes and apartments, radiators may sit directly under the windows where you want to grow orchids. This situation can be turned to an advantage by hanging a shelf over the radiator or placing a table that is taller than the heating unit over it. (Be sure to cover the tabletop to prevent damage to the surface.) Then outfit the surface with one or more pebble-filled humidity trays.

The more the heating unit is used, the more water evaporates from the trays into the air surrounding the orchids. Thus they enjoy both gentle bottom heat and a pleasantly moist microclimate.

(See Orchid Resources on page 216). They are a wise, moderately priced investment.

Modifying temperature

Many people customarily turn their thermostats down at night to 55° or 60° F to conserve energy. In addition to reducing the heating bill, this practice also satisfies the cool-night requirements of orchids. In a well-insulated house, however, the temperature may not drop enough. If this is the case, consider opening a window to cool the plants. Ideally, a room in which orchids are grown can be separated at night from the rest of the house by a closed door. The temperature in that room can then be allowed to drop without chilling the rest of the home.

Be sensitive to any hot or cold drafts blowing directly on your orchids, from heating and cooling units or from open windows and doors. Also be on the watch for microclimates, growing spaces where temperatures are cooler or warmer than elsewhere in the same room or space. Use a maximum-minimum thermometer to remove any guesswork.

TEMPERATURE TIPS

Temperatures can vary considerably within a growing area.
■ At night, the temperature is coolest next to the windows and near the floor. During the day, especially in fair weather, the air next to window glass is the warmest in the room. You can take advantage of these small-scale variations or eliminate them by mixing the air with a fan. When in doubt, place a maximum-minimum thermometer in the area so you will know precisely what temperatures your plants are experiencing within a 24-hour period.
■ Place orchids with lower temperature needs closer to the floor and those with higher temperature needs on shelves above them. Those on the top shelf will likely experience the highest temperatures.

■ Hang plastic curtains around windows to create microclimates that are cooler at night and warmer during the day.
■ Keep plants from touching windows in winter in cold regions.
■ Use a fan to circulate warm air or bring cool air in from another part of the house, depending on the time of day.
■ Be on the alert for any hot or cold drafts that may blow directly on your orchids.

Humidity and Air Circulation

Most orchids grow best in a relative daytime humidity of about 40 to 70 percent. Humidity is moisture in the air, not water on the plants or in the growing medium. Airborne moisture keeps plants from drying out in bright light and warm air, without encouraging fungi and bacteria that can infect wet plants.

A hygrometer can help you provide adequate humidity for your orchids. Below, an automatic misting system raises humidity around orchids in a greenhouse

Measuring humidity

An experienced orchid grower can tell whether the humidity is right by sniffing the air—or so some claim.

Hygrometers (instruments that measure humidity) are usually more reliable. The simplest and least expensive hygrometers have a dial that shows the percentage of relative humidity. Digital models are also available. A fibrous material connected to the needle shrinks and swells, depending on the humidity. More accurate (and more expensive) hygrometers are a combination of two thermometers. One of the thermometers measures the wet bulb temperature—the temperature of evaporating water. The other measures the dry bulb—or air temperature. By consulting a table, you can convert these temperatures to relative humidity. For most hobbyists, the inexpensive dial-type hygrometer is sufficient. Many orchid supply companies carry hygrometers. See Orchid Resources on page 214 for names and addresses.

Raising humidity

Relative humidity falls as the temperature rises. The simplest way to keep plants from drying out is to raise the humidity around the plants. Try growing them on water-filled trays or saucers filled with water and pebbles.

Choose trays that are watertight; plastic and fiberglass are the most reliable. The tray should be a minimum of 1½ inches

deep, filled to the rim with ¼- to ½-inch pebbles. Keep the water level in the tray within ½ inch of the surface. This allows the pebbles to remain moist but keeps the water from saturating the bottoms of the pots. The air circulating through this layer of moist pebbles provides humidity for the plants.

Raising the humidity by using pebble trays is not always effective—especially if the air is extremely dry or if there is too much air movement around the plants. The moist air from the trays may dry quickly or be circulated away too soon to be of much help. A solution may be to drape a plastic sheet around the collection. Avoid making it airtight; some air circulation is required.

Many types of trays are offered by indoor gardening suppliers. (See Orchid Resources, page 216.) Trays lined with sections of plastic grid instead of pebbles are easier to clean and carry. A grid pattern inside the tray holds the pots above the water. You can also place a sheet of ½-inch

Use a turkey baster to remove excess water from evaporation trays after you water your plants.

HUMIDITY TIPS

There are many ways to increase the humidity in a growing area. These pointers explain care of evaporation trays and give ideas for maintaining the moisture in the air around your plants.

■ Remove the pebbles from your evaporation tray every two or three months and wash them in a weak bleach solution to remove accumulated salts and algae. Keep bleach or algaecide out of water in the trays when they are in use.

■ Use a turkey baster to remove any excess water from the evaporation trays after you water your plants.

■ If you choose to mist your plants, do so only if they will have enough time to dry off before nightfall.

■ Group your plants to create an attractive display and humid microclimate, but avoid setting them so close together that air circulation is restricted.

plastic lighting-diffuser grate in the bottom of a tray to create your own gridded plastic effect. Also, diffuser grates are available at most do-it-yourself stores.

Plants themselves are effective humidifiers. By arranging your orchids in groups with ferns and other moisture-loving plants, you can raise the humidity and create an attractive display at the same time.

Ordinary cool-vapor room humidifiers and the more high-tech ultrasonic humidifiers are a reliable way to maintain humidity in a plant room or in the area near a plant grouping, perhaps in a fluorescent-light garden. Be consistent about cleaning the humidifier and replacing the filter as necessary. This prevents harmful bacteria from taking up residence in the humidifier and being transmitted into the air.

Misting, although commonly practiced, probably provides more enjoyment for the grower than humidity for the plants. If your plants are in an eastern window, a morning spritzing might raise the humidity enough to carry them through the bright morning hours. But in most cases, misting provides only five minutes of relief for a 24-hour problem. Try to mist just the foliage, not the flowers. And never wet the foliage near nightfall. It would dry too slowly and create ideal conditions for fungal problems. Check leaf centers or other crevices to prevent water from pooling.

Humidity and Air Circulation
(continued)

Provide your orchids with moving air that circulates freely by using an ordinary fan.

You can help maintain humidity by keeping heating vents from blowing directly on your orchids. Draping plastic over a light garden can boost humidity inside.

Aquariums

Growing plants in aquariums is another way to maintain good humidity. You can use an aquarium tank, buy an aquarium-type enclosure built especially for orchids, or make your own. (See Orchid Resources on page 214 for enclosure vendors.) Orchids of many types—flowering plants, mounted specimens, seedlings, and new arrivals—can be grown in an aquarium turned into a terrarium. Some units are utilitarian, with shelves and small pieces of wire mesh for mounting orchids, while other growers transform the interior of the case into a miniature landscape, combining the orchids with rocks, sphagnum moss, or small branches.

Whether you buy one, or make your own, be certain the aquarium is waterproof. Setting the pots on a shallow layer of pebbles will raise the pots above water and also allow the water to evaporate and add humidity to the case. You need a good light source, the correct temperature, and air circulation that can be created by including a small fan in the design. Much like Wardian terrariums used decades ago for ferns, these contemporary orchid cases alleviate the humidity problem while providing an attractive way to showcase plants, making them perfect for display in a living room or elsewhere in the home.

Air movement

One of the best things you can do for your orchids is to provide them with fresh, moist air that circulates freely. Gentle air movement helps your orchids in many ways. Moving air cools the leaves, allowing the plants to tolerate higher light intensities without burning. It also evaporates water from the surfaces of the leaves and the cracks between them, reducing the risk of infection by fungi and bacteria. A gentle breeze eliminates pockets of cold air that may form next to windows or along floors.

The need for ventilation is often emphasized in orchid books written for energy-conscious greenhouse growers but is less of a problem for home hobbyists. Still, if your home is well sealed, indoor pollutants from pilot lights, cooking, smoking, and aerosol sprays can build up to levels that will damage orchid flowers.

Obviously, the easiest way to ventilate a windowsill garden is to open the windows. Be cautious about opening them wide, though, as strong drafts can rapidly dry the plants and a gust of wind could knock them over. Double-hung windows, which can be opened from the top, work well because they allow air to circulate through the room without creating drafts directly on the plants.

If it is too hot or too cold to open the windows, circulate the air with a small fan, directed away from the plants. Ceiling fans are quiet, inexpensive to run, and ideal to keep the air healthfully activated.

The air movement produced by a ceiling fan mimics the gentle breezes in the leafy canopy of a tropical cloud forest.

An ordinary oscillating fan placed in the vicinity of your collection is an easy, efficient way to keep the air moving.

Orchids will thrive in a well-lit aquarium or grow case.

Greenhouses and Other Indoor Areas

Even in yards with limited space, you can usually find a spot to squeeze in a greenhouse.

Allow about 1 square foot of bench space for each potted orchid.

Most orchid enthusiasts begin with a growing area that is readily available, such as a windowsill in a kitchen or a bathroom. But as you buy more and more plants, it becomes necessary to develop growing areas that can accommodate a burgeoning collection.

For many orchid lovers, greenhouses are the ultimate dream come true, a place to pamper your plants while also providing a haven for you. If this is your idea of orchid paradise, you may be joining the 2 million other owners of hobby greenhouses in the United States.

Greenhouses are ideal to build on sheltered patios. Many are attached to existing buildings. Some stand alone. The New York Botanical Garden spent $21 million to cover 36,000 square feet of space with glass, but you could spend as little as $20 to wrap plastic sheeting

around your back porch. Your choice of a greenhouse and its location will be influenced by the climate where you live, the number and type of plants you own, the amount of space you have available, and how much you can afford to spend.

If you are handy and have the tools, you can build your greenhouse of materials that are readily available. Plans for greenhouses can be purchased from specialty bookstores or on the Internet. Or, you can buy a greenhouse kit with all the parts ready for assembly from one of the vendors listed under Orchid Resources on page 214.

A professional greenhouse builder will be able to erect a fully operational greenhouse for you. Check advertisements in horticulture magazines, look in your local Yellow Pages, talk to greenhouse owners, or go online to search the Internet for greenhouse builders. Request their catalogs showing styles and prices. You might also watch your local newspaper's classified ads for a greenhouse for sale or advertise to buy one.

Size

Before building or buying, think about how many plants you will want to fit inside the greenhouse. In making your plans, allow about 1 square foot of bench space for each pot. Calculate the size of benches required to support that number of pots, and determine the amount of floor space you will need.

For example, miniature cattleyas will need far less vertical space than tall dendrobiums, and mature vandas need even more head room than that. Plan for sufficient vertical space to accommodate the plants you hope to grow.

Location

The correct amount of light is essential to ensure healthy growth and abundant flowers. In June, the average light range on a cloud-free day is 10,000 to 12,000 foot-candles during the brightest part of the day. Orchids need 500 to 4,500 foot-candles, depending on the genus (see chart on page 44), or 50 to 80 percent shade. Position your new greenhouse in a partially shaded area. Otherwise, you will need shade cloths or lattices to filter light, fans to provide constant air movement, and, perhaps, air-cooling devices. On the other hand, if you live where low light levels are common, you may need auxiliary lighting for certain plants.

Where you position the greenhouse will influence how much light will reach the plants. If possible, situate a lean-to greenhouse along a south-facing wall to capture the most sunlight. Freestanding greenhouses have the advantage of exposing all the plants to about the same amount of sunshine throughout the day. However, a freestanding greenhouse will cost more to build than a lean-to. It will need its own utility lines, for example, whereas utilities for a lean-to may be borrowed from the house. A lean-to greenhouse has some disadvantages.

The building wall it leans against will be exposed to water and fertilizers, which can damage paint and wood.

Foundation

Your greenhouse needs to be built with care from the ground up, beginning with the foundation. Greenhouse walls ideally should be fastened to a solid foundation to prevent shifting. Consider pouring a narrow concrete perimeter base for it. Grass and soil inside the base may be removed and replaced with a layer of sand. On top of that, lay gravel, bricks, or ground cloth to make a floor. One disadvantage of a ground-level foundation is that weeds, ants, and slugs can find their way inside. To discourage them, build a low brick wall on the base to a level of 2 to 3 feet. Anchor the greenhouse's sides to that.

Materials

One challenging aspect of building a greenhouse is determining what materials to use. For the frame and rafters, use redwood or cedar lumber, which is less subject to rot. Many professional builders prefer aluminum frames. Steel, once preferred for its strength and permanence, is expensive and seldom used today. Glass remains the covering of choice for many hobby greenhouses for its clarity and permanence. Do-it-yourselfers often prefer fiberglass, which can be purchased in panels of varying lengths and widths and cut with shears to fit. The sheets can then be nailed to the frame. Fiberglass is subject to sun damage, so choose a brand that has been treated with a protective coating. Although initially more expensive, panels of double-walled polycarbonate are light and sturdy. They will outlast fiberglass, while reducing the cost of heating and cooling.

Use care when installing utilities. You can bring water into the greenhouse with a garden hose attached to an outside tap. But electrical connections for lights, fans, and heaters should be installed by an electrician using waterproof outlets and switches. Piping for natural-gas-fueled heaters is also a job for a professional. Contact the gas utility.

Greenhouses built with wood, unlike those built of metal, are subject to rot, but they have a warmth that steel and aluminum can't match.

Glass is still the material of choice for many home greenhouses.

Greenhouses and Other Indoor Areas
(continued)

Display

Think about how you will display your orchids. Planning can help you develop a design that provides effective growing spaces for the plants while creating a pleasant environment in which to water, repot, and enjoy them.

Choices are abundant. Wooden stair-step benches provide more space than flat benches for plants and let a grower observe and reach them more easily. Ready-to-assemble step benches of sturdy plastic are a quick, inexpensive solution..

A popular bench-building design involves concrete blocks stacked to support a wooden frame surrounding a screen of galvanized pig wire.

Builders of prefabricated greenhouse install aluminum frames with wire mesh fastened directly to the sidewalls or suspended from aluminum rafters.

Hanging plants may be suspended from electrical conduit pipes or plastic water pipes fastened to bench fronts or rafters. Mounted orchids can be hung on sheets of hardware cloth or wire mesh stretched onto vertical frames.

Whatever shape your greenhouse takes, there is one immutable law of orchid collecting: It will be too small.

Windowsills

Windowsills provide an obvious place on which to grow orchids. There your cherished plants can take advantage of natural light to grow and flower.

Think about where in your home you would like to see the plants growing—bathroom, living room, kitchen, bedroom, great room, study—and where it will be most convenient for you to provide water and a periodic application of fertilizer. With a small investment, it's easy to transform an ordinary window into an orchid garden.

THE RIGHT LIGHT: Providing the correct amount of light is paramount; insufficient light is the main reason orchids fail to flower. Choose a window with a well-lit exposure that offers bright, but not direct, sun. A northern window will seldom suffice. Choose an east- or west-facing window. Conditions that satisfy one orchid might spell disaster for another. If there is too much light for your plants, move them away from the pane or hang a sheer curtain between the glass and the plants (remembering to move it out of the way when less natural light is available). When light is inadequate, try another window or consider installing supplemental lighting to provide the correct illumination. The quality of the glass may also impact the intensity of the light. Frosted glass diffuses light and offers some protection from the sun.

SET-UP SUGGESTIONS: To make watering easier and impart a finished and uniform look to the window, invest in plastic trays that fit snugly inside the window. These come in various sizes and colors, and can be purchased

An orchid grouping complements this windowsill and ceiling display.

with sections of grid that will hold the bottoms of containers above the water, keeping the growing media from being soggy.

There are also trays that can expand to cover the width of the sill. You could even pull a table close to a windowsill to take advantage of the light. In the absence of trays, use saucers (plastic or clay with glazed interiors) under the containers to prevent drips and marks on the surface of the windowsill.

To expand the growing area, glass shelves can be fitted inside a window frame to add layers.

Hooks can be installed in the ceiling above a window to accommodate hanging orchids (choose hooks that rotate), each in a container with an attached saucer to catch drips.

A windowsill orchid garden can even serve as a window treatment, providing growing space for the plants and privacy for you.

SEASONAL CARE: During the summer, open the windows on warm days to provide ventilation. Better yet, take your plants outdoors for the summer. Move them outdoors only after all danger of frost is past and the evenings are warm.

Before bringing them indoors in the early autumn, inspect plants for damage and remove any insects you find on them.

To protect your orchids on chilly winter nights, pull plants back from the glass or slip a sheet of cardboard between the plants and the pane. Some growers temporarily adhere a sheet of bubble wrap to the glass to offer the plants relief from the cold.

If you live where cold nights are frequent or you keep the thermostat set low, consider collecting cool-growing orchids that will grow and flower at lower temperatures.

Watering may consist of hauling plants to a sink or bringing water to the plants. Slender coiling hoses, 50 or 75 feet long, are an efficient option.

LIGHT GARDENS

■ Ready-made light gardens for orchids are available. Multitiered stands and carts with built-in humidity trays and fluorescent lights come in a variety of sizes, providing an easy solution to a lack of light. Simple units consisting of a fixture and frame are designed to light a small table or shelf.

■ If you are a do-it-yourselfer, you will find it simple to build your own light garden with the components offered by lighting supply stores and mail-order suppliers. See Orchid Resources on page 216 for companies that specialize in this equipment.

■ The smallest practical hand-built light garden uses a reflector 24 inches long with two 20-watt fluorescent tubes over a 12- by 24-inch shelf. Suspend the lamp so that the tubes are 12 to 15 inches above the shelf's surface. Small orchid plants with beautiful foliage such as *Ludisia discolor* and *Macodes petola* can be accommodated in such a space, along with miniature gloxinias, African violets, begonias, and earth-star bromeliads *(Cryptanthus)*.

■ To grow abundant orchids under lights, install four evenly spaced 40-watt tubes in one or two reflectors 18 inches above a bench measuring 2 feet by 4 feet.

■ Another option is to install four evenly spaced 74-watt tubes in one or more reflectors 18 to 24 inches above a table or plant bench measuring 3 feet by 8 feet. This provides 24 square feet of growing space, equal to a standard-size bench in a home greenhouse. This configuration can be stacked as a double-decker (48 square feet of growing space) or triple-decker (72 square feet of growing space) on only 24 square feet of floor space.

Growing and Caring For Orchids

Orchids, like other plants, need to be repotted when they outgrow their containers.

Now that you have found or created a place in your home to grow your orchids—on a modified windowsill, under lights, or in a greenhouse—it's time to turn your attention toward their cultural needs. From potting and dividing to watering and fertilizing, orchids have many of the same basic care elements as other houseplants. Some special requirements, however, set orchids apart. Develop the variations that allow you to raise your orchids your way—and savor success.

You can begin with the suggestions that follow. Then as you build confidence, embellish them with ideas gleaned from local hobbyists and commercial growers in your area.

Be on the lookout at your orchid society for advice that might work for your orchids at home. Be willing to explore and discover new ideas—and experiment.

One word of caution: Try a new technique or product on a few plants to make sure it works before applying it to your entire collection.

Potting Orchids

Every orchid needs repotting at some point. Like other houseplants, orchids should be moved to larger pots as they grow. Repotting is also the first step in nursing an overwatered orchid back to health. Often, repotting is necessary before the orchid has outgrown its container because the growing medium has decayed, restricting the flow of air to the orchid's roots. In this case, the plant is often potted back into its original container with fresh medium.

The type of container and growing medium you choose will affect how you care for your plants.

Some supplies for repotting include clay pots, slat baskets, stakes, and pieces of tree fern.

The right container

Some orchids are grown in plastic or clay pots. Plastic pots are inexpensive, lightweight, absorb no toxic salts, and retain moisture. Some people prefer the natural look of unglazed clay. Porous clay pots allow the medium to dry out more quickly than it would in a plastic pot—an advantage if you are inclined to overwater. The salts in hard water can accumulate in the walls of clay pots and burn the roots. Among plastic pots are mesh-type pots that allow for greater air circulation, and others made from clear plastic that may aid you in viewing the health of roots. Plastic pots come in many sizes, including tall, narrow ones especially well suited to the needs of cymbidiums. There are also plastic foam pots, although tall plants may topple if planted in these lightweight containers.

Slat baskets, with their rapid drainage, are popular for epiphytic orchids. They're great for outdoors since watering can be a bit messy.

The roots of some orchids, such as miniature oncidiums, cannot tolerate the moist conditions of a pot. They grow beautifully either on slabs of cork, wood, and tree-fern fiber or on branches, as in their natural habitats. Colonies of related species are often grown together.

TESTING THE SIZE OF A POT

A new pot for a sympodial orchid will need to accommodate two years' growth. Judge by placing the oldest pseudobulb against the rim to see if there is enough room in front for the youngest shoot to expand. For a monopodial orchid, use a pot just large enough to hold only the roots without bending or breaking them. Be sure to avoid using too large a pot.

When to repot

Unless you are trying to save a sick or damaged orchid, wait to repot until after flowering, the time most orchids begin a cycle of root growth. Orchids repotted at this stage are quick to reestablish. The new roots in sympodial orchids are usually obvious, at the base of the new growths when the shoot is a couple of inches long, or from the newest part of the plant before the new shoot appears. New roots in monopodial orchids may not be as readily apparent, but they usually begin growing as soon as flowering finishes. In any case, repot when the new roots first appear. After the roots have grown more than ½ inch, they are easily broken during transplanting. Once a root's tip is injured, the root will stop growing.

This angraecum is ready to repot.

Potting Orchids
(continued)

How to repot

When you repot an orchid, remove all the growing medium from the roots, leaving them bare. This may seem to be an overly drastic treatment, but if you do not remove all the mix from the roots, it will continue to decay and could eventually lead to root rot.

You will need a sharp, sterile knife with a long blade, sterile pruning shears, a blunt dowel or stick, and the potting mix. It is important to sterilize all cutting tools to prevent the spread of viruses.

Before working on each plant, hold the blade in a flame, such as from a propane torch or dip it in a weak bleach solution. Another precaution is to wear a fresh pair of disposable plastic gloves for each plant you pot, especially if you are dividing it.

FIRST WATER: A thorough watering makes the roots easier to handle.

REMOVE THE ORCHID: Before you begin to remove a plant from its container, lay a stack of opened newspapers on the potting bench or work surface.

Each time you repot an orchid, remove a sheet of paper and repot the next orchid on its own sheet of paper. Using fresh sheets of paper will help prevent the spread of viruses.

Lay the pot on its side, grasp the plant at its base and tug gently. The root ball of a terrestrial will usually slide right out, but the roots of epiphytes often cling to the container. If the plant will not come out with a gentle tug, work a long-bladed dull knife around the inside, between the pot and the roots. Then turn the pot back on its side, grasp the plant as before and gently tug the plant out of the pot.

If it still resists—sometimes the case with cymbidiums in clay pots—wrap the pot in a few pieces of newspaper and break it by tapping it lightly with a hammer. Once the pot is shattered, unwrap the bundle and pick out the pieces of clay pot.

CLEAN THE ROOTS: Shake the old potting medium from the roots. Wash away the clinging bits with water. Using a sterilized cutting tool, sever any rotten roots (they will be black or dark brown; some portions may have sloughed away, leaving only the threadlike center).

Leave the pale, healthy roots intact unless they have grown outside the pot

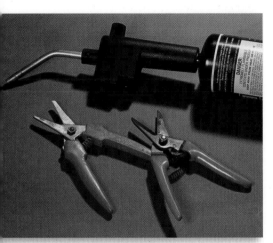

Sterilize your tools with a propane torch before working on your orchids. Or dip them in a solution of 1 part chlorine bleach to 9 parts water.

Center a monopodial orchid in the pot with the bottom of the lowest leaf at the bark's surface, ½ inch below the pot rim.

Position a sympodial orchid plant with the oldest pseudobulbs against the rim and the newest growth aimed at the rim on the opposite side of the pot.

POTTING TIPS

Potting an orchid lets you hold the plant, look at it from all sides, and prune and wash the roots. Here are some tips to help you master this enjoyable process:

■ Sift or wash the splinters and dust out of fir bark or tree fern before use. Otherwise, the smallest particles will settle to the bottom of the pot and clog the air spaces.

■ Always sterilize tools before working on each plant to avoid spreading viral diseases from one plant to another.

■ Before adding synthetic material such as plastic peanuts or cubed plastic foam to a pot, cover a few with water and let them stand overnight. Some material may dissolve inside the pot and cause problems for the roots. Some growers fill the bottom third of containers with plastic materials to reduce the amount of medium needed. The foam may create a lighter container, so this method is best used for orchids that are not top-heavy.

■ Avoid using ordinary all-purpose potting soil for epiphytic orchids.

■ Label plants immediately after potting them.

■ Bend and twist cymbidium pseudobulbs apart to separate them, then cut through the rhizome with a knife.

■ Place a plastic bag over a newly potted plant to help maintain humidity. To allow some air flow, do not close the bag completely, and cut a few small holes in the plastic on all sides of the plant. Keep direct sunlight from striking the covered plant; the trapped heat would roast it.

---

and would be broken off in repotting. If this is the case, cut them back to 3 or 4 inches long.

POT THE ORCHID: Sympodials. Hold the plant in position with the older pseudobulbs against the rim. Adjust the height of the plant in the pot so that the base of the rhizome is about ½ inch below the rim. If the new growth is higher than the old pseudobulbs, position the plant at an angle so that it is growing parallel to the bottom of the pot. Fill in bark or potting medium around the roots, firmly tamping it in with your fingers or a dowel. After

Settle the new growing medium around an orchid's roots by tamping and poking gingerly with a dowel. Your fingers are even more sensitive—and convenient.

adding a few handfuls, lift the pot and thump it back down to settle the bark. Continue adding bark until it covers the sides of the rhizome. Thump the pot again.

Monopodials. Center the plant in the pot (if it is tall, place a stake next to it at this time). Position the plant so the bottom of the lowest leaf is at the surface of the bark—about ½ inch below the rim of the pot. If the lowest leaf does not have at least three healthy roots on the stem below it, strip off one or more of the bottom leaves until there are healthy roots that you can anchor in the bark. Cut off the bottom of a stem if it does not have roots on it. Fill in with medium around the roots, tamping it with your fingers or the dowel.

After each handful or addition, thump the bottom of the pot against the table to settle the bark.

Continue adding medium until it reaches the bottom of the lowest leaf. Thump the pot again to settle everything in place.

SUPPORT THE ORCHID: Top-heavy orchids such as cattleyas need the support of a stake. Other orchids with large root systems can stand on their own. Metal stakes that clip to the side of the pot work best. Clip the stake to the pot at the back of the plant and tie the pseudobulbs to it using raffia, garden twine, or plastic-coated telephone wire. Rhizome clips designed to anchor the plant in the medium are available from orchid supply companies. (See Orchid Resources, page 216.)

Rhizome clips help anchor a plant in its growing medium.

Potting Orchids
(continued)

Raffia in a bow tie.

Staking

At its simplest, staking is a useful means of protecting a developing spike of orchid flowers. But when done well, it is a marriage of art and science that results in a subtly beautiful presentation at flowering time. Orchid growers use galvanized wire stakes in a variety of preformed configurations that suit the various habits and sizes of the most commonly cultivated orchids. There are three types made out of wire.

One type of stake is a length of straight wire, usually 12 to 18 inches long, with its top bent into a U-shape. The "U" holds the flowering spike. The effect of the stake is based on its angle and positioning in the growing medium.

A second type of stake is a wire with one end shaped to clip over the rim of the pot, above which a length of straight wire—usually about 5 to 8 inches tall—extends. The upper end of the wire is formed into a circle that can be up to 8 or 10 inches across. This circle is intended to cradle a group of mature cattleyas or similar orchid growths.

Another type of stake is actually a wire pot clip, little more than a horizontal length of wire, usually 4 to 8 inches long. It bends at one end to clip over the pot rim. This simple piece of equipment is used primarily to secure sympodial orchids after they are first potted, until the roots become established.

Then there are the stakes that orchid growers create themselves. Commercial growers use bamboo, which can be thin and reedlike or as thick as a pencil. Sometimes these stakes are inserted only to protect the orchid during shipping with no particular concern as to whether the size is aesthetically pleasing.

On other occasions, the bamboo cane that comes with a purchased orchid needs only to have utilitarian plastic ties or twist-

Three staking systems (left to right): wire, cane and raffia, and twig.

ties replaced with more graceful and organic raffia.

Be gentle when tying an orchid to a stake. Use a figure-eight tie, first wrapping the raffia tightly around the stake, then loosely around the orchid's stem.

Twigs are a popular material for orchid staking, and most people have a ready supply right in their backyard. Twigs are often cut and trimmed so that a "Y" or "U" already present in the branch can gently cradle the orchid's spike, showing off its beauty to maximum advantage.

When you are installing a stake, the medium often resists your attempts to insert it. Be firm but take care—you could hurt yourself or damage the buds and flowers of the orchid plant if you push too hard.

When you are staking orchids to help guide developing flower spikes, such as on phalaenopsis, insert or attach the stakes just as the spikes are beginning to emerge. As the spike grows, attach it at several points along the support, being careful not to snap it off. Taking the time to guide and secure the spike will contribute to the best presentation of the flowers.

For symmetrical growth, tie cymbidium leaves individually but connect them all with one long piece of raffia.

Growing Media

Many potting media for orchids are available. Over the years, growers have tried everything from exotic fibers to common gravel and from simple mixtures of fir bark and perlite to elaborate combinations of many ingredients. Despite the variety, most growers use fir bark alone or as the main ingredient in a mixture. Commercially prepared mixes are the most convenient for beginners, and many of today's nurseries and big-box stores offer several mixtures catering to the needs of the main groups of orchids, such as vandas and paphiopedilums.

Choosing the best medium

FIR BARK: Inexpensive and easy to handle, fir bark pieces have rough surfaces that can supply the right combination of air and water to the roots of epiphytic orchids.

Fir bark chips are available in three grades: fine, medium, and coarse. Fine bark (⅛- to ¼-inch pieces) is used for seedlings or mericlones and for mature plants with fine roots, such as miltonias. Medium bark (¼- to ½-inch pieces) is best for most epiphytic orchids. Coarse bark (½- to 1-inch pieces) is right for vandas and large phalaenopsis. Avoid ungraded bark, because the small pieces fill in the spaces among the large, resulting in poor aeration. Although fir bark can be used alone, many growers add coarse perlite to increase its water-holding capacity.

When you put fir bark in a pot, it is already breaking down. This is its main drawback. As the bark decays, the pieces shrink and settle in the pot. As the pieces get smaller, the spaces between them get smaller, too, causing the medium to retain more water and less air. The roots will rot if the plant is not repotted. Generally, plants in medium and coarse fir bark need repotting every two years. In humid, warm climates, the bark breaks down rapidly and may need to be replaced annually. Fine fir bark generally lasts about a year but breaks down in warm, humid climates far too rapidly to be useful. Most orchid growers in Florida use a more stable medium such as tree-fern fiber.

The organisms responsible for the decay of bark use a great deal of nitrogen. If there is insufficient nitrogen to accommodate both the decay organisms and the plant, the plant suffers. Stopping the decay is impossible, but you can easily compensate for it by using a high-nitrogen fertilizer, such as 30-10-10, to fertilize plants potted in fir bark.

Fir-bark chips

TREE-FERN FIBER: The second most popular potting medium for orchids is tree-fern fiber. Its resistance to decay and excellent aeration make it the preferred medium in Florida, where the year-round warm temperatures and high humidity quickly rot fir bark. Tree fern costs more than fir bark and needs to be watered more often. To alleviate these problems, many tree-fern users mix in some coarse fir bark.

Because tree fern breaks down slowly, balanced fertilizers such as 23-19-17 or 20-20-20 are recommended.

Tree fern is becoming increasingly difficult to find. Many tree-fern populations are endangered in their native habitats, inspiring the conservation-conscious orchid grower to experiment with alternative potting media.

REDWOOD BARK: Although it's similar to fir bark, redwood bark offers the advantage of decay resistance. Although it comes from California, most redwood bark is used in Florida, where it lasts even longer than tree fern. It is often used as a component in mixtures. Use a balanced fertilizer for plants in redwood bark.

OSMUNDA FIBER: This fiber comes from the roots of ferns in the genus *Osmunda*. At one time, it was the most popular medium for orchid culture. It has become so expensive that few use it anymore. Fir bark seems to work as well, is easier to handle, and is much less expensive.

An orchid planted in tree-fern fiber.

A tree-fern totem, plaque, and container.

Osmunda fiber

Growing Media
(continued)

Coconut-husk fiber

Coconut-husk chips

Charcoal

Aliflor

COCONUT-HUSK FIBER: This by-product of coconut processing is relatively plentiful and, when dry, lightweight, so it can be shipped efficiently. The pale reddish-brown color flatters the green of orchid plants and looks attractive in either clay or plastic pots.

Coconut-husk fiber works well as the sole medium for epiphytic orchids. It is slow to decompose. Balanced fertilizers such as 23-19-17 or timed-release 14-14-14 work well with coconut fiber. For easier handling, soak overnight and use as a potting medium, to line hanging baskets, and to wrap around the roots of epiphytic orchids tied to mounts.

COCONUT-HUSK CHIPS: Available in several grades, this natural product—from the chipped husks of coconuts—can be used alone or in a mix. However you use it, soak the chips overnight and then rinse them to remove any dust and salts. They decompose slowly.

CHARCOAL: Hardwood charcoal (not the pressed-powder briquettes you use for barbecuing) is added most often to cork or redwood bark, both of which produce acid. Charcoal absorbs the acids. It is also a common component of commercially packaged mixes. Like lava, charcoal collects salts and should be avoided if you have hard water. In Florida, growers of vandas and ascocendas sometimes place chunks of horticultural charcoal around the roots of the plants inside wood-slat baskets.

GRAVEL: Although it does not decay, gravel is rarely used because it retains little water and few nutrients, is heavy, and can tear the roots from plants when they are repotted.

LAVA ROCK: Plants growing in lava rock can remain undisturbed for many years because lava does not decay. Lava is well aerated and retains water well, though not as satisfactorily as fir bark. One disadvantage is its tendency to accumulate salts; avoid lava if your water contains large amounts of

dissolved minerals. Lava is most commonly used in Hawaii, where its low cost and high resistance to decay make it the medium of preference. A 20-20-20 fertilizer works well with lava.

AGGREGATES: These include a variety of products artificially made from clay or shale that have been fired to form nuggets of a porous material similar to lava rock. Two examples are Solite and Aliflor. Expanded clay is most commonly used in Hawaii, with a balanced fertilizer such as 20-20-20. Aggregates are structurally stable because they are inorganic. They come in various grades and can be incorporated into a mix or used alone.

PERLITE: This processed volcanic material is used as an additive to other potting media.

FAVORITE COMBINATIONS

Growing Medium A is typical all-purpose medium sold for epiphytic orchids. It consists of 1 part perlite, 1 part coarse sphagnum moss 6 parts coniferous bark (fir, for example), and 1 part horticultural charcoal chips.

Growing Medium B is designed for terrestrial orchids grown in pots, cymbidiums for example. It consists of equal parts sterilized garden loam, sphagnum moss, and clean, sharp sand. An alternative is to mix together by volume 2 parts of a purchased soilless medium such as Pro-Mix with 1 part bark chips.

Growing Medium C is a finer version of Mix A, for seedlings and orchids having delicate roots. Mix 6 parts fine bark chips, 3 parts sphagnum moss, and 3 parts chopped live sphagnum moss.

Perlite's low cost, high water-holding capacity, and decay resistance make it a popular additive to use with fir bark.

When working with dry perlite, wear a mask to avoid inhaling the fine dust, which can also hurt your eyes. Wash perlite before use to remove the tiny dustlike particles and make it safer to work with.

SPHAGNUM MOSS: This comes in several forms—long or short fibers, alive or dried—

Lava, plastic foam, clay pot fragments

and grades that last for different lengths of time. Live sphagnum is the best for orchids—and the most expensive. It is green and, if not overwatered or over-fertilized, will continue to live and grow after it is placed in the pot. It is used most often as an additive to other potting media, though some growers use it alone to set special plants in small pots or to nurse ailing plants back to health.

If you use dried sphagnum moss, it needs to be moistened first. Submerge the moss in a bucket of water and leave it there until no more air bubbles surface. Remove the moss, squeeze it to remove the excess water and tease the moss apart. To pot, tuck it in among the roots of an orchid. Wear gloves when working with sphagnum moss. It is known to occasionally harbor a fungus that can cause serious illness in humans.

CORK: Crushed cork is usually mixed in nearly equal parts with charcoal for potting orchids. It has a small but loyal following. Whole wine corks are too large and dry for use as a potting medium.

PEAT MOSS: Peat moss has a greater water-holding capacity than sphagnum moss, but it decomposes more rapidly. Coarse peat was once a favorite ingredient in orchid mixes. It is rarely used now because of its scarcity and its expense. It should not be mixed with tree fern, cork, or osmunda fiber, but may be blended with fir bark or charcoal. Coarse peat moss contains few nutrients and breaks down slowly, so balanced fertilizers are recommended. Horticultural peat is too fine and dense for orchids.

SOILLESS MIX: Many orchids sold at larger nurseries and in big-box stores are grown in soilless mixes that provide support and drainage for the plants, but no nutrients. Plants growing in soilless mixes need to be fertilized regularly. Soilless mixes break down at various rates depending on the ingredients used. Soilless mixes are sold under various trade names, or you can make your own.

ROCKWOOL: This artificial material has a neutral pH, retains water, and does not break down. It's made by spinning molten rock that cools into fine strands resembling fiberglass. Before using, rinse rockwool well. Wear a mask to avoid inhaling the particles. Keep rockwool moist once you begin using it because it is hard to wet again if it dries out. Although undesirable moss can grow on the surface of rockwool, a number of growers prefer it.

Coarse perlite

Sphagnum moss

Cork

Peat moss

Rockwool

Beyond Containers: Mounting Orchids

**Brassavola nodosa
growing on a tree branch**

One of the most fascinating ways to grow orchids is to attach the plants to slabs of cork bark or tree-fern fiber. Until the roots of the orchid become established, it is necessary to secure the plant to the mount with monofilament fishing line, twine, wire, staples, or even instant glue. Electrician's staples work well; their flat edges make them easy to press into the wood or cork. A layer of rust will soon form, causing them to blend into the background.

In addition to fishing line, staples, or another means of attaching the orchid, you will need sphagnum moss or coconut fiber, as well as a fresh slab of cork bark or a piece of wood.

If you use lumber, a shingle, or a branch, wash it to remove any salts. Always wear gloves when handling sphagnum moss. Before starting to work with the mount, make sure it has a hook attached to it to make hanging possible.

Start the mount by making a small, slim pad (about the same diameter as the plant's base) out of the sphagnum moss. Staple the pad to the mount and lay the plant's base on top of it, arranging the roots so they extend outward.

Fasten the roots to the mount, putting small rolled-up pieces of moss between them and the staples or wire. In humid or wet conditions, the plants can be attached directly to the slab without the bottom pad of moss.

Keep the plants lightly shaded and water them infrequently (see page 71) until they

10 ORCHIDS TO GROW ON SLABS

Brassavola nodosa
Dendrobium
Encyclia
Epidendrum
Masdevallia
Oncidium
Ornithocephalus
Psygmorchis pusilla
Sophronitis acuensis
Trichocidium Elvena

become established. This usually takes six to eight weeks.

Most mounts last a long time. You will not need to transplant the orchids until they begin to hang off the sides. Even then, if the mount is in good condition, you can allow the plants to continue growing undisturbed by attaching the overgrown slab to the center of a larger

one of the same material. If the oldest parts of the orchid plant begin to die off in the center, it is time to salvage the healthier parts and establish them on fresh mounts.

Mounted orchids generally do best if situated where the air is full of moisture. They tend to become too dry in the window of an average home. Better suited interior situations include sunrooms and other plant-dedicated rooms, window and home greenhouses, and conservatories.

Attaching sphagnum moss

Arranging roots on moss

Wiring roots in place

Wire mounting

When mounting ascocendas and other vandaceous orchids, some hobbyists use a piece of heavy-gauge wire for the mount. There is no cork or other organic support, just the piece of wire. Growers take an 18-inch length of wire and, using a pliers, create a hook at the top so it can be suspended. A length of ascocenda stem with some roots and a growing point is fastened to the stiff wire, with the orchid cutting positioned so its base is near the bottom of the wire. (The top of the plant should be lower than the top end of the wire.) Although there is no moss or other medium around the ascocenda, the plant will grow and flower when provided with the correct amounts of water, fertilizer, and light. Because the water drains rapidly away, plants grown this way may need to be drenched more often. (See page 71.)

Post-planting care

When you finish potting and staking any orchid or attaching it to a mount, move the plant to a slightly shadier location than it grew in before. Make sure the air is adequately humid, but withhold water or water only sparingly for one to two weeks to give the roots and stems a chance to heal. Water the plant less frequently than usual for the next two months to stimulate root growth, and fertilize it lightly when you water. After four to six weeks, you can move the orchid back into brighter light and begin to treat it as usual.

Watering

Once you put the right orchid in the right light in the right growing medium in the right range of temperatures, all that remains for a resounding success are the right watering and fertilizing practices. The one inviolate rule about watering is never to leave an orchid standing in water. Another is to avoid overwatering the plants.

Beginning orchid growers, assuming that tropical plants need to be kept continuously wet, often overwater their orchids. Although it is true that the forest habitats of many of the most treasured orchids are moist, the plants grow in some of the driest spots in these forests—in the trees. Because there is no soil to hold moisture for them between rainstorms, epiphytic orchids have evolved special roots that enable them to capture and retain the water that briefly falls on them. These roots are sheathed with velamen, a white, spongy material that absorbs moisture like a sponge from rain or dew and holds it until it is drawn into the pseudobulbs and leaves.

Orchid roots need more than just water—they also need air. When the velamen on a root remains saturated for too long, the inside of the root suffocates and begins to rot. Thus, while velamen performs a positive function for a plant on a tree, it can be a liability for a plant in an overwatered pot.

Some beginning orchid growers are alarmed to find their plants sending roots straight out into the open air. This is natural, especially for vandas, ascocendas, dendrobiums, and other epiphytes growing in wood-slat baskets. The roots may look a bit unruly, but they add to the plants' charm. Refrain from cutting them off, forcing them into the medium, or otherwise disturbing them.

Sharpen a pencil to expose new wood. Insert it into the medium about 1 inch deep and twist a few times. If the wood comes out damp, no water is needed. If it is dry, you probably need to water the plant.

When to water

There are many variables when it comes to watering orchids. Some types of orchids require more water than others, and some have rest periods when they should receive little or no water. These specifics are described for each type of plant in the Orchids A-Z listing beginning on page 96. Also, the type of pot and the growing medium will influence its need for water, as will the light intensity and other environmental factors. Despite these exceptions, a few general guidelines apply.

Epiphytic orchids with pseudobulbs or orchids with succulent leaves should be watered when the potting medium is almost completely dry.

To test for dryness, press your finger about one knuckle deep into the medium.

This orchid may seem to be in need of water. In fact, its roots have all died from overwatering. It may not be salvageable.

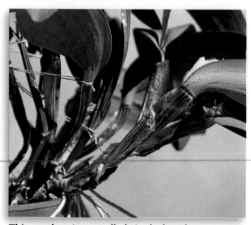

This cattleya's overall shriveled and shrunken state means it has been habitually underwatered. Gradual, slow rehydration could save it.

If it feels moist, wait a day or two and test it again before watering it. If it is dry to the touch, the plant should be watered.

If you prefer to keep your fingers out of the pot, use a pencil. Sharpen the pencil to expose new wood, then insert it into the medium and twist it a few times. If the wood is damp, hold off for now on watering the plant.

Take care when using this testing method, because inserting a pencil into the medium can damage roots. It may also be difficult to insert the pencil into some types of media, such as pieces of bark or aggregates.

Avoid letting orchids that lack pseudobulbs or succulent leaves, such as paphiopedilums and phalaenopsis, dry out completely between waterings. Test these plants before watering them as you would an epiphytic orchid, but water them when the medium is still slightly moist.

High temperatures, bright light, low humidity, and air movement will, singly or in combination, increase an orchid's need for water. By keeping an eye on your plants' growing conditions, you will soon learn how frequently you need to water them. You will probably find that you will water most of your plants about once a week in winter and twice a week or more in summer, especially if they are outdoors.

Orchids on slabs need a brief shower from a kitchen sink hose sprayer or from a hose, if they're in a greenhouse.

How to water

When it's time to water an orchid, water it thoroughly. If possible, take the plant to the sink or bathtub and liberally pour water through the potting medium. Even when you first see the water draining out of the container, continue to water more so the medium and roots are drenched. This thorough soaking will flush any accumulated salts out of the pot and will provide the even moisture that encourages large, healthy root systems. Use room-temperature water if possible. Cold water

WATERING TIPS

Here are some suggestions to help you master this all-important aspect of orchid care.

■ Before you water a plant, lift the pot to see how much it weighs. With some practice, you will be able to tell whether the plant needs water simply by holding it.

■ Water your plants in the morning so that the excess water will evaporate rapidly.

■ All other things being equal, plants in clay pots or small pots will generally require water more often than will plants in plastic pots or large pots.

■ You can tell if a pseudobulbous orchid is receiving enough water by looking at the pseudobulbs. The youngest pseudobulb should remain plump, but the older ones may shrink slightly between waterings without harm.

■ As a potting medium ages, the air spaces in it shrink, making it retain more water. Thus, newly repotted plants need to be watered more often than those that have been in the same growing medium for a while. In a collection of many plants, it will help at

watering time if those in aged potting medium are separated from those plants that have been recently potted.

■ Avoid allowing water to collect in the center of the plant, such as in the crown of a phalaenopsis. If water does gather, roll up a paper towel and use it to dab the water out of the plant's center.

■ If you dunk a basket or pot into a container of water, do not immerse more than one plant per vessel of water. Otherwise, you run the risk of transferring a virus from one plant to another.

shocks plant roots and can damage the leaves of orchids such as phalaenopsis. If the water in your area is hard—that is, full of dissolved minerals—flush the plants with distilled water (or rainwater) occasionally to keep the minerals from building up in the potting medium. Avoid using water that has been chemically softened—the sodium in the water will quickly kill the plants.

When watering an orchid, it is vital that water be applied over the entire exposed surface area, rather than in one spot. The media used to grow orchids are relatively coarse and less likely to wick water throughout the pot than houseplant potting soils that contain peat moss and other humus. Try grouping pots by size and kind of orchid. Sometimes a collection will grow haphazardly with little pots jammed next to big ones, where they can easily be overlooked at watering time (and possibly robbed of light). Similarly, when orchid plants of different kinds and sizes, in different types of pots—clay, plastic, wood slat—are mixed together on a table or bench, you may be tempted to water them all the same way at the same time. Such a practice may prevent the production of uniformly beautiful and thriving orchid plants.

Hydroponics

In the commercial orchid farms of Singapore and Thailand, orchids have long been grown hydroponically. Cut-flower farmers hang their vandas and renantheras from racks over a shallow trench filled with water and fertilizer. It's not high tech, but it qualifies as hydroponics. The long ropy roots grow downward into the mix, soaking up the nutrients they require. Growers in the 17th century discovered that plants can readily absorb suitable nutrients dissolved in water. Today, hydroponic agriculture produces a significant and growing percentage of the world's vegetables, fruits, and flowers.

Orchids lend themselves well to hydroponic culture. As epiphytes, they thrive naturally without soil. Even terrestrial orchids, which appear to grow in the ground, merely use the soil as an anchor for their roots, just as tree-bound epiphytic orchids fasten themselves to their host's bark.

In one form of hydroponics, plants dangle above water, as in the Singapore farms. A second method provides an inorganic anchoring medium, such as gravel, sand, porous clay balls, or rockwool, through which water circulates.

Plants receive a constant supply of all the nutrient groups they need in carefully measured amounts. Insects and disease agents are screened out. Repotting becomes unnecessary. Less water and fewer nutrients are needed, as these are recycled continuously through the system. With all their needs met with precision, plants can grow faster and, in the case of floral crops, produce more and larger flowers.

A working hydroponics system requires an investment in pumps, motors, pipes, timing mechanisms, thermostats, mixing tanks, and containers. For the homeowner, making an elaborate system work is dauntingly complex. Hobby growers with a few plants and a small growing space can opt for individual units that can be bought with all of the materials in a kit. Each unit holds one plant, and the containers may even come in different colors that allow for coordination with your interior design. These containers easily fit into a growing area and, because they need little attention, are a boon for those who travel and want to be able to leave their plants alone from time to time.

To learn more about hydroponics, search the Internet for "hydroponics floriculture" and choose among scores of companies specializing in the drip systems, bubbler systems, water and air pumps, plant nutrients, and net pots developed for the hydroponic gardener. See Orchid Resources on page 216 for vendors that sell hydroponic units.

Healthy plants are a reflection of correct watering practices.

Fertilizing

In the wild, epiphytic orchids obtain nutrients from the decaying organic debris that collects around their roots. Terrestrial orchids obtain nutrients from the organic matter on the ground. Neither type of plant absorbs nutrients directly from organic matter. The plants depend on bacteria to break it down and liberate its constituents in simple forms they can readily absorb. As long as the temperature is warm enough to keep the bacteria active, they produce a continuous, though dilute, supply of nutrients. Your orchids will grow best if you mimic this natural process by fertilizing them frequently with a dilute fertilizer solution.

Dry or blackened leaf tips are a sign of too much fertilizer. To prevent further damage, drench the medium with fresh water several times to rinse out excess fertilizer salts.

Types of fertilizers

Fertilizers may be organic (derived from plants and animals) or inorganic (derived from minerals). The nutrient content of both types is described by a set of three numbers on the label. These numbers indicate the percentages of nitrogen, phosphorus, and potassium—in that order—in the fertilizer. For example, a fertilizer labeled 15-5-5 contains 15 percent nitrogen, 5 percent phosphorus, and 5 percent potassium. Some fertilizers also contain trace elements such as iron and zinc. These are as important to healthy growth and flowering as nitrogen, phosphorus, and potassium, but plants need only traces of them.

The type of fertilizer you choose depends mainly on the medium in which your plants are growing. Orchids growing in bark need much more nitrogen than phosphorus and potassium because the bark decays so rapidly. The bacteria that break down the bark take most of the nitrogen for their own use, leaving little for the orchids. For this reason, orchids planted in bark should be nourished with a fertilizer such as 30-10-10 or 15-5-5. These formulations have the same ratio of nitrogen, phosphorus, and potassium (3:1:1). The first formulation is twice as concentrated.

Fish emulsion is a popular organic fertilizer for orchids grown in a greenhouse, but its odor may make it unsuitable for home use. Plants growing in tree-fern fiber or other relatively stable materials do well

An orchid such as this *Cattleya bicolor* var. *measuresiana* will have more and larger flowers if the plant is well nourished.

with a balanced inorganic fertilizer such as 20-20-20 or 23-19-17. These are offered by many companies; the best also contain iron and other trace elements.

Many growers alternate fertilizers, switching to a low-nitrogen, high-phosphorus fertilizer (such as 10-30-20) to stimulate flowering when the plants complete their vegetative growth. While not required, this practice may improve the quality and number of flowers.

Time-release fertilizers can be used when conditions are stable, such as for orchids growing outdoors in summer, in a greenhouse where temperatures are controlled thermostatically around the year, or in fluorescent-light gardens where the amount of light is constant and not influenced by the time of year or by periods of cloudy weather. Osmocote 14-14-14, for example, is excellent for orchids growing in tree-fern fiber or other stable materials. Read the product label so you will know when to re-fertilize; some pellets release nutrients over 90 days, others for 120 days. Scatter the pellets uniformly over the surface of the growing medium, avoiding a concentration in one spot.

Research is revealing new approaches to the materials and methods for fertilizing orchids. The knowledge gained from these studies may result in formulas that further enhance orchids' health and productivity.

How to fertilize

"Weekly, weakly" aptly describes the constant fertilizing regime that works best for orchids. It is also the easiest way to make sure your plants are adequately fertilized. Each time you water your plants, or with one watering each week, give them a half-strength fertilizer solution. (Half-strength is one half the rate recommended on the label for potted plants.) However, if you have hard (highly alkaline) water, add fertilizer to the water every other time you water. The alternating plain waterings flush out excess minerals.

If you are growing orchids on bark mounts, remove them from where they hang and dip the plant, mount and all, in a pail of fertilizer solution. Dip up and down a few times, remove, let the excess drip off, and then hang the plant back. If you are afraid of spreading disease by dipping more than one plant in the solution, an alternative approach is to spray bark-mounted orchids with fertilizer solution. If you have only a few plants, use a hand-operated pistol-grip mister. If you have many, in a greenhouse or outdoors, for example, use a pressurized sprayer dedicated to this use, one in which a weed killer has never been used.

How to promote flowering

Most orchids will flower on their own without any special treatment, as long as they are receiving adequate sunlight and proper temperatures. Some species, such as deciduous dendrobiums, need seasonal treatments to promote flowering. These usually involve cutting back on water and fertilizer to respect the plant's resting period (the period following a cycle of vegetative growth). It is impossible to generalize about how long the resting treatment should last in terms of weeks or months; the requirements of the different species and the conditions under which they can be grown vary. Generally, you should allow the orchid to rest from the time its newest growth has matured until it starts to produce new growth or flower spikes. For specific recommendations on the rest requirements of orchids, look under the genus in question in Orchids A-Z, beginning on page 96.

The orchid on the right has been fertilized regularly. It will also flower sooner with more blossoms than the undernourished plant on the left.

A pressurized fertilizer sprayer

FERTILIZER TIPS

Most fertilizer problems result from too much rather than too little fertilizer. If the tips of the leaves become dry and blackened, you may be overfertilizing. Cut off the burned tips with sterilized scissors, and flush fresh water through the medium to remove the excess fertilizer. If the symptoms are severe, repot the plant with fresh medium regardless of the time of year. Keep in mind that in the wild, orchids grow in a lean environment.

■ Fertilize year-round, but more when plants are actively growing. In other words, fertilize depending on0 the season.
■ Always use a measuring spoon when adding fertilizer; guessing leads to overfertilizing.
■ Hold off on fertilizing plants suffering from too little water or damaged roots. Water them with plain water until they recover.
■ Water plants immediately before fertilizing to prevent injury from fertilizer salts. Resist the urge to push your plants with extra fertilizer. Extra fertilizer actually stunts plants.
■ It is generally thought that it is better to fertilize orchids with nitrogen derived from sources other than urea. If in doubt about the source, check the label on the container.
■ Until you settle on one or more fertilizers that give you the results you want with your orchids, try products labeled specifically for orchids or purchase fertilizers sold by orchid specialists.

Propagating Orchids

Orchids can be propagated both sexually and asexually. Division is the simplest and most popular method for sympodial orchids and, because it is asexual, it is a reliable way to produce more plants of a favorite orchid that will grow up identical to the parent plant. Division is typically done at repotting, although there is no rule against impulsively offering a division of an admired plant to a friend if the orchid has multiplied to the point of being divisible. Depending on the growth habit of the orchid, the offset may be removable along with a promising set of roots without disturbing the parent. One of the advantages of orchids is that the offset, or keiki, can simply have its roots and rhizomes or pseudobulbs wrapped loosely in moistened paper towels and the whole placed in a plastic bag for transport to its new home and potting up.

Other ways of propagating orchids are keikis, cloning, and seeds. These more complicated methods are used by commercial growers.

Before repotting a division, cut out any dead, rotted, or broken roots. Remove old leafless, shriveled pseudobulbs.

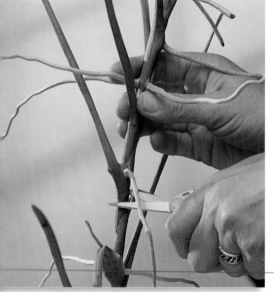

Propagate a monopodial orchid by cutting off the plant's top beneath several aerial roots and potting it up separately. The old plant will sprout again as well.

How to divide orchids

Many orchids are easily propagated by division, a process of splitting a plant into two or more actively growing pieces. At repotting time, dividing the plant is optional. If it is growing in a fine, symmetrical pattern and is producing new growth from several points, you may put off dividing it because it is on the way to becoming a spectacular specimen. But if it has grown in a straight line across the pot, died out in the center, or has some other defect, you can improve its appearance and stimulate new, more promising growth by dividing it.

The techniques for dividing sympodial orchids are different from those used for monopodial orchids.

SYMPODIALS: To divide a sympodial orchid plant, cut it into sections by slicing through the rhizome (the horizontal stem joining the pseudobulbs) with a sterile knife or shears. Leave at least three leafy growths on each section, preferably four or five.

Normally, if you are dividing the orchid at repotting to develop a specimen plant or to improve the habit of the plant, you will remove and discard all of the leafless, shriveled pseudobulbs and preserve all the healthy ones. The pseudobulbs supply food to the rest of the plant and may sprout new growth.

If you are dividing and repotting to propagate a sympodial orchid into as many new growths as possible, start by following the directions for repotting. Then, divide the plant into portions containing a minimum of three leafy pseudobulbs. Plant these divisions in separate pots of appropriate sizes.

In this case, however, retain the dormant pseudobulbs you removed from the active growths; these can be used to make new plants. Strip away any old leaf bases and plant the pseudobulbs (also called back-bulbs) in moist, live sphagnum moss or fine bark with the "eyes" (dormant buds) above the surface of the medium. Place them in a warm area and keep the moss or bark moist but not soggy. When the buds sprout new growth, gradually acclimate the plants to the growing conditions of the mature plants. They will reach blooming size in one to three years.

Old pseudobulbs can be rehabilitated in any growing situation where temperatures are comfortably warm (65° to 80° F) and light is bright but there is not much direct sun. A warm fluorescent-light garden where the air is moist can be ideal, as would a propagation corner set aside in a home greenhouse.

SIMILAR ORCHIDS: Paphiopedilums lack pseudobulbs, but their growths are connected by a rhizome. Divide paphiopedilums in the same manner

as you would a sympodial with pseudobulbs, cutting through the rhizome to create divisions with at least three leafy growths each.

Two orchids that are grown for their beautiful leaves, *Ludisia discolor* and *Macodes petola,* are described as terrestrial and growing from creeping rhizomes. Neither is called "sympodial," though technically they may be. Pieces of stem from ludisias, if broken off and inserted in live sphagnum moss and perlite, and kept moist and in high humidity, will root and form new plants. This is unusual for an orchid but shows the possibilities within this varied family.

MONOPODIALS: Because sympodial orchids multiply into clumps that resemble common garden plants such as bearded iris, they often seem easier to propagate than monopodial orchids, such as vandas and ascocentrums. However, monopodials can also be multiplied in a variety of ways. Determine which to use by observing what is going on with each plant.

Typically, an older monopodial plant will grow tall and somewhat leggy with a portion of leafless stem toward its bottom. The plant can be shortened by cutting off its top immediately below a node with well-developed aerial roots (use a sterilized cutting tool). The upper part is then potted separately while the old plant, though leafless or nearly so, is returned to where it has been growing. It will usually produce new growth at the top of the cut stem, which you can later remove and plant. Or, it may sprout new growth at the base of the stem. If that happens, cut off the old stem once the new growth is well established.

If an older, leggy monopodial orchid plant is lacking aerial roots, try air-layering: Wrap a handful of moist, live sphagnum moss, or thoroughly moistened dry sphagnum moss, around a portion of the bare stem, covering at least two or three nodes where leaves once grew. Enclose the moss in plastic. When roots have begun to grow actively into the moss, cut the stem directly beneath the air-layer and pot the plant.

When to divide

Avoid dividing and repotting an orchid while it is actively growing, in the process of sending up flower spikes, or flowering. The ideal moment for dividing an orchid is at the outset of a new growing season, when the new roots are barely beginning to appear. Orchids reach the perfect stage for repotting at different times. Some are better repotted in the autumn, others in late winter or spring. When you attain a sizable collection, the differing needs of orchids will help you spread your work load through the seasons.

If you find it necessary to repot an orchid after it is well along in new growth or a spike has begun to emerge, proceed with caution: New shoots on orchids, whether leaves or flowers, are extremely tender and vulnerable to the slightest bruise or misplaced movement. It is almost impossible to keep from breaking off a part if you try to divide and repot an orchid that has advanced into fully active growth.

Young orchid plants often benefit from being moved to a pot that is a size or two larger at the beginning of each growing season. Most mature orchids need repotting only once every two years, or before the growing medium seriously decomposes. Cymbidiums and restrepias are examples of orchids that may require repotting as infrequently as once in three or four years. The leafy calanthes and phaius may benefit from repotting almost every year.

This sympodial orchid has been in the same pot for so long that it has multiplied around the edges. The dead center indicates a need for dividing and repotting.

When a sympodial orchid has outgrown its pot, it needs dividing into as many as three or even six new plants to prevent long-term decline.

A sympodial orchid that has grown in an almost straight line across the pot can be divided and repotted to produce a more attractive, rounded plant.

Propagating Orchids
(continued)

Repotting records

It is important to keep records for each orchid plant with details of its repotting. Use indelible ink on a label placed in the pot. If you are a meticulous record keeper, further notes may be kept by assigning a master number to each orchid plant that corresponds to a number kept in a notebook or in a computer data file. In your database, you can list the orchid's full name, the date it was obtained, from whom, and any other information you may have gleaned about it. Computer programs are available for generating labels and maintaining data for an orchid collection, such as when a plant was acquired, repotted and flowered, as well as other details. Some growers still document such information in a notebook or on index cards, with each plant in the collection being represented by its own card.

The records you keep in a notebook or your computer are likely to be more reliable than what is placed in the pot. Plastic labels grow brittle from exposure to sunlight and hot and cold temperatures. Typically, one will snap in two when you are busy caring for the orchid. In haste, you push the two pieces together between the growing medium and the wall of the pot. Before long, unless you are highly disciplined in caring for your growing area, the pieces will become separated. You then have to become something of a sleuth to figure out everything you would like to know about the orchid's family tree. Assigning a number to the orchid will make it easier to keep track of the plant. You may even write the number on the bottom of the pot with a bold, permanent marker. The ultra-fine-point permanent markers that many growers use

SEPARATING AIRBORNE PLANTS

One of the marvels of monopodial orchids such as vandas, ascocendas, ascocentrums, and trudelias is that mature plants or those with damaged growing tips will often sprout plantlets along the main stems. These resemble the keikis associated with phalaenopsis in that they form new plants with leaves and roots in the air on the old stems. Because they are genetically identical to the parent plant, these offsets (often called offshoots) will have the same characteristics—such as flower color, substance, number per spike—important when propagating a named and awarded cultivar.

When these offsets are large enough to handle, with at least 2-inch-long roots, they can be cut from the parent stem with a sterilized knife or single-edge razor blade or merely removed by hand with a slight twisting or downward movement. Then, the plantlet is ready to be set into its own small pot of fresh growing medium. It will likely reach flowering size in one to three years, and the flowers will be exactly like those of the parent plant. The ideal time to remove such an offset from a monopodial orchid

is at the beginning of the most active growing season, usually in late winter or early spring. The parent may yield more offsets later if it is encouraged to grow.

Sympodial orchids such as epidendrums and dendrobiums often produce new offsets that stand above the old growths, with their roots extending down all around. In the case of dendrobiums, platelets form along the old canes. In fact, if nobile-type dendrobiums are haphazardly cared for in the autumn—watered when they should be dry or kept warm when they need to be cool—the flower buds will often abort and become new plants. When these growths have a promising set of roots and the leaves are expanding rapidly, they can be cut or broken from the parent and potted separately. Late winter and spring are usually the times to take advantage of these growths, although they can be successful at almost any season in a fluorescent-light garden where temperatures and humidity are always favorable. They will reach flowering size in about two seasons, and the offsets will produce leaves and flowers exactly like those of the plant from which they were taken.

are less reliable for labels. Although the ink is indelible, repeated exposure to the elements fades the ink over the months, until your writing becomes illegible.

Avoid overcrowding

One of the most fundamental rules for success in developing an orchid collection is one you may rarely find elsewhere: You must be disciplined about the number of plants you try to house in the space you have. Many collections have been spoiled by overcrowding. Overcrowding thwarts air circulation, keeps adequate light from reaching some specimens, prevents the orchid plants from developing symmetrically, and encourages insect pests and diseases. The work involved with caring for too many plants can also have a depressing effect on the orchid grower.

There are two main ways to end up with too many orchids. One is that you buy indiscriminately and end up with excess plants in the autumn, when all frost-tender plants must come inside. The other is that you cannot bear to discard any divisions or keikis when repotting, staking, and grooming. If you want a beautiful and soul-satisfying collection of orchids, you must discipline yourself to buy only those plants you truly want. Refrain from acquiring one more plant unless you have a place where it will have the chance of growing to perfection. You can control the size of your collection by periodic culling, taking excess plants to your plant society's sale table, or giving them to budding orchid growers.

Another practice that will help you have a successful, pleasing collection is to arrange orchids of one kind together, as well as to arrange them by type and size of pot. These practices are visually calming in their repetitiveness and help you give better care to your orchids. If different kinds and sizes are mixed together, the hodgepodge is visually chaotic, and proper care is almost impossible, especially when it comes to watering and fertilizing.

You will enjoy the work of dividing and repotting your orchids more if you organize a potting bench that suits your height and work habits. Back and shoulder aches as well as tendonitis (tennis elbow) are aggravated by work surfaces that are mere inches too high or too low.

The quality of your work and the pleasure you take in it will also be enhanced by having good light and, if you need it, a magnifying glass. Air circulation and a pleasant temperature help create a productive work area. Add to these basics a supply of clean, fresh pots in different sizes, growing media, staking and tying materials, sterilized shears and single-edge razor blades, plastic gloves, and a supply of newspapers.

Keikis

Offshoots, commonly called keikis (Hawaiian for children, pronounced key-keys), are small plants produced at the base or along the stems of monopodials, or from the pseudobulbs of some sympodials. The leaves of keikis form first, followed by the roots. When the roots are between 1 and 2 inches long, twist or cut the keikis off and plant them separately in fine bark. Under good growing conditions, a keiki will reach flowering size within two years. Phalaenopsis plants sprout keikis from buds along the flower stem. Because they do this commonly, it is a capability associated more often with them rather than the orchid world at large. These fledgling plants can be removed from the parent phalaenopsis when they have well-developed roots. Treat them like other keiki types. If the roots are slow to develop, encourage them by bending the flower stem down and planting the keikis in a pot of bark. Once the keikis have rooted into the bark, sever them from the flower stem with a sterilized cutting tool, using a freshly sterilized tool for each keiki. The plant will rapidly develop.

Although keikis provide a good way to propagate plants, their formation may indicate the parent

A new orchid can be propagated from a keiki.

Using sterilized pruners, cut or break a keiki, or offshoot, from the stem of a phalaenopsis when it is well-formed.

Set the keiki in fresh potting mix.

Propagating Orchids
(continued)

Cut off at the base a mature dendrobium cane that has not flowered.

Cut the cane into 4- to 6-inch sections, each with two or three nodes where leaves once grew.

plant is under stress. If one plant produces several keikis or multiple plants in your collection grow these offshoots, check your cultural conditions to be sure you are providing a stress-free environment. Sometimes the production of keikis indicates changes are needed in your plant-care regimen to meet the plant's needs.

Cloning

The techniques of propagating by division and by keikis work on a small scale. They are too limited for commercial nurseries that need to produce as many plants as possible as quickly as possible. Cloning (usually referred to as "mericloning'" or "meristemming'") is a tissue-culture technique that allows growers to produce thousands of plants from a single specimen.

The two most important events in the 20th century world of orchids were the discovery that seeds could be grown in a sterile agar solution and the advent of tissue culturing. Before these two events, orchids were propagated so slowly and so mysteriously that there was little likelihood of their becoming one of the world's most popular flowers, as they are today. Fine orchids would still be rare and expensive.

Although mericloning is complicated and requires some expensive equipment, the basics are fascinating and worth knowing. Most hybrid plants are produced this way, starting out as tiny lumps of tissue swirling in flasks of sterile nutrient solution.

To start the process, the plant is taken to an antiseptically clean laboratory where the one shoot tip is removed. Working with a scalpel and microscope in a clean room designed to exclude airborne fungi and bacteria, a technician carefully strips the embryonic leaves from the shoot tip. Removing the tiny leaves reveals the meristem, a primal lump of actively growing cells less than ½ millimeter in diameter. Meristems are like embryos, capable of growing and changing into the cells that form leaves, stems, roots, and flowers.

The meristem is placed in a flask of nutrient solution, which is then put into a climate-controlled chamber where it is gently agitated by a machine. The lump grows other lumps, which are removed and placed in other flasks. These lumps generate more lumps, which are also removed and put into flasks. This process of orchid fission continues until hundreds, sometimes thousands, of embryonic orchids are swirling in flasks.

Dip stem cuttings of dendrobium in fungicide before laying them horizontally on sterile sphagnum moss to root.

greater vigor, more compact growth, or better foliage. All of these possibilities are taken into consideration before an orchid grower goes to the expense of meristemming. Among the thousands of plants propagated from a single meristem, one may show a variation, perhaps in flower color, substance, or number of flowers per inflorescence. Although rare, these variations offer collectors a chance their new plant may develop into something new and worthwhile.

Orchids from flasks

Some nurseries offer flasks of orchid seedlings growing in nutrient jelly (sterile agar). Although they are relatively inexpensive, they are extremely tender and a challenge for even a veteran orchid grower. If, however, you have a greenhouse or space under fluorescent lights, you may find it rewarding to obtain a flask of seedlings and grow them, transplanting them first to community pots, then to individual pots. It may take three to five years for the first blooms to appear. Depending on the cross, it is possible you will find a winner among your flasklings.

While meristemming has been produced, they are planted into flasks containing solid nutrient medium. There they develop into tiny plants with leaves, stems, and roots. Eventually the plants grow large enough to be transplanted into the open air. Several years later, these clones may be found flowering on windowsills and in greenhouses around the world.

The practice of meristemming has led to a new way of selling orchids. Typically, a flowering specimen will be displayed in the greenhouse sales area surrounded by myriad small pots of clones. While the flowering plant is for display—or sale only at a high price—the clones are reasonably priced. The purchaser can safely assume that most will grow to be as fine as the parent.

Mericlones of an orchid species are often made from a choice selection that is finer than a common example of the type. It may have larger and more numerous flowers,

While mericloned orchids are almost always from superior parents, orchid seedlings result from sexual propagation and can be anywhere on the spectrum between inferior and extraordinary.

Sprout tiny seeds in flasks of sterile agar. Patience is needed: the seedlings will take two to seven years to reach flowering size.

Orchids growing outside have sufficient air flow when hung next to lattice panels and fencing with spacing between the boards.

Growing Orchids Outdoors

Orchids can be grown outdoors year-round in some regions of the country. South Florida, the Gulf Coast, coastal regions of Southern California, and Hawaii are areas where many plants can simply be tied to the trees in the backyard. Californians grow cymbidiums in pots on the patio or at the entryway, and San Franciscans and other fog-dwellers have an ideal climate for cool-growing orchids such as odontoglossums and a host of fascinating small masdevallias.

Across much of the country, orchids can spend the summer outdoors, provided they stay inside until the weather is warm and settled, and they are brought back indoors before night temperatures drop below 50° to 60° F. You can safely move orchid plants to where they will spend the summer at about the time you plant tomatoes,

eggplants, peppers, and okra outdoors. Cymbidiums are an exception to this rule. When you bring them inside in autumn, wait until night temperatures hover around 38° to 42° F. Chilling will set flower buds.

Summering

In areas with warm, humid summers, most orchids will benefit from being placed outdoors, provided they are carefully positioned to receive healthful amounts of light and given adequate protection from insects and other pests, such as slugs and snails. As for your indoor growing area, you will need to study how much direct sun reaches any given area in the garden. Orchids suited to low light (see chart on page 44) will adapt well in bright, open shade or on the north side of a wall where the only direct sun is early or late in the day. A site that receives sun in the morning is suited to orchids that thrive in medium light levels, while direct sun through midday and into the afternoon is generally too much even for those tolerant of high light levels. Plants will need some protection from the sun's hottest rays. Shade trees, shade cloth, or lattice screens also protect leaves and flowers from being damaged by falling debris. Avoid moving any orchid directly outdoors into full sun; gradually increase its exposure over several days.

Accommodating orchids outdoors

While it is possible to hang orchids from tree branches where they will receive dappled sunlight and shade as breezes blow through their leaves, small pots or a large collection can be better managed if you grow the orchids on benches. The ideal bench is slatted and then covered with ¼-inch wire hardware cloth to allow excess water from rain or the hose water to rapidly drain off. This arrangement also facilitates the sort of free air circulation orchids are accustomed to in the rain forest. A raised lip around the edge of the bench will keep plants from being easily knocked off the bench. If tall dendrobiums and epidendrums tend to topple, slip the containers inside clay pots to hold the plants upright. Make sure the pots have drain holes so water will drain freely.

For maximum comfort, build the benches at a height that suits yours. A tall bench for a short gardener—or a short bench for a tall gardener—causes physical stress and also diminishes the pleasure of growing orchids. Some growers set the pots in flats (with drainage) on top of the benches to group plants together and keep plants from tipping over. Depending on the size of your collection and the various sizes and habits of the plants themselves, you may elect to build some benches in the style of staging, like bleachers for plants. The lowest may be 12 inches off the ground, the next stepped back at 24 inches, a third at 36 inches. This arrangement works well set against a wall. Consider installing a shelf on the wall itself about 2 feet above the top bleacher-type shelf. This makes an inviting place to arrange a collection and, even though it is essentially an orchid nursery, there is a certain appeal in the orderliness of the arrangement.

Setting orchid plants directly on the ground is a sure way for the pots to become infested with slugs, snails, sowbugs, and other creatures that love the moist environment under the plants and that make a meal of your plants in the night.

Avoid leaving an orchid standing outdoors in a saucer or cachepot, which can collect rainwater. Unless you immediately empty the excess, the roots will perish and the plant will topple from rot.

In the absence of regular adequate rainfall, you will need to water your orchid plants outdoors with the same devotion you show when they are housebound. Also, maintaining a consistent schedule for fertilizing the plants is vital while the orchids are growing outdoors in warm weather. Otherwise, you may lose an opportunity for stronger growth that helps them prepare to put on the best flower show ever in the next regular blooming season.

Phalaenopsis can be problematic outdoors. The plants are vulnerable to sunburn and damage from hard rains and gusty winds. If you have a sheltered porch—ideally, a screened one—it is a perfect place to summer phalaenopsis

outside, along with florist gloxinias and gesneriads such as African violets. Leave the phalaenopsis on the porch until night temperatures fall to between 50° and 55° F. This slight chill will help the plant set buds for a big show of winter and spring flowers.

Before bringing plants inside, check each one for insects. Inspect the leaves, especially the undersides, and also along flower spikes and down among the pseudobulbs. Decant one or two plants and inspect the rootballs, checking to see if any slugs, snails, or insects have crawled into the pot. Trim away any dead leaves and spikes before bringing plants indoors to ensure the future health of your collection. Likewise, remove any leaves or debris from other plants that may have fallen into the container or the crown of the plant.

This shaded garden features phalaenopsis and cattleyas in wall-mounted baskets. Quick drainage is essential for orchid pots outdoors.

Display flowering orchids in a sheltered spot when the weather is warm and frost-free.

Orchid Troubleshooting

Orchids are tough plants, tolerant of pests such as insects and diseases, and capable of enduring a considerable amount of environmental stress. But if a plant's natural defenses are weakened by adverse growing conditions, it may succumb to opportunistic pests. The key to growing healthy orchids is to avoid stressing them.

In addition to minimizing stress, you can prevent problems by keeping orchids and the growing area clean. Certain fungi can produce millions of spores on dead leaves and flowers, so remove any dead material as soon as you notice it. The papery sheaths covering pseudobulbs provide a perfect place for scale insects and mealybugs to reside. Remove leaf sheaths on new growths as soon as they dry out, peeling them away from the pseudobulb. Remove dead leaf tips with sterilized cutting tools, making the cut ¼- to ½-inch into healthy tissue.

The color break on this cattleya indicates a virus.

Diagnosing problems

Your first step in diagnosing a problem is to inspect an ailing orchid and then compare its needs to its situation. You often can predict the cause of a problem. Inspection will help you sort out whether the problem results from an insect, a mite, a disease, or improper cultural practices. Inspect your orchids with a 10× magnifying glass, which will show small insects and mites. Also check the roots of ailing orchids.

When treating plants, be aware that few pesticides are registered for use on indoor plants. Check the pesticide's label; you may have to take orchids outside to spray them. If temperatures are warm enough, leave them outside until the spray has dried. Also check labels to ensure that pesticides can be used on orchids to control the pests in question. Obtain pesticides for use indoors from orchid suppliers and retailers who specialize in houseplants. If you spray indoors, take precautions to provide adequate ventilation and keep people or pets out of the vicinity. Follow manufacturers' specifications for preparing any mixtures and protect yourself by wearing goggles and gloves. Prepare only as much pesticide as you will use at one time. Before applying any pesticide, know the location and phone number of your local poison control center. (See Orchid Resources on page 216.)

Recommended treatments for insects, mites, fungi, and bacteria change periodically. Check with a professional resource to make sure a particular chemical is approved for orchids. To better educate yourself about orchid ailments, the correct identification, and treatment, consult with professionals. Your local county extension service may be able to help. A local nursery may also offer advice and identify what is ailing your plant. Some local plant societies run orchid health-care clinics, while others may offer programs during the year on orchid ailments and their treatment. Ailment identification services for most states can also be found on the Internet. In addition, a list of specialists who deal in plant pathology and plant nematology is maintained jointly by the American Phytopathological Society and the U.S. Department of Agriculture. (See Orchid Resources on page 216.)

Insects and Mites

Mealybugs

DESCRIPTION: These oval to elliptical, cottony-appearing insects have threadlike protrusions around a horizontally ridged body.

SYMPTOMS: Mealybugs quickly form colonies on leaf and petal undersides, in crevices between leaves, and inside bud sheaths, causing stunted growth and yellowing leaves.

TREATMENT: Physically remove mealybugs using a cotton swab dipped in 70 percent denatured or rubbing alcohol. Repeat every five to seven days until control is obtained. Weekly sprays with insecticidal soap, acephate (Orthene), malathion, or horticultural oil are also effective.

Aphids

DESCRIPTION: Aphids are small (less than 1/8 inch) slow-moving soft-bodied green, yellow, or pink insects that cluster on new growth, flowers, or flower buds. Cymbidiums are especially susceptible.

SYMPTOMS: Buds, flowers, and tender new growth look pitted or stunted. Honeydew, a sticky fluid secreted by the insects, attracts ants and provides a growth medium for sooty mold fungi.

TREATMENT: Spray with insecticidal soap, acephate (Orthene), malathion, or horticultural oil. For minor infestations, remove insects by washing plants with warm water and mild detergent. (Many

Mealybugs have a cottonlike appearance.

This orchid leaf is infested with scale.

detergents may be toxic to orchids; however, mild forumlations such as Ivory and Dr. Brommer's Peppermint Soap, work well.

Scale insects

DESCRIPTION: Mature scale insects appear as hard-shelled elliptical to round 1/16- to 1/8-inch-long immobile brown, white or gray bumps attached to leaves, stems, pseudobulbs, and flowers. Several types of scale insects attack orchids, including brown soft scale and Boisduval scale.

SYMPTOMS: Severe infestations can cause leaf yellowing and stunt the plant. Like aphids, soft scale insects secrete honeydew, which attracts sooty mold fungi and ants.

TREATMENT: Remove scale with a swab dipped in 70 percent denatured or rubbing alcohol. Inspect plants regularly, removing insects as you find them. Control severe infestations by spraying with insecticidal soap, acephate (Orthene), malathion, or horticultural oil. Spraying is most effective on the tiny young scale (crawlers), which have no hard covering and move about the plant or from one plant to another. Spray plants weekly for several weeks to kill crawlers as they emerge from eggs.

Spider mites

DESCRIPTION: Mites appear as green or red specks on lower or upper leaf surfaces. It takes a 10× magnifying glass to see them.

SYMPTOMS: Stippling is found on the leaves; sometimes also on the buds and flowers. Fine webbing may be present when infestation is severe.

TREATMENT: Mites thrive in hot, dry, dusty conditions, so keep leaves clean.

Spider mites stipple leaf undersides and create gossamer webbing.

Aphids are drawn to new growth and flower buds.

Insects and Mites
(continued)

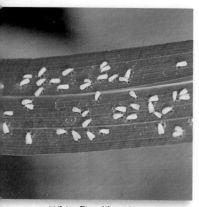
Whiteflies like plant sap.

To prevent outbreaks, occasionally wash plants with warm water and mild detergent (see above), remembering that many detergents may be toxic to orchids. For infested plants, spray leaves, especially the undersides, with insecticidal soap. Treat plants weekly for several weeks to kill mites as they emerge from eggs. To avoid introducing mites to your collection, carefully inspect new plants before bringing them in.

Whiteflies

DESCRIPTION: Approximately $\frac{1}{16}$ inch long, whiteflies are sucking insects that feed on plant sap. They are found primarily on the undersides of leaves. These insects have a white powdery wax over the body and wings.

SYMPTOMS: Weakened specimens appear damaged, with unhealthy new growth. Yellow, mottled leaves may drop. Leaves covered with honeydew attract ants and sooty mold fungus. A cloud of tiny white insects may rise from an affected plant.

TREATMENT: In greenhouses, use predatory insects, parasitic wasps, and insect pathogens. Weekly applications of systemic insecticides such as imidacloprid and acephate (Orthene) may be effective. Indoor growers may prefer contact insecticides, including insecticidal soaps, horticultural oils, and insect-growth regulators.

Thrips

DESCRIPTION: Thrips are $\frac{1}{16}$- to $\frac{1}{3}$-inch-long yellow, brown to black winged insects that reproduce rapidly, especially in warmer temperatures.

SYMPTOMS: Most common on dendrobiums and vandas, thrips suck the sap from orchid plants. Their damage to leaves, stems, and flowers appears as brown or chlorotic spots, streaks, and discoloration of plant tissues. Eventually the leaves drop and the plant's growth may be stunted.

TREATMENT: For indoor growing areas, including windowsills, try insecticidal soap for controlling thrips. Outdoor or greenhouse hobbyists may prefer malathion, acephate (Orthene), or spinosad applied at weekly intervals. They may also use the predatory mite *Amblyseius cucumeris.*

Fungus gnats

DESCRIPTION: Adult fungus gnats are $\frac{1}{16}$ to $\frac{1}{8}$ inch long with long legs and antennae, dark bodies, and dark wings. The larvae are white, transparent or slightly translucent, legless, and $\frac{1}{4}$ inch long.

SYMPTOMS: Adults are visible flying above the surface of the potting medium. Larvae remain below the surface, feeding on decaying plant material, medium, orchid roots, and orchid seedling tissues. Their presence indicates overly moist growing conditions or broken-down growing medium.

TREATMENT: Pot orchid plants in mixes using charcoal, coconut fiber or chunks, perlite, Aliflor, or lava rock. Allow the medium to dry between waterings. Biological controls include bacteria,

Right: Left untreated, thrips can deform plant growth. Far right: Fungus gnats are a sign of too much moisture or poor growing medium.

parasitic nematodes, and predatory mites. Drenches of imidacloprid may control larvae.

Slugs and snails

DESCRIPTION: The presence of soft-bodied slugs and hard-bodied snails is revealed by the trail of slime they leave behind.
SYMPTOMS: Plants have chewed leaf and petal margins and holes in buds. Slime trails lace flowers and other surfaces.
TREATMENT: Physically remove slugs or snails and place in a container of soapy water. Check under pots and rims; remove all debris. Use slug bait for large outbreaks, but keep bait away from pets. Diatomaceous earth or iron phosphate

The orchid blossom midge damages buds and flowers.

(Sluggo) may be placed around the base of orchids to prevent slug and snail attacks. Iron phosphate is safe to use around pets.

Orchid blossom midge

DESCRIPTION: Orchid blossom midge larvae are small and white, while the adult flies are about ½ inch long with banded legs, large eyes, long antennae, and spotted wings.
SYMPTOMS: The larvae are hidden in and feed on orchid buds and flowers, preferring dendrobiums and vandas. They cause bud blast, with damage to and deformity of developing floral tissues.
TREATMENT: Spray acephate (Orthene), with a penetrant such as LI-700, on the foliage and buds of orchids weekly for three to four weeks to control adults and larvae. If the infestation is severe, it may be necessary to remove all of the inflorescences before applying an insecticide.

Cockroaches

DESCRIPTION: Cockroaches are adaptable and hardy, and they reproduce prolifically. Variable in color, they range from 1 to 2 inches long, with a broadly oval body shape and chewing mouthparts. In addition to damaging orchids, cockroaches are a health hazard, carrying disease-causing bacteria that can affect humans.
SYMPTOMS: Cockroaches enter orchid pots through drainage holes. They come out to feed at night. Their presence is often noticed only after damage—such as nibbled flowers, roots, and new growth—occurs.
TREATMENT: To keep cockroaches out of the growing area, seal cracks and crevices, and keep everything clean. Insecticidal soap is a natural repellent, while diatomaceous earth is a contact desiccant. Cockroach baits and traps are useful, as is borax. All baits should be kept away from pets and children.

Lubber grasshoppers

DESCRIPTION: The bold colors, markings, and large size (2 to 3 inches at maturity) of lubber grasshoppers makes these voracious grasshoppers easy to spot.
SYMPTOMS: Young lubbers (nymphs) usually travel in large numbers, swarming and devouring orchids. They can quickly cause widespread damage to an orchid collection.
TREATMENT: Chemical control is effective only against the nymphs, and insecticides labeled for grasshoppers are unavailable for use on orchids. The best treatment is to prevent their access to orchids. Lubbers are slow moving and harmless to humans; they can be removed by hand.

Above left: Slugs have chewed this flower.
Above: Cockroaches can harm both orchids and humans.

Diseases

Orchids are usually resistant to diseases. However, if they are crowded so that air cannot freely circulate among plants, they're more likely to have problems. Orchids growing in decorative cachepots without drainage holes are especially vulnerable to root rots. Avoid problems by setting the orchid in its pot on a small, overturned pot in the bottom of the cachepot or by placing a layer of pea gravel in the bottom of the container and setting the pot on the gravel. Any excess water will then accumulate below the orchid's roots.

Providing sanitary growing conditions is the key to avoiding diseases on orchids indoors. As with insecticides, few fungicides are available to the home orchid grower and even fewer fungicides can be used indoors. When selecting a fungicide, read the label carefully to ensure that it is labeled for indoor use on orchids and that it controls the disease(s) in question.

Black rot fungus

(Phytophthora cactorum or *Pythium ultimum)*
DESCRIPTION: Cattleyas and phalaenopsis are especially susceptible to black rot fungus. Dendrobiums, oncidiums, and vandas can also get this disease, as can any orchid left standing in water or in decomposing growing medium.
SYMPTOMS: Soft, rotted areas begin on leaves or new growth, then spread into rhizomes and roots if unchecked. Infected leaves are initially purplish brown, then turn black. The outer margins of the infection site are yellowish.
TREATMENT: Remove infected areas, cutting ½ inch into healthy tissue. Sterilize cutting tools after each cut. Take the plant outside and drench it with a fungicide containing etridiazole. Isolate the plant in a low-humidity area to dry off. Water carefully until the plant recovers. Repot with fresh growing medium.

Treat black rot fungus as soon as you notice it.

Root rot fungus spoils the roots and spreads through the pseudobulbs until the foliage shrinks and yellows.

Root rot fungus

(Fusarium oxysporum cattleyae or *Rhizoctonia solani)*
DESCRIPTION: These fungi usually enter through the roots, causing roots to rot. Plants may be in decline for up to a year before dying, although they may also perish only a few months after being infected.
SYMPTOMS: Orchids are stunted and wilted. Brown, discolored to black areas may extend from the roots into the rhizomes. Leaves become yellowed and twisted.
TREATMENT: Cut off all rotted roots and discolored rhizomes, sterilizing cutting tools between cuts. Repot the plant using new medium and a sterile pot. Take the plant outside and drench it with a fungicide. Follow the instructions on the label.

Bacterial brown spot

(Pseudomonas cattleyae)
DESCRIPTION: Bacterial brown spot is the most common disease of phalaenopsis and is known to infect other types of orchids.
SYMPTOMS: A sunken, water-soaked lesion develops on the leaf, which eventually turns brown or black. The lesion exudes a dark liquid.
TREATMENT: Remove badly infected leaves, sterilizing tools between cuts. Spray the plant with a bactericide such as copper A. Because the exudate contains bacterial spores, isolate infected plants to keep the disease from spreading. Discard plants if crowns are infected.

Bacterial brown spot turns leaves yellow, then brown.

Typically, leaf spot fungus begins on a leaf's undersides. As they darken, the spots become visible on both sides.

Leaf spot fungus

(*Cercospora, Colletotrichum* and other fungi)
DESCRIPTION: The leaves, especially injured ones, are attacked. The damaged spots are well-defined round or irregularly shaped brown, sunken areas.
SYMPTOMS: Spots start out as yellow areas on the undersides of leaves. As they develop, they become visible on both sides of the leaf and turn purplish brown or black.
TREATMENT: Spray plants using a fungicide. Remove badly damaged leaves.

Petal blight

(*Botrytis cinerea*)
DESCRIPTION: Botrytis is a common disease in both indoor and outdoor environments. It's usually only a problem on orchids in humid greenhouses, especially on the flowers of phalaenopsis.
SYMPTOMS: Small circular pinkish to tan spots appear on sepals or petals after flowers open.
TREATMENT: Cut off and destroy all affected flowers. Increase air circulation and lower humidity. Clean up plant debris that may harbor the fungus. Avoid getting flowers wet when watering orchids.

Viruses

DESCRIPTION: Many viruses infect orchids, but diagnosis can be difficult because symptoms can resemble problems such as nutrient disorders.
SYMPTOMS: Black, red, or yellow spots or streaks appear on leaves. Flowers may have white or brown streaks or mosaic patterns. Symptoms will vary depending on the orchid species infected.
TREATMENT: Viruses are incurable; destroy infected plants. Plants may carry viruses without symptoms, so sterilize cutting tools between uses. Space plants to keep them from touching. Some private and university-based laboratories will test to determine if an orchid is infected with a virus. However, since viruses in orchids are uncurable, it is best to discard infected orchids and start over with virus-free plants.

5 WAYS TO PREVENT THE SPREAD OF VIRUS

■ Choose plants that appear healthy. Check them closely for viral symptoms. You can't remedy viruses.

■ When removing a leaf or flower or dividing a plant, always cut with a clean cutting tool. This may be scissors or pruners sterilized between uses (plunge into boiling water), or a single-edged razor blade. Once a blade is used, discard it.

■ Wear clean latex gloves when handling plants. Put on a new pair to handle each orchid you repot or divide.

■ Avoid dunking plants in the same bucket of water when irrigating them. Instead, water orchids individually and refrain from pouring runoff onto other orchids.

■ When repotting orchids, work on a pile of opened newspapers. Repot each orchid on its own sheet of paper, then discard the sheet.

Far left: Petal blight causes spots, blotches, and browned petal and sepal edges. Left: Virus symptoms can appear on flowers or on leaves as in this example.

Underwatering has stressed this orchid, attracting scale to its leaves.

are shriveled and growing slowly or not at all. When inspecting the roots, you will find evidence of root rot from overwatering. The treatment is to reduce watering or, if the medium has decayed, to repot. Keep the plant shaded in a humid area until new roots become established. Sometimes overwatering can be the result of planting in a pot that is too large and in which the medium has begun to decompose. Again, the solution is to repot, this time into a smaller pot, using fresh growing medium.

Underwatering

The second most common problem with orchids is underwatering. The symptoms of underwatering are the same as overwatering with one important exception: the roots will be firm and white when you inspect them as opposed to brown and decayed. The treatment in this situation is to water the orchid until the growing medium is saturated. Pseudobulbs should plump up in a day or two. In the future, water more frequently. If an orchid is completely dried out, the roots may not adequately take up new water. As a result, frequent watering of a previously dry specimen will lead to root rot. Certain growing media, such as sphagnum moss, are difficult to rewet. It is important to keep them from drying out completely.

Overfertilization

This condition can occur from applying fertilizer too frequently or from haphazard measuring. Symptoms include leaf edges and tips that are burned and roots that are withered, especially at the tips. Treat by pouring several gallons of deionized water through the growing medium to leach out the excess fertilizer salts.

Scaly or powdery white mineral deposits

White deposits found on the rims and exterior walls of clay pots and on the

Problems in the Environment

Probably no one who successfully grows orchids has done so without solving some problems along the way. It helps if you can get into the role of a detective. To do this, you will need a good 10× magnifying glass.

To be an orchid problem-solver, practice being a keen observer. Examine the troubled orchid in strong light, the sort a dentist or doctor uses. To comprehend what you see, you need to know the growing conditions required by the type of orchid you are inspecting.

Overwatering

Often cited as the most common orchid problem, overwatering results in pseudobulbs (and leaves, if succulent) that

Scaly mineral deposits are visible on clay pots.

APPEARANCES CAN BE DECEIVING

Within the orchid world, some species have such an unusual appearance that they can fool you into thinking something is amiss. Consider the *Restrepia xanthophthalma*, whose tiny 1-inch flowers appear on top of the leaves. You can use a magnifying glass for exploring this plant's unique features— which is a rewarding pastime.

surface of the media indicate that your water contains high concentrations of minerals or that orchids are being overfertilized. Leaf tips may show signs of burning by excess salts, and new growth may be stunted. The solution is to pour several gallons of plain or deionized water through the growing medium to leach out the excess salts, or to repot the orchid in fresh growing medium. When you water, thoroughly soak the entire surface of the growing medium, not just one location. If your water is hard, mix it with deionized water or rainwater to reduce the mineral concentration.

Top-heavy plant in a small pot

There are obvious visual clues that it's time to divide and repot an orchid. Symptoms include gradual, even yellowing of leaves with the oldest ones affected first. Foliage has an overall dull appearance. New growth is stunted. The pseudobulbs extend over the edges of the pot or are beginning to grow on top of each other.

Sunburn or too much light

Sunburn appears as scorched blotches on leaves and exposed surfaces of pseudobulbs, or as a general, overall yellowing of the plant. In extreme cases, the flower buds may be deformed. Provide less light, more shade, and lower daytime temperature, or increase humidity and improve air movement to prevent heat buildup.

Too little light

Inadequate light results in foliage that is unnaturally dark green but otherwise healthy. Orchids fail to bloom. Increase light gradually over a period of a month. If orchids are growing under fluorescent lights, increase the number of lamps or replace them if they have been in constant use for a year or more. Raise the orchids so that they are closer to the light, or increase the number of hours the lights are turned on each day. Avoid lighting the plants for longer than 16 to 18 hours a day.

Restrepia xanthophthalma

This orchid leaf suffers from sunburn.

Problems in the Environment
(continued)

Air pollution negatively affects orchids.

Air pollution

Certain types of air pollution can be a problem. Gases in the air—ethylene from ripening fruit, sulfur dioxide from smog, and other gases from pilot lights, stoves, or heaters—can result in flower damage ranging from drying and discoloring of the tips of the sepals to rapid wilting of the flower. Buds may fall off or abort. Sheaths may yellow and dry before buds appear. Refrain from leaving flowering orchids in a closed room with ripe apples or hyacinth flowers, which give off ethylene. Improve ventilation and properly adjust and maintain gas appliances.

Bud drop

Temperature fluctuations, reduced humidity, a change in environments, and air pollution are all causes of bud drop. A large fluctuation in temperature for a brief period, for example 20° F or more, is one of the common causes of bud drop. Also, moving an orchid in bud from ideal light, moisture, and temperatures such as in a greenhouse, sunroom, or light garden, to a relatively dark, dry home condition may result in buds shriveling and dropping. It's better to wait until flowers have opened before moving orchids.

Pleated leaves

Pleated leaves are a signal of inadeqaute watering, low humidity, or poor lighting. This occurs on orchids with relatively thin leaves such as miltoniopsis. Orchids are generally weak, stunted, and shriveled.

If the growing medium dries too much between waterings, roots fail to become sufficiently established to boost vigorous growth. They are merely surviving. To avoid this condition, water more often and be consistent. Once leaves become pleated, no amount of water will cause the wrinkles to disappear. You may need to add a cool-vapor humidifier to your growing area during the time of the year when the heating system is being used, because the heat dries the air. Another solution would be to add fluorescent or other supplementary lighting. Check the chart on page 44 to be sure your type of orchid is getting enough light.

Temperature fluctuation is a common cause of bud drop.

Accordion-pleated leaves indicate a lack of water.

Lack of rest

Not getting enough down time can keep orchids from thriving in the same way it can cause humans to malfunction. Lack of rest is more likely to be a problem if plants are growing under lights. Use a timer to assure they receive uniform amounts of light and dark over a 24-hour period. Continuous lighting is as detrimental to the orchids as leaving them in total darkness for a similar period.

Potted too high

When an otherwise healthy plant develops shriveled leaves, particularly if it is a phalaenopsis, doritis, or doritaenopsis, be sure that it is set correctly in the growing medium. If the lowermost leaf is an inch or more above the surface of the medium, replant so that the bottom leaf emerges from the stem at the surface of the medium rather than above it. Remove the orchid and repot; it is futile simply to push it down into the existing growing medium.

If your orchid shows shriveled leaves, you may have potted it too high.

Weeds

Several types of weeds may bother potted orchid collections. *Oxalis acetosella* is one; another is a small acanthus with big roots, such as a *Chameranthemum*. Fern spores that land and germinate in orchid media become fern rhizomes that can compete with an orchid, depriving it of fertilizer and water.

The best solution for weeds is to pull them by hand, along with their roots, as soon as you notice them. The roots must be removed, or the weeds will grow back.

Always pull out the roots when removing weeds, such as this oxalis, which can grow even among potted orchids.

Orchid Pest Controls

An adult ladybug can devour more than 5,000 aphids.

nontoxic to humans, animals, and beneficial organisms such as ladybugs, spiders, and earthworms.

When sprayed onto orchids, these oils suffocate insect and mite pests by smothering their breathing pores. They work against aphids, mealybugs, spider mites, scale, thrips, and whiteflies. They are also effective against certain fungi and mildews.

Follow the label directions exactly when applying the horticultural oil. Shake the solution intermittently during application to keep the ingredients well mixed. Cover all plant surfaces completely for maximum effectiveness.

Rubbing alcohol

An easy way to control a light infestation of mealybugs, aphids, or scale is to wet or remove the insects with a cotton swab dipped in rubbing alcohol (70 percent isopropyl). This method dissolves the insect's waxy covering. Using the swab enables you to reach pests hidden deep within sheaths and leaf crevices.

Another approach is to spray rubbing alcohol, or a 50-50 mixture of water and alcohol, with a misting bottle or small pump sprayer. Mix in a few drops of gentle, plant-safe liquid soap to the alcohol solution for this to work. Alcohol may also be combined with insecticidal soaps, but not with oils.

Avoid applying excessive amounts of alcohol, as it may burn sensitive orchids, particularly those in bud and flower. Alcohol may overcool and damage plant tissues, leaving the orchid susceptible to bacterial or fungal infection. On warm or breezy days, wipe off residual alcohol with a tissue instead of allowing it to evaporate.

Orchid growers are always on the hunt for new methods to keep their orchids strong and free of ailments. The best line of defense is taking the time to regularly inspect plants, removing dead leaves and spent flowers, and checking for any insects lurking in crevices, at the bases of leaves, or along flower spikes. By inspecting orchid plants periodically, you can prevent many ailments.

Horticultural oils

Natural and synthetic horticultural oils are an effective method of pest control and are generally harmless to humans, animals, and plants. Those most often used are neem oil, superfine oils (paraffin- or petroleum-based, highly refined oils), and mineral oil. Neem oil is extracted from the seeds of the neem tree, *Azadirachta indica,* also called Indian lilac or margosa. Neem is effective against insects and mites but relatively

Botanical insecticides: pyrethrins and rotenone

Botanical insecticides are derived from natural sources. Pyrethrins are extracts of chrysanthemum flowers, while rotenone is derived from the roots of plants in the legume or pea family. Both are available as dust, wettable powder, and emulsifiable concentrates. They are also used in some insecticidal spray solutions, either alone or in combination with other insecticides.

Pyrethrins attack the nervous system of a wide range of insect and mite pests, including ants, aphids, beetles, caterpillars, fungus gnats, mealybugs, cockroaches, scale, spider mites, thrips, and whiteflies. Rotenone inhibits respiration, asphyxiating insect and mite pests. It is useful for control of aphids, mites, thrips, and whiteflies.

Always take precautions to handle these insecticides in accordance with the manufacturer's safety instructions provided on the label. Rotenone has low toxicity to humans, warm-blooded animals, and the environment but is extremely toxic to fish.

Whichever formulation is chosen, these insecticides should be applied three times at weekly intervals to suppress successive generations of insect and mite pests.

Natural predators

Green lacewings and ladybugs are beneficial insects for use in enclosed growing spaces like greenhouses. The larvae of green lacewings are voracious predators, consuming the eggs and immature stages of soft-bodied insects that attack orchids, including aphids, mealybugs, scale, spider mites, thrips, and whiteflies. Ladybug adults and larvae favor aphids, and can consume more than 5,000 aphids each. They also eat other pests, including mites and scale. In addition, they consume insect eggs.

Beneficial insects can be purchased and released into your greenhouse. To keep them around, provide food such as flowering plants and water. Many beneficial insects prefer to feed on plants with tiny flowers that offer both pollen and nectar. A tray of wet pebbles supplies drinking water. Bug chow is sold as a food supplement for lacewings and ladybugs.

If you apply pesticides, use horticultural oil, insecticidal soaps, and insect growth regulators as many pesticides are harmful to beneficial insects.

Insecticidal soaps

Insecticidal soaps are derived from the potassium salts of fatty acids. Of the variety of fatty acids, only certain ones have insecticidal properties. This is based on the length of the carbon-based fatty acid chains. Most soaps with insect and mite activity are composed of long-chain fatty acids (10- or 18-carbon chains) whereas shorter chain fatty acids (9-carbon chains or fewer) have herbicidal properties and can kill plants. Oleic acid, an 18-carbon fatty acid present in olive oil and other vegetable oils, is effective as an insecticidal soap.

Insecticidal soaps are widely available from garden centers and nursery suppliers as premixed spray solutions. Soaps kill insects and mites by removing or breaking down their protective coating.

Insecticidal soaps are useful against soft-bodied insects and mites such as aphids, mealybugs, scale crawlers, spider mites, thrips, and whiteflies. For soaps to be effective, complete coverage is essential. The spray must make contact with the insects and mites. The soaps have no residual properties, so repeated applications at weekly intervals may be necessary to reduce pest populations below damaging levels.

When treating your prized orchids, use caution. Orchids, especially the flowers, may be sensitive. Repeat applications may burn foliage, particularly the tender new tissues, or damage blooms, especially when mixed with hard water. To prevent injury, orchids should be shaded until the spray residues dry.

Although generally regarded as safe for use around humans, animals, and plants, soaps can stimulate allergies and respiratory problems and should be applied with care.

Apply insecticidal soaps to completely cover all surfaces of the plant.

Orchids A–Z

In the following section, you will find some of the best orchids for growing in windows, light gardens, greenhouses, and outdoors. To help you choose wisely, each orchid has been rated as to its suitability for a beginner, intermediate, or advanced grower. The rating depends on the adaptability of the orchid, that is, how easily it will forgive underwatering or overwatering, too much or too little light, and temperatures that vary from the ideal. The exacting seasonal treatments required by a few of the orchids (such as the late autumn and winter drying-out required by deciduous dendrobiums) may earn them an advanced rating.

The entries in this guide are organized alphabetically by genus. Most genera contain many more species than you will encounter when you visit orchid shows and festivals and begin to correspond with other growers online. The species included here offer a starting point on your journey into the wonderful hobby of growing orchids and assembling a collection of plants that offer delightful colors, shapes, and fragrances year-round. Occasionally, as in the case of *Cattleya labiata,* the species is now rarely grown, although hybrid progeny are found in collections all over the world.

When you visit nurseries and big-box stores, you will find most of the orchids offered for sale are hybrids. Every year, more hybrids are introduced. You can expect to see the traditional plants that have stood the test of time alongside new specimens that offer fresh choices. In most genus descriptions there are highlights of the work of the orchid breeders, describing both new hybrids as well as some popular classics.

Each orchid entry begins with a quick, care-at-a-glance section that includes a pronunciation guide for the botanical name. The next line gives the abbreviation for the genus as accepted by the Royal Horticultural Society, which maintains the official register for orchid hybrids. Following the abbreviation is a growth note that identifies the plants in the genus as monopodial or sympodial. (See pages 14 to 16.) This information gives an overall impression of how the plants grow and is helpful during dividing and repotting.

Next are the orchid's requirements for light and temperature—two of the most critical factors. Light needs are described as low, medium, or high. (See Ideal Light Ranges on page 44.) Temperature requirements are given as cool, intermediate, or warm. These terms are defined in degrees on page 50. Next, the flowering season is listed. In some genera, especially ones with many species and hybrids, the flowering seasons are so variable that it is impossible to identify a precise flowering time. By considering natural bloom time in selecting orchids, you can assemble a collection that blooms every month of the year. The last line rates the genus as best for a beginner, intermediate, or advanced grower, assuming the growing environment meets basic light, temperature, and water requirements.

The entry text describes the genus in more detail, explains its cultural needs, and gives the commonality of species within the genus. Other information includes historical details and native habitat. Orchids may be listed under more than one name in orchid literature, catalogs, and Internet entries. In those cases, synonyms provide keys to the plants' identity.

Throughout this guide to orchids, care has been taken to include species and hybrids that reflect what is currently available on the market as well as orchids which have remained popular for decades. The choices are seemingly endless, especially when you consider there are more than 120,000 registered orchid hybrids and more than 25,000 named orchid species. Visit a nursery or garden center to find types ideally suited for the beginner. As you gain experience and an appetite for the odd and unusual, attend orchid shows, festivals, and sales to gain access to orchids that require more care but deliver new growing challenges. When you shop the Internet, e-mail orchid hobbyists, and chat in online forums, you will be welcomed among enthusiastic orchid growers who are as diverse and interesting as the plants they grow.

Month after month and year after year, your interests will shift as new orchids catch your eye. By starting with some of the selections in this gallery, you can gain an appreciation for the diversity found within the orchid family and select those species and hybrids that bring satisfaction— and abundant orchid blooms.

Cymbidium
Lamplighter

ANGRAECUM

an-GREE-kum

Abbreviation:	Angcm.
Growth:	Monopodial
Light:	Low to high
Temperature:	Cool to warm
Flowering:	Varies
Care:	Beginner to advanced

Orchid enthusiasts with a penchant for white flowers will want to investigate *Angraecum* and its relatives, which offer amazing variations on a single color theme. The genus *Angraecum* is made up of about 200 species from Africa and Madagascar, with more than half of the species from Madagascar. The plants vary in size from a tiny tuft of a plant only a few inches tall to giants that can reach 6 feet. Likewise, the flowers range from ½ inch to a foot or more across. The largest flower on the African continent is reported as *Angcm. infundibulare.* Only a few of the 200 or so species of *Angraecum* are widely distributed in cultivation. Many are threatened in their natural habitats by deforestation, habitat conversion, and other human pressures.

Angraecum is the most typically encountered genus for a group of orchids called angraecoids, which number about 750 species in 50 genera. Most of the angraecoids come from Africa, Madagascar, and the surrounding islands, although there are some genera in tropical America, including the famous ghost orchid (*Dendrophylax lindenii* on page 13). Other commonly grown angraecoid genera include *Aerangis* (ay-er-RANG-giss), *Aeranthes* (ay-er-AN-theez), *Jumellea* (joo-MELL-ee-ah), and *Mystacidium* (miss-ta-SID-ee-um). Most of the angraecoids are moth pollinated and have white, star-shaped flowers with a nectary (or spur), and sweet, enticing fragrances at dusk or dawn. Just as Charles Darwin was drawn to the handsome flowers of *Angcm. sesquipedale* (page 99), so will orchid fans be lured to these orchids that have long held fascination for the discerning hobbyist.

In the United States, much of the recent popularity of angraecoids can be traced to Fred Hillerman and his California-based nursery, the Angraecum House, which operated from 1975 until 1999. Hillerman was an endless champion of angraecoids. More and more of these species are being grown from seed. Hobbyists can now obtain the plants they want without threatening plants in their native habitats.

Culture

The majority of angraecums are not difficult to grow, making them suitable for novice growers with a sense of adventure as well as for the more sophisticated hobbyist. Most will do well under an intermediate to warm temperature regime—daytime temperatures of 68° to 80° F with minimum night temperatures of 60° F—in moderate light without direct sunlight. A few species that grow at higher elevations, among them *Angcm. magdalenae*, will need cooler conditions, especially during the winter.

Most angraecums benefit from drying out slightly between waterings. It is important to use water with a low salt content. Maintain humidity above 50 percent. The species as well as the hybrids will do well potted in bark-based mixes, although any mix that drains freely and dries evenly will work. Many of the species will also grow well when mounted onto supports. Some with pendent inflorescences require mounting.

Angraecums, as well as angraecoids in general, are not difficult to grow but can be slow to mature. Good water quality, humidity above 50 percent, and careful care of the plants' roots will lead to lush growth and lovely flowers.

Species

■ **Angraecum didieri:** Perfect for any growing area where space is at a premium, this small plant puts out showy 2-inch starlike flowers. The pristine white lip almost sparkles, while the 3- to 6-inch-long greenish spur uncoils as it matures. Medium light and either potting in a well-drained mix or attaching to a slab are recommended for this epiphyte. It does well under lights, on a windowsill, or in the greenhouse. Native to Madagascar.

Angraecum didieri

Angraecum leonis

Angraecum sesquipedale

■ **Angraecum leonis:** The fascinating sickle-shaped foliage makes this small- to medium-sized epiphyte appealing even when not in flower. Pure white flowers with short curved spurs are borne in clusters. This plant can be grown mounted or in a container. In either case it's essential to meet the plant's moisture needs. If it is on a mount, make sure it does not dry out. While it is in a pot, prevent the medium from remaining too wet. Native to Madagascar and the Comoros Islands.

■ **Angraecum sesquipedale:** A large plant with fans of stately dark green leaves, this epiphyte, which can reach 3 feet tall, is best suited to growing in greenhouses or, in the subtropical or tropical garden in a container or attached to a tree. Under-lights and windowsill growers who covet this king of the angraecums will see these small plants begin to flower when the plants are less than a foot tall. Found in hot lowlands in its native habitat, this species is best grown in intermediate to warm conditions. Take care not to damage the roots when repotting adult plants. Native to Madagascar.

Hybrids

■ **Angraecum Orchidglade (sesquipedale × giryamae):** Jones & Scully, an important South Florida firm, registered this hybrid in 1964. This plant reaches 42 inches tall. Upright spikes carry up to a dozen 5-inch-tall flowers that are white with a green spot in the nectary and a heavy, sweet fragrance in the evening. Bright light, intermediate to warm temperatures, and frequent applications of a dilute fertilizer coax plants to flower.

■ **Angraecum Veitchii (eburneum × sesquipedale):** Widely available, this 30-inch-tall plant bears 5-inch-wide ivory to white star-shaped flowers with a 6-inch-long nectary. It was an introduction of the esteemed English orchid nursery Veitch & Sons, which registered the hybrid in 1899. More than 100 years later, it remains a favorite of orchid enthusiasts because it's so easy to grow. It makes a good companion for growing with cattleyas, laelias, and epidendrums.

Angraecum Orchidglade

Angraecum *continued*

Relatives

■ **Aerangis citrata:** (Abbreviation: Aergs.) The specific epithet *citrata*, meaning lemon-scented, is appropriate for this small species that bears cream-colored to yellow,

Angraecum Veitchii

Aerangis citrata

fragrant flowers on slender inflorescences that grow about 10 inches long. It may flower several times during the year. The 4- to 5-inch-long leaves are dark green. Although most aerangis grow best on mounts, this one is suggested for pot culture where its moisture demands can be more easily met. Rewarding to grow and floriferous even in low light, it's a good candidate for the beginner. Native to Masdagascar.

■ **Aerangis luteoalba var. rhodosticta:** Extremely popular for its long sprays of white or cream flowers with a red column, this small-growing epiphyte will flower in low light.

The narrow leaves can reach 3 inches in length. An intermediate to cool grower, it can be attached to a mount or tucked into a thumb pot in a medium with good drainage. Native to East Africa.

Aerangis luteoalba var. rhodosticta

■ **Aerangis modesta:** This small plant looks like a bright green phalaenopsis with a leafspan—the measurement from one leaf tip to the opposite leaf tip—that rarely reaches 10 inches. Pendent spikes bear up to 15 crisp, white six-pointed, star-shaped flowers that are about 1 inch across. The 3-inch nectary or spur hangs down. Flowering primarily in the autumn, this species may also bloom in the spring. A sweet, hyacinthlike fragrance is obvious in the evening. Mount rather than pot, but take extra precautions to keep the plant from drying out. Low light, intermediate to warm temperatures, and regular applications of a dilute fertilizer are beneficial. Native to Madagascar.

■ **Jumellea comorensis:** (Abbreviation: Jum.) *Jumellea* is a genus of about 50 species of lithophytes and epiphytes. Like other angraecoids, jumelleas are members

Aerangis modesta

of the Vanda Alliance. This relationship is seen in the leaves and their arrangement along the stems, as well as in their flowers and their shared DNA. *Jumellea comorensis* is a small-growing evergreen orchid with leafy stems.

It stays in flower most of the year. Each inflorescence bears a single 2-inch-wide green flower with a spur up to 10 inches long, adding an elegant touch to the presentation. Grow it in intermediate to warm temperatures either on a mount or in a pot, and water often. Native to the Comoros Islands.

■ **Jumellea major:** One of the larger members of the genus, this plant has dark

Jumellea major

green leaves that are folded at the base where they clasp the main stem. Each of the single-flowered inflorescences puts forth an intensely white 3- to 4-inch nocturnally fragrant flower. Provide intermediate to warm temperatures and grow in a pot or on a mount, always being sure to provide rapid drainage. As specimens age and develop stems, you may need to cut away lower leaves. To protect the health of the plant, remove leaves with a sterilized cutting tool to prevent the spread of viruses. Native to Madagascar.

Jumellea comorensis

BRASSAVOLA

bra-SAH-vo-la

Abbreviation: B.

Growth: Sympodial

Light: Medium to high

Temperature: Intermediate to warm

Flowering: Summer to autumn

Care: Beginner

The genus *Brassavola* is composed of 17 Latin American epiphytes, distributed for the most part in lowlands and closely related to cattleyas and laelias. Their star-shaped flowers are deliciously fragrant at night, but the scent becomes almost imperceptible shortly after daybreak. In addition to the popular *B. nodosa*, the lady of the night orchid, this genus once contained *B. digbyana,* which botanists have moved to the genus *Rhyncholaelia.* (See page 103.)

Culture

Easily grown with cattleyas and laelias, brassavolas demand abundant light but tolerate humidity as low as 40 percent. They are rapid growers, quickly filling a pot or basket—wood-slat, wire, plastic mesh, even tree fern. Provide a well-draining medium and allow the plants to dry slightly between waterings. *Brassavola* species can also be grown on bark mounts, particularly in tropical and subtropical climates where they can be hung outdoors most of the year. The plants will live indefinitely in low light. In order to thrive and bloom regularly, they need strong light and good air movement.

During active growth, fertilize these plants regularly to develop robust new growths and bountiful flowers. These plants benefit from being placed outdoors during the summer, provided they are brought back indoors in the autumn. The plants are easily propagated by division after flowering. Young plants begin to flower at an early age.

Some species can be brought to bloom twice or more yearly by alternating periods of freely watering and fertilizing with periods of maintaining plants on the dry side and withholding fertilizer. For this reason, they are considered worthwhile plants for the indoor gardener who must make every inch of growing space count.

Brassavolas thrive in a wide range of temperatures, from cool to warm, and bloom successfully in window or fluorescent light. Their tolerance for relatively low humidity makes them choice houseplants and noteworthy confidence builders. Indeed, they are almost foolproof orchids that offer profuse flowers in exchange for meeting a few cultural needs.

Species

■ *Brassavola cucullata:* This orchid has longer (8 to 18 inches), narrower leaves than the more commonly grown *B. nodosa*. Carl von Linné first described it in 1763 as *Epidendrum cucullatum.* When another orchid fancier introduced the genus *Brassavola* in 1813, he made *B. cucullata* the type for the genus. The orchid's decorative, spidery, nocturnally fragrant flowers bloom from summer into winter. These attributes, along with its robust growth, have made *B. cucullata* popular with breeders. The sepals and petals are pale yellow (straw colored) to white on the inner surface, attractively blushed with reddish brown on the outside, also called reverses. Native from Mexico to northern South America and into the West Indies.

■ *Brassavola nodosa:* Commonly called the lady of the night in Latin America for its exquisite evening perfume, the 3-inch-long flowers of *B. nodosa* may be white with tiny

Brassavola cucullata

Brassavola nodosa

Brassavola subulifolia

purple dots on the lip, greenish-white, or cream. There is variation in the fragrance, too. The foliage is upright and ranges in height from a compact 4 inches tall to 12 inches. Unlike *Rhyncholaelia digbyana* (formerly *B. digbyana*), *B. nodosa* does not need a dry rest period. It grows and flowers year-round. In subtropical and tropical gardens, it can be attached to trees, where it grows and flowers with little care. Native from Mexico through Central America to Peru and Venezuela, it is also found in the West Indies.

■ **Brassavola subulifolia (syn. B. cordata):** Although smaller than *B. nodosa*, this 20- 24-inch epiphyte resembles it in many aspects, including its slender leaves that may be upright or hang out from the support. The 1¾-inch flowers of *B. subulifolia*, though smaller than those of *B. nodosa*, are produced in greater quantity, with each leaf putting forth 5 to 8 flowers. John Lindley, the father of orchid taxonomy, described it in 1836. Since then, the name *B. cordata* has been used by the Royal Horticultural Society when registering hybrids. *Brassavola subulifolia* can be grown in a pot or on a mount in bright light and warm temperatures, similar to those provided for cattleyas. Native to Jamaica.

■ **Brassavola tuberculata (syn. B. perrinii):** This large epiphyte or lithophyte was first brought into flower near Liverpool, England, in 1828. The spidery, airy, nocturnally fragrant flowers are palest yellow to lime. They appear in great numbers on an established plant, which is often seen on a slab of cork or other mount. The elliptically shaped lip is white and may be flushed green in the throat. The flowers sometimes fail to open fully. The sepals in some plants have blood-red spotting. While current authorities list this brassavola as the species *B. tuberculata*, it has been known as *B. perrinii* in fairly recent times. Native to Brazil.

Brassavola tuberculata

Hybrids

■ **Brassavola David Sander (cucullata × digbyana):** An early hybrid of *Rh. digbyana* (syn. *B. digbyana*) and *B. cucullata*, this orchid has narrow, pinkish-white petals and a broad, perfectly fringed lip. It has shiny, pencil-sized leaves. It grows 18-inches with 5- 6-inch flowers and benefits from intermediate to warm temperatures, bright light, and regular water and fertilizer when in active growth. Pot in an open, well-drained growing medium.

Brassavola David Sander

Brassavola Little Stars

■ **Brassavola Little Stars (nodosa × subulifolia):** When given proper culture, loads of beautiful, pale greenish-white 2-inch blooms burst forth from this 12-inch primary hybrid to perfume the night. A good beginner orchid, *B. Little Stars* is fairly tolerant of a wide range of conditions. Bright light, copious water, and regular applications of dilute fertilizer during active growth bring out the best in this charming hybrid.

Brassavola *continued*

Brassocattleya Maikai

Intergeneric hybrids

■ *Brassocattleya* Maikai (*B. nodosa* × *Cattleya bowringiana*): (Abbreviation: Bc) Another popular and fairly easy-to-grow hybrid, *Bc.* Maikai adds a splash of color to any collection. There are many clones of this plant awarded by the American Orchid Society. Its cream-colored blossoms are heavily spotted rich purple, even on their reverse. With its prolific nature and tendency to form specimen plants, this grex handsomely rewards even novice hobbyists who provide the same growing conditions as for cattleyas.

■ *Brassolaelia* Morning Glory (*B. nodosa* × *Laelia purpurata*): (Abbreviation: Bl.) This grex earns its name with its clusters of ethereal pale white flowers, their petals faintly flushed lavendar,

Brassolaelia Morning Glory

with a lip boldly flushed and striated magenta. The *B. nodosa* parent contributed its floral shape and enchanting perfume, while *L. purpurata* has painted accents into every flower. Give it abundant light to bring forth its best blooms.

■ *Brassolaelia* Richard Mueller (*B. nodosa* × *L. milleri*): *Bl.* Richard Mueller's flowers suggest the airy, spidery blooms of its parent *B. nodosa*. It gets its bright gold color and compact growth habit from its *L. milleri* parent, and its cheery bright red spots from *B. nodosa*. This is another brassavola hybrid that fills a pot or basket quickly and easily. It flowers several times each year.

Brassolaelia Richard Mueller

■ *Brassolaeliocattleya* Everything Nice (*Blc.* Memoria Helen Brown × *B. perrinii*): (Abbreviation: Blc.) Clones of this fragrant and compact grex are available in a range of lovely hues from cool ice green to

Brassolaeliocattleya Everything Nice

sunny yellow, some with magenta accents in the lip. Given proper care, this hybrid blooms twice a year in intermediate temperatures with bright light, regular watering, and fertilization during active growth.

■ *Brassolaeliocattleya* Goldenzelle (*Blc.* Fortune × *C.* Horace): With its classic cattleya shape, beautiful colors, and enticing fragrance, *Blc.* Goldenzelle is a well-known and popular hybrid among fanciers. Most clones have the golden hues the grex was named for, with contrasting shades of reds accenting its lip. This orchid will benefit from typical cattleya culture: lots of bright light (but protected from direct afternoon sun) and good air circulation.

■ *Brassolaeliocattleya* Momilani Rainbow (*Lc.* Mari's Song × *Blc.* Orange Nuggett): Both parents of this hybrid have earned many awards and have passed on their

Brassolaeliocattleya Goldenzelle

finest qualities to *Blc.* Momilani Rainbow. It requires good light in an eastern, southern, or shaded western exposure, intermediate temperatures, copious water, and dilute fertilizer when in active growth. This lovely splash-petaled hybrid perfumes the late spring and early summer air with its delicious fragrance.

Brassolaeliocattleya Momilani Rainbow

Relatives

■ *Rhyncholaelia digbyana (syn. Brassavola):* (Abbreviation: Rl.) Two epiphytic species once placed in the genus *Brassavola* have been moved into their own genus, *Rhyncholaelia* (rink-oh-LAY-lee-ah), although they are still listed in some catalogs as brassavolas. *Rhyncholaelia digbyana* was first introduced into cultivation from Honduras and first brought into flower in England in 1845 by Edward St. Vincent Digby. Botanist John Lindley named the species in Digby's honor the following year. Subsequently it was moved for a time to the genus *Laelia,* until 1918, when Rudolf Schlecter determined that it belonged in a separate though closely related genus and henceforth should be known as *Rhyncholaelia digbyana.* For orchid hybrid registration purposes it is referred to as a brassavola, the name that continues to be seen in catalogs and literature.

Whatever the name, it is a popular parent in crosses with cattleyas and laelias, giving the large flower size and prized fringed lip to many cattleya hybrids. It is also worth growing in its own right for its 4- to 6-inch greenish white flowers with a lacy labellum and lemony fragrance. The 8- to 10-inch-long narrow silvery leaves are succulent. Respect its rest period by watering lightly and withholding fertilizer for several months after it flowers. This plant needs warmth and high light.

Rhyncholaelia digbyana

It often does better bark-mounted instead of potted to assure that the roots are never soggy. Native from Mexico to Guatemala.

■ *Rhyncholaelia glauca (syn. Brassavola):* Growing only 10 to 12 inches tall, this epiphyte's 4- to 5-inch flowers combine narrow green sepals and petals with a wavy white waxy·lip. Unlike *Rh. digbyana,* the lip is not fringed. When used in hybrids, *Rh. glauca* imparts to its progeny pink hues and a waxy substance. Grow this orchid in bright light, allow it to dry between waterings, and place plants in a container or attach to a mount, such as a piece of cork. Use a vertical mount or attach the plant to a horizontal mount, similar to a raft. Native from Mexico to Honduras.

Rhyncholaelia glauca

BRASSIA

BRASS-ee-ah

Abbreviation: Brs.

Growth: Sympodial

Light: Medium

Temperature: Intermediate

Flowering: Late spring to early summer

Care: Beginner

Orchids in the genus *Brassia* are among the many orchids commonly called spider orchids. In this case, the name is descriptive. The slender, pointed sepals and petals of the flowers resemble spiders' legs. The lip is shaped much like a spider's body. The extraordinary blossoms of some forms can stretch more than 16 inches from top to bottom.

Although brassias come in a limited range of colors, their hues are appealing and, to some collectors, irresistible. Most are gold to green, speckled or banded with brown, purple, or maroon. Fragrant flowers are a signature of almost all of the 30 species native to regions from Florida and the West Indies to Mexico and into South America. Well-grown plants may bear literally hundreds of blossoms, perfectly spaced on gently arching spikes. Each large, flattened pseudobulb bears two or three long, leathery leaves. Most plants grow to about 2 feet tall, though some may reach 3 feet.

Culture

Treat brassias like cattleyas, but avoid letting them dry out completely when they are actively growing. They will grow well in any standard, all-purpose orchid bark mix. Young plants may benefit from being transplanted yearly to a size or two larger pot each time. After the first flowering, you may need to repot only every two years (before the growing medium begins to degrade).

If grown outdoors, brassias require slightly less light than cattleyas. Indoors, they are suited to a half-sunny window, such as one receiving direct sun from the east or south. Plants grown in the hot, western sun require more shade. Brassias will grow with artificial light under banks of four to six 40- or 74-watt tubes burned 16 hours out of every day.

Avoid letting brassias dry out severely between waterings. When grown with a steady hand, they are capable of beautiful foliage that rises above smooth green pseudobulbs. Enhance the effect by cleaning the leaves and pseudobulbs with fresh lemon juice to remove any spray or hard-water residue. This treatment gives leaves a natural, attractive sheen.

Brassia gireoudiana

Species

■ **Brassia gireoudiana:** The large, flattened pseudobulbs and leathery leaves of this species are typical of the genus. The fragrant flowers measure up to 12 inches from top to bottom. The sepals and petals are greenish yellow, blotched near their bases with shiny black or brown markings. The large, pale yellow lip spreads widely at the tip. It has a few brown spots near the center. *Brs. gireoudiana* flowers in late spring to summer. Native to Costa Rica and Panama.

■ **Brassia maculata:** This species is similar to *Brs. gireoudiana*, except that the flowers are smaller (5 to 8 inches long) and are spotted with purple. They also last a long time, up to a month and a half. *Brs. maculata* blooms at any time between autumn and spring, sometimes blooming twice a year. Discovered in Jamaica,

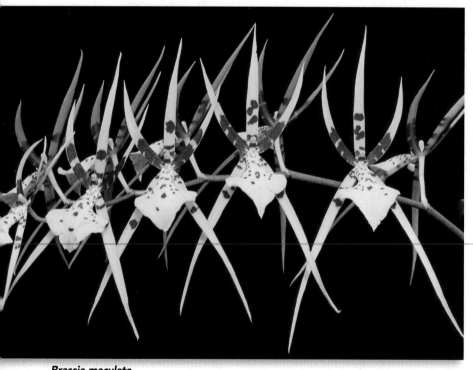

Brassia maculata

Brs. maculata was first flowered in cultivation at the Royal Botanic Gardens, Kew, in 1813. It is a large, robust epiphyte that occasionally grows as a lithophyte. It is easy to grow and useful in breeding work to create hybrids. Native to Guatemala, Honduras, Venezuela, Cuba, and Jamaica.

■ *Brassia verrucosa:*
Upright spikes carry large flowers with pale green sepals and petals spotted dark green. The showy greenish lip is spotted near the base, imparting a dramatic touch to the floral composition. Each oval pseudobulb is topped with two leaves. Plants can be somewhat large, making them ideal for growing in pots and slat baskets in sunrooms and greenhouses, or outdoors

Brassia Rex

in subtropical and tropical gardens. Easy to cultivate, they respond favorably to copious quantities of water and fertilizer when actively growing. Native to Mexico and Venezuela.

Hybrids

■ *Brassia Rex* **(***verrucosa* × *gireoudiana***):** King of the spider orchids, *Brs.* Rex was registered in 1964 by legendary Hawaiian breeder W.W.G. Moir. This primary hybrid remains popular today. Not only is the original cross still on the market, but *Brs.* Rex has also given rise to new hybrids with improved traits. *Brs.* Rex is cherished for its arching sprays that carry overlapping 8- to 10-inch-tall greenish flowers with brown bars near the base of the sepals and petals. A few markings also appear on the showy, wavy pale green lip. This robust orchid flowers several times a year and grows well under the same conditions provided for cattleyas and laelias.

Brassia verrucosa

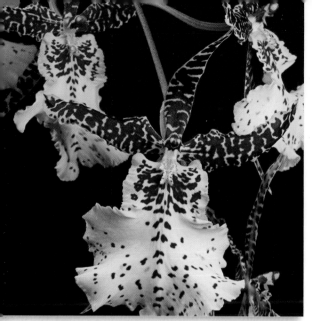

Aliceara Sweetheart Jonel

Brassia *continued*

Intergeneric hybrids

■ *Aliceara* **Sweetheart Jonel** **(*Miltassia* Cartagena × *Oncidium* Enderanum):** (Abbreviation: Alcra.) Combinations of three genera—*Brassia, Oncidium,* and *Miltonia*—result in *Aliceara* hybrids. These plants bear dozens of enormous flowers in combinations of rich gold and maroon, yellow and chocolate, orange and yellow, and green and white. One awarded clone of the hybrid *Aliceara* Sweetheart Jonel is 'Vin-Mar', AM/AOS, which has been cloned and is widely available; it puts forth 4-inch flowers with a large speckled, ruffled pale creamy yellow lip. The color theme is carried to the sepals and petals, which are much narrower and heavily barred with mahogany. A crystalline texture offers an added attraction to these flowers that rise above lush, dark green leaves. Guarantee success by providing good air circulation, medium light, and a well-drained potting medium that will still retain moisture.

■ *Brassada* **Orange Delight (*Ada* aurantiaca × *Brs.* Mary Traub Levin):** (Abbreviation: Brsa.) If you want a spider orchid in vivid orange, this hybrid is for you. The star-shaped flowers, which measure a generous 4 inches tall, are bright orange with a yellow, red-marked lip. The ada parent imparts the vivid color, while the brassia provides the distinctive shape. It's common for each spike to bear 10 to 12 flowers, or more. Each pseudobulb often will put out two inflorescences. Plants of this cross begin flowering at a young age. Easy to grow, the plants like intermediate temperatures, good air circulation, medium light, and a porous mix.

Brassada Orange Delight

■ *Degarmoara* **Kramer Island** **(*Mtssa.* Aztec × *Odontonia* Lake Harbor):** (Abbreviation: Dgmra.) Hybridizers are constantly tinkering with orchid genes in the pursuit of creating new and improved hybrids. The oncidium Alliance, of which brassia is a member, holds particular appeal because of the floral diversity and the ease with which species and hybrids match successfully. *Miltassia*—a cross between *Brassia* and *Miltonia* that is abbreviated *Mtssa.*—has been paired with other genera to yield new results. The genus *Degarmoara*, in which the third partner is *Odontoglossum*, is one example. A flurry of activity in

Degarmoara Kramer Island

hybridizing this genus of showy orchids has generated some degarmoaras with names that convey their beauty and the fun of growing orchids, among them *Dgmra.* Tutti Frutti (*Brs.* Spider's Gold × *Odontonia* Norcut) and *Dgmra.* Winter Wonderland (*Mtssa.* Cartagena × *Odontoglossum* Gledhow). With *Dgmra.* Kramer Island, the influence of *Odontoglossum* is introduced through the *Odontonia* parent, which is itself a combination of *Odontoglossum* and *Miltonia*. *Dgmra.* Kramer Island flowers well in a 4-inch pot with each upright inflorescence bearing about six of the showy, 4½-inch-tall flowers composed of cream-colored sepals and petals with burgundy blotches. The wavy-edged white lip is tinted rose. Shown here is an awarded clone of *Dgmra*. Kramer Island called 'Everglades,' AM/AOS. A flurry of flowers will reward growers who provide medium light coupled with a fast-draining mix in a clay or plastic pot, and frequent applications of dilute fertilizer.

Forgetara Everglades Pioneer

■ *Forgetara* **Everglades Pioneer (Mtssa. Aztec × Aspasia principissa):** (Abbreviation: Fgtra.) Here, *Miltassia* is mixed with another orchid— *Aspasia* (ah-SPAY-zee-ah), a genus of eight species—to generate the intergeneric hybrid *Forgetara*. A standout in this genus is *Fgera*. Everglades Pioneer, which brings *Aspasia principissa* into the heritage of these captivating hybrids. Light green, narrow sepals and petals barred with brown markings contrast with the large white lip. The 4-inch flowers—including those of the clone 'Dottie Kone,' HCC/AOS, shown above—have a glistening texture. Allow the media to dry slightly, but not entirely, between waterings. Pot in a porous medium that retains moisture but lets excess water drain.

■ *Miltassia* **Charles M. Fitch (Brs. verrucosa × Milt. spectabilis):** Orchid hybridizers often add some brassia in a cross with other genera to increase flower size and plant vigor. Miltonias are crossed with brassias to form the intergeneric hybrid *Miltassia* that is favored for its generous production of star-shaped flowers with ruffled lips. Miltassias are easy, flowering and growing in a wide range of temperatures and forgiving the beginner's sometimes-unsteady green thumb. One of the best known is *Mtssa*. Charles M. Fitch, named to honor photographer, horticulturist, orchid hybridizer, and educator Charles Marden Fitch.

■ *Miltassia* **Royal Robe (Mtssa. Erachne × Milt. Seminole Blood):** More hybrids, including this one, are being mericloned for mass propagation and distribution through the nursery trade. A benefit of buying mericloned orchids is that the name tells you exactly what you are purchasing. (Seed-grown plants may show variation in flower color, size, markings, and fragrance.) When shopping for plants of *Mtssa*. Royal Robe, look for the clone 'Jerry's Pick,' AM/AOS, with cheery large raspberry-colored flowers that come with a delightful fragrance. Eight to ten flowers are borne on each spike. Like other iltassias, it should not be allowed to dry completely and benefits from ntermediate temperatures and regular applications of weak fertilizer.

Miltassia Charles M. Fitch

Miltassia Royal Robe

BULBOPHYLLUM

bulb-oh-FILL-um

Abbreviation: Bulb.

Growth: Sympodial

Light: Low to medium

Temperature: Intermediate to warm

Flowering: Spring to autumn

Care: Intermediate to advanced

With more than 1,200 named species, *Bulbophyllum* is among the largest genera in the orchid family. These epiphytes have one or two leaves per pseudobulb and exhibit tremendous diversity in size, ranging from quite substantial specimens to those best observed with a magnifying glass. Bulbophyllums offer some of the most wonderfully quirky flowers in the orchid kingdom, among both the species and the hybrids. One of the more noteworthy features of the flowers is their fragrances. Many species are fly pollinated. To attract their pollinators, they emit scents mimicking carrion and other fragrances appetizing to flies. In addition, the flower lip (labellum) is hinged at the base of the column, allowing it to wiggle, jiggle, and bob in the slightest breeze.

Orchid taxonomists disagree on whether some of the orchids identified as bulbophyllums are members of that genus or should instead be assigned to smaller, closely related genera, the most common of which is *Cirrhopetalum* (seer-oh-PET-al-um). As a result, growers may find many species and hybrids labeled as either *Bulbophyllum* or *Cirrhopetalum* in catalogs, at nurseries, on the Internet, and at plant shows and sales.

Hybrids within the genus *Bulbophyllum* expand options for orchid growers. In addition to named hybrids that are registered with the Royal Horticultural Society, some unnamed hybrids are available.

Culture

Bulbophyllums offer something exotic for every orchid enthusiast, from those who raise plants in greenhouses to those who raise their specimens under lights in a basement light garden. Because of the variety of species in the genus and the habitats from which they originate, these cultural recommendations are necessarily general. Overall, bulbophyllums benefit from low to medium light—bright shade to gentle early morning sun—sufficient humidity with good air circulation, regular applications of weak fertilizer, and copious amounts of water when the plants are actively growing. Warm temperatures—daytime highs of 85° F and nighttime lows of 60° F—suit bulbophyllums. Bulbophyllums are fine in pots, but some are equally at home when grown in slat or mesh baskets or even on mounts.

Bulbophyllum affine

Species

■ **Bulbophyllum affine (syn. Bulb. kusukusense, Phyllorchis affinis, Sarcopodium affine):** Native to the lower altitudes in its original habitat, this plant reaches about 9 inches tall at maturity and bears single, light yellow to white blooms with red veining on 2½-inch-tall inflorescences growing from the base of the plant. Warm to intermediate growing conditions in bright shade agree with this summer-blooming species. Grow in a well-drained mix that is allowed to dry slightly between waterings. Native to northern India, Nepal, China, and Taiwan.

■ **Bulbophyllum graveolens (syn. Cirrhopetalum graveolens, Crphm. robustum):** A larger member of the genus, *Bulb. graveolens* can grow to 30 inches tall and put forth 8-inch-long inflorescences bearing umbels of nine long-lasting, sunny yellow flowers, each with a reddish, hinged lip. Native to lower elevations, this species is a warm-temperature plant. It can be cultivated in a large pot. It grows best with partial shade, high humidity, and copious water during active growth. Native to Papua New Guinea.

Bulbophyllum graveolens

■ *Bulbophyllum lobbii (syn. Bulb. lobbii var. siamense, Phyllorchis lobbii):* This medium-sized member of the genus reaches 12 inches in height and has a rambling growth habit with the pseudobulbs spaced about 3 inches apart along the rhizome. One of the few pleasantly scented members of its genus, *Bulb. lobbii* has single 2¾-inch flowers from pale yellow to bright gold with red, brown, or purple-red stripes. It will benefit from warm temperatures, bright shade, plentiful humidity, and a well-drained medium. Native to Thailand, Malaysia, Borneo, and the Philippines.

Bulbophyllum lobbii

■ *Bulbophyllum medusae (syn. Cirrhopetalum medusae, Phyllorchis medusae):* An oddly beautiful member of the genus, this intriguing species was named for the mythological Medusa, who bore a head full of writhing snakes in place of hair. This compact-growing plant

Bulbophyllum medusae

reaches about 9 inches, with large blooms for the plant size. It's easy to see why this curious species attracts attention: Its umbels of ghostly, pale cream-colored flowers reach nearly 5 inches in length. Grow in warm to hot temperatures with bright shade, high humidity, and plenty of water. Native to Thailand, Malaysia, Sumatra, Borneo, Singapore, and the Philippines.

■ *Bulbophyllum phalaenopsis (syn. Bulb. giganteum):* One of the largest members of the genus, this striking species has leaves that reach 3 feet tall at maturity. This species' deep

Bulbophyllum phalaenopsis

red flowers covered in light yellow protrusions mimic maggot-infested rotting meat in both appearance and scent, attracting flies and repelling humans when in bloom. Dedicated orchid enthusiasts should grow this species in shaded conditions, warm to hot temperatures, and high humidity with good air circulation and drainage. It does well in a hanging basket, which allows its leaves to be displayed gracefully. Native to New Guinea.

Hybrids

■ *Cirrhopetalum Elizabeth Ann (longissimum × rothschildianum) (syn. Bulbophyllum):* (Abbreviation: Crphm.) Registered as a *Bulbophyllum* in 1969, this orchid is also listed in catalogs and orchid literature under the genus name *Cirrhopetalum*. It is a popular hybrid displaying the best of both species parents. *Crphm.* Elizabeth Ann has taken numerous awards for its long umbels (up to 7 inches tall) of cream-colored blooms heavily striped a deep, rich reddish pink. Grown in intermediate to warm temperatures in light shade with regular waterings, this handsome hybrid rewards good cultivation with many impressive flowers.

Cirrhopetalum Elizabeth Ann 'Buckleberry', AM-FCC/AOS

CATASETUM

kat-a-SEE-tum

Abbreviation: Ctsm.

Growth: Sympodial

Light: Medium to bright

Temperatures: Warm

Flowering season: Variable

Level of care: Intermediate

About 100 species of *Catasetum* are native to the New World tropics, where they occur in seasonally dry habitats as epiphytes on the trunks of trees and palms, although some also grow as lithophytes. In cultivation, the plants will be lush and green during their growing season and deciduous during their dormant phase.

During this time the leaves drop; only a grouping of pseudobulbs remain in the container. Catasetums can put forth male or female flowers. In a few cases both flower sexes are borne on the same plant, sometimes even on the same inflorescence. In cultivation, the showier male flowers are most often produced, although female flowers are seen.

Catasetums have a surprising pollination mechanism. When you touch the flower, the pollinia shoot into the air. In nature, the pollinia attach to pollinators that carry the pollen to other flowers of the same species.

In addition to hybrids within the genus *Catasetum,* there are intergeneric hybrids between *Catasetum* and other genera, such as *Catamodes* (*Ctsm.* × *Mormodes*) and *Catanoches* (*Ctsm.* × *Cycnoches*). Some of these expand the color range, including *Catamodes* Black Magic (*Morm. sinuata* × *Ctsm.* Orchidglade). Registered by JEM Orchids of Delray Beach, Florida, in 1987, this hybrid features incredibly dark flowers, as the name Black Magic indicates.

Culture

Originating in hot tropical regions with distinct wet and dry seasons, these epiphytes require a growing period alternating with dormancy. In the autumn, when leaves begin to fall, start withholding water and then water sparingly during the winter months, as the plants rest. When new growths appear in spring, wait until they are 1 or 2 inches long before resuming regular watering. Although the new growths need plentiful water to develop and to store in their fast-growing pseudobulbs, keep water out of the crown of leaves, especially on young shoots. Catasetums are touchy about watering. One of the quickest ways to succeed with them is to master the art of watering.

Provide catasetums with medium bright light and warm daytime temperatures of 80° to 90° F. During their growth, fertilize regularly so the newly developing pseudobulbs will reach their maximum size. Provide ample humidity and good air circulation at all times. When the plants are actively growing, mites can be a problem. To keep them under control, maintain high humidity or spray with a miticide approved for use on orchids.

When potting catasetums, choose a porous, fast-draining medium and use a plastic or clay pot. Some growers set the plants inside wood-slat baskets, with or without a few large pieces of cork, bark, or horticultural-grade charcoal. Securely anchor the plant inside the container to prevent wobbling. Repot in the spring as new roots are forming, taking care to avoid injuring emerging roots. Catasetums benefit from being placed outdoors during the summer, where they receive both fresh air and bright light.

Species

■ *Catasetum fimbriatum:* The specific epithet *fimbriatum* refers to the fringed lip of the 2-inch-tall flowers that were chosen as the emblem of the Brazilian Catasetinae Growers Association. The male flowers are produced on graceful inflorescences. They are green to yellow with varying amounts of red-brown spotting and have a strong, pleasant fragrance. Some shade is necessary to induce the male flowers on this catasetum. It is tolerant of various cultural conditions, although a well-drained mix and ample air movement are recommended. Native to Brazil, Paraguay, Uruguay, Argentina, and Bolivia.

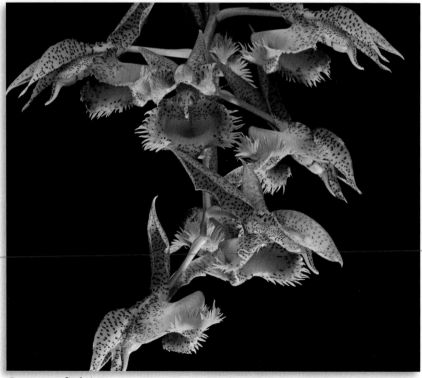

Catasetum fimbriatum

Catasetum maculatum

■ **Catasetum maculatum:** This robust species flowers in the summer. About 10 flowers, which are green-spotted maroon or even solid maroon, are borne toward the middle and end of the 20-inch-long inflorescence. A good subject for the greenhouse grower, it can be raised on a mount or in a wood-slat basket positioned in bright light. Native from Panama south to Costa Rica, Colombia, Venezuela, and Brazil.

Catasetum pileatum

■ **Catasetum pileatum:** This was the national flower of Venezuela until 1921. Common names such as mother-of-pearl flower and white rooster convey the beauty of the flowers, which are typically pure white, although yellow forms are known. Male flowers reach 3 inches in diameter. They are gracefully arranged in an overlapping manner along the 12-inch-long inflorescence. This summer- and autumn-flowering species can bloom at other times of year, too. A good choice for someone just starting to grow this genus of epiphytes, it benefits from a well-drained medium, bright light, and plentiful water and fertilizer during active growth. Native to Trinidad and Tobago, Venezuela, Brazil, and Colombia.

Catasetum tenebrosum

■ **Catasetum tenebrosum:** The handsome flowers of this species convey an understated elegance. A yellow-green lip contrasts with dark wine red sepals and petals. Unlike most catasetums, the rest period for *Ctsm. tenebrosum* is brief. This easily grown species benefits from some shade and does best on a mount or in a wood-slat basket that will provide the aeration necessary to avoid rot. Native to Ecuador, Peru, and Brazil.

Hybrids

■ **Catasetum Susan Fuchs (expansum × Orchidglade):** Registered in 1982, this hybrid is named for Susan Fuchs, the younger sister of Robert Fuchs, world-famous hybridizer and owner of R. F. Orchids in Homestead, Florida. In September and October, the green or bright chartreuse flowers are often speckled mahogany and may grow as large as 3 inches, often with more than a dozen flowers on each of the pendulous inflorescences. *Ctsm.* Susan Fuchs is easy to cultivate, provided the new growths are protected as they emerge. Never allow water to collect in the crown of the new foliage. When the leaves have fallen, keep the plant dry during the dormant period, with only occasional watering, perhaps every 10 days to 2 weeks. Stop fertilizing.

Catasetum Susan Fuchs

CATTLEYA

KAT-lee-ah

Abbreviation: C.

Growth: Sympodial

Light: Medium to high

Temperature: Intermediate to warm

Flowering: Variable

Care: Beginner

When most people think of an orchid, they think of a cattleya, the prom-night corsage. Important in orchid history, the genus was named after William Cattley, the English horticulturist who first brought these beautiful plants into flower outside of their native habitat. Cattley was growing plants shipped to him from South America by a plant explorer named Swainson. In preparing his shipments, Swainson included plants of the undescribed orchid. Upon their arrival, his curiosity piqued by the odd plants, Cattley potted them up. When the plants started flowering in 1824, Cattley showed them to John Lindley, a famous botanist. Lindley recognized that these gorgeous flowers were new to science. He named the genus *Cattleya* and the species *labiata,* in reference to the flower's impressive lip. Word of the discovery spread quickly, inciting orchidmania. To this day, cattleyas reign as queen of the orchids. Fifty species in the genus *Cattleya* offer a great variety from which to choose and form a solid foundation from which hybrids and intergeneric hybrids have been developed.

In fact, thousands of cattleya hybrids have been produced. Most involve crosses with plants in other genera, for example: *Brassolaeliocattleya (Brassavola × Laelia × Cattleya), Epicattleya (Epidendrum × Cattleya), Laeliocattleya (Laelia × Cattleya), Potinara (Brassavola × Cattleya × Laelia × Sophronitis)* and *Sophrolaeliocattleya (Sophronitis × Laelia × Cattleya).* These are discussed under Intergeneric Hybrids, page 120.

The range of colors, patterns, and fragrances found in hybrids is astounding. Flowers in rose, pink, and lavender may have lips of vivid chartreuse with yellow markings in the throat. Yellow flowers may be pure gold or tinged with green and have red markings on their lips. The green forms with yellow- or red-marked lips often have lemony fragrances. Whites and semi-whites usually have contrasting lips marked with red, purple, or yellow.

Culture

Cattleyas are among the easiest orchids to grow. Their thick pseudobulbs enable them to withstand periods of drought. Attentive growers may need to avoid overwatering. The growing medium needs to dry out almost completely—but not quite—between waterings. Cattleyas growing in fir bark need to be watered about once a week when they are in active growth. After flowering, cattleyas may enter a resting phase lasting a month or two. During this time of semidormancy, often during the shorter days of winter, increase the intervals between waterings and fertilizer. Generally, the plants will take longer to dry between waterings because of the cooler temperatures and shorter days. Too much water or fertilizer during the winter can lead to weak, spindly growth that is more susceptible to disease, and plants are less likely to flower in the appropriate season.

Species cattleyas may be more seasonally oriented in their culture than hybrids. It is important to be ready to pot when new roots are initiated from developing growths, as this may be the only time during any given year that new roots are formed. Plants potted at the wrong time languish and may die because of the lack of new roots. Plants potted at the appropriate time grow robustly and present no problems.

It's a fallacy that plants normally initiate new roots from freshly emerging growths, as many believe. Rather, the new roots come from

Cattleya aurantiaca

the base of the growth when it is anywhere from half-developed to recently flowered, depending on the species. The grower must observe the plants over a period of time and notice when new roots form.

Pot when the medium has decomposed—most commonly used media seldom last more than 24 months—and the plant is making new roots. Keep watch between the two equinoxes—around March 20 and September 22. Avoid repotting when the days grow shorter than 12 hours.

When potting, firmly anchor the plant in the container, placing the rhizome level with the surface of the medium. Choose a container that is large enough but not too large— it should allow for a maximum of two years' growth. Another good rule: Pot for the bottom rather than for the top. That is, choose a pot according to the size of the root ball and ignore what seems to be in proportion with the foliar mass. Top-heavy plants with few roots may fit into a relatively small pot and will need to be staked well until new roots anchor the plant in the pot. If the plants still fall over, set their containers into larger clay pots or vessels with drainage holes to keep the plant upright. To reduce stress after repotting, especially for poorly rooted plants, place the plants where they will receive more shade and humidity until roots appear. When

roots emerge, gradually increase watering and resume fertilizing.

Cattleya flowers can last from two to four weeks on the plant. Cut flowers last about a week. To make them last as long as possible, avoid cutting the flowers until they have fully expanded and ripened—about three to five days after they open. Although they may be richly fragrant on the plant, the flowers lose their fragrance when cut. Touching the flowers may cause them to age prematurely as a result of oily hand residue.

Species

Species cattleyas were once secondary to hybrids, but there are many superior species newly available. Cattleyas are divided into two groups according to the number of leaves arising from the pseudobulbs: unifoliate and bifoliate.

Unifoliate cattleyas have a single leaf on each pseudobulb and grow between 1 and 2 feet tall. The flowers, generally borne one to five per stem, are between 2 and 7 inches across. Hybrid flowers may be larger. Their large, ruffled lip is often marked with colorful patterns. Unifoliates may also be called labiates in reference to *C. labiata,* the most important species in the group. Labiate species were once the standard cut flowers, imported en masse from Central and South America. Rarely seen in collections

for many years, species of this group are making a comeback in availability and popularity as select seed-raised populations of superior or unusual types.

Bifoliate cattleyas have two or sometimes three leaves atop long, slender pseudobulbs. The bifoliates range from 15 inches to 5 feet tall. The flowers, which are generally thicker and smaller than those of the unifoliates, are borne 10 to 25 per inflorescence and usually last longer than those of the unifoliates.

■ *Cattleya aurantiaca:* Bifoliate. This winter-flowering species grows 18 to 24 inches tall. The clustered flowers are thick, bright orange or orange-red, and 1 inch across. It flowers in late winter, often in late February to March. Flower sheaths formed in summer can often be dry and brown by the time the flowering season arrives and may impede flowering if they are not carefully removed. This species rapidly makes large specimen plants and is a good choice for the subtropical and tropical garden where frost does not threaten. Commonly used in hybridizing, *C. aurantiaca* is an ancestor of many hybrids with orange and red flowers. Native to Mexico, Guatemala, El Salvador, Honduras, and Nicaragua.

■ *Cattleya bicolor:* Bifoliate. The thin pseudobulbs may reach 4 feet

tall. The fragrant flowers, four to seven per inflorescence, spread up to 4 inches across. The sepals and petals are golden green with a coppery tinge and a brilliant purplish-red, narrow lip. *C. bicolor* flowers in autumn. Pot only when new roots are forming, generally when the new growths are at least half developed. This species demands space to reach its full potential. Native to Brazil.

■ *Cattleya bowringiana:* Bifoliate. This species can be one of the showiest of all cattleyas, with big clusters of bright lavender medium-size flowers offset by a darker lip. The plants can reach massive proportions, with the individual pseudobulbs growing more than 30 inches tall and even modestly sized plants requiring an 8-inch pot. However, when the heads of blooms appear in the autumn, growers fall in love with this fine orchid. *C. bowringiana* is also the progenitor of a race of outstanding multifloral lavender- and purple-flowered hybrids that are rare but well worth the search. Native to Honduras, Belize, and Guatemala.

Cattleya bowringiana

Cattleya bicolor

Cattleya gaskelliana

Cattleya guttata

Cattleya *continued*

■ **Cattleya gaskelliana:** Unifoliate. *C. gaskelliana* flowers in early summer. Typically a lighter rose than *C. labiata,* it has a splash of darker color in the trumpet-shaped lip. *C. gaskelliana* has become more available recently as select sibling crosses from Venezuela. You can acquire a variety of different colors.

When a plant needs repotting, wait until the plant has finished flowering and new roots are emerging from the ripening growth. Native to Venezuela.

■ **Cattleya ×guatemalensis:** Bifoliate. The natural hybrid of *C. aurantiaca* and *C. skinneri,* this plant has also been remade many times in cultivation with superior parents, resulting in plants with flowers showing off a broad range of sherbet colors from cream through peach, rose, and orange. The hybrid's growth habit is intermediate between the two parents. It is common for the plants to grow 24 inches tall. They flower freely late winter through spring with showy clusters of 2- to 3-inch flowers. *C. ×guatemalensis* is an excellent specimen and is ideal for garden culture in mild winter areas. Native to Guatemala.

■ **Cattleya guttata:** Bifoliate. Usually about 3 feet tall, this species flowers from late autumn to winter. Vigorous forms of *C. guttata* may grow to 5 feet tall. The fragrant yellow-green flowers are heavily blotched with wine-red to brown. The lip is usually magenta and may have white side lobes. *C. guttata* has been used by hybridizers to produce popular novelty hybrids with heavily spotted flowers. This is another species that must be repotted at the right time of year. Monitor plants and make sure new roots are emerging before repotting. Native to Brazil.

Cattleya ×guatemalensis

Cattleya labiata

■ *Cattleya lueddemanniana:*
Unifoliate. A superb, large-flowered species, it is set apart from its closely related species by an exceptional brilliance and depth of rose color, highlighted by a diamond-dust texture.

In January and February, two to four flowers, 7 inches wide, appear on relatively compact plants that seldom grow more than 24 inches tall. Plants of this spectacular orchid are increasingly available to growers. Pot after flowering when the new roots emerge. Native to Venezuela.

■ *Cattleya labiata:* Unifoliate. This plant grows up to 2 feet tall and represents the typical corsage orchid. Its rosy flowers have excellent proportions and a fine texture. The large, ruffled lip—for which the species is named—is deep rose lavender with dark lines leading to a pair of yellow spots in the throat. The long-lasting flowers are fragrant. The plants flower in autumn in response to shorter days. A lamp left on in the evening during autumn will prevent flowering. Native to Brazil.

Cattleya lueddemanniana

■ *Cattleya luteola:* Unifoliate. *C. luteola* is a dwarf species, usually no more than 8 inches tall. It can even flower when only 2 inches tall. It has been valuable in breeding miniature hybrids. The 2-inch-wide winter flowers come in shades of yellow, often with red in the tubular lip. Like *C. walkeriana,* this species does best on mounts or in baskets. Native to Brazil, Peru, Ecuador, and Bolivia.

Cattleya luteola

Cattleya maxima

Cattleya continued

■ **Cattleya maxima:** Unifoliate. There are two distinct plant forms of this species: One is quite large, growing to more than 3 feet tall, while the other is more compact, often less than 24 inches tall. Although individual flowers may seem less attractive than those of some of its labiate relatives, they are borne on imposing, upright spikes of 12 or more, giving an outstanding display. Generally, the flowers are rose lavender with darker veining in the tubular lip. Native to Peru.

■ **Cattleya mossiae:** Unifoliate. This spring-flowering plant has given horticulture a group of hybrids that form the basis of the cut-flower industry. *C. mossiae,*

like many of its cousins, comes in a range of colors from the typical lavender to white with a yellow or rose-veined lip to nearly blue. The most common shade is lavender, which may have a special rosy glow that sets it apart. The flowers are highly perfumed. *C. mossiae* can have some of the largest of all cattleya flowers, up to 8 inches across. When plants have outgrown their containers, repot them after flowering. Well-grown plants of *C. mossiae* make excellent specimens, branching freely and giving tall inflorescences of up to seven blooms. Native to Venezuela.

■ **Cattleya percivaliana:** Unifoliate. More compact than most of its close relatives—growing to only about 12 inches tall—this cattleya flowers at Christmas. Closer to a true lavender than most, *C. percivaliana* is easily recognized by the distinctive golden yellow background in its trumpet-

Cattleya percivaliana

shaped throat, overlaid with darker rose. The musky scent is considered attractive by some hobbyists. Plants of this species easily and rapidly grow into fine specimens because of the free-branching nature of the rhizomes. Pot plants after flowering. Native to Venezuela.

■ **Cattleya skinneri:** Bifoliate. The 3-inch-wide flowers of this species vary from rose to purple to a less common white, with a glittery texture and a faint fragrance. This 2-foot-tall plant has an excellent habit and makes many new growths every year. It flowers from late winter to spring. Although the flowers are shorter-lived than other *Cattleya* species, it remains a favorite because of the tremendous show it puts on. It is the national flower of Costa Rica. Native to Mexico, Guatemala, Honduras, and Costa Rica.

Cattleya skinneri

Cattleya mossiae

Cattleya trianaei

■ *Cattleya trianaei*: Unifoliate. Some find this winter-flowering species to be the most lovely of the unifoliates. The large broad-petaled flowers give an impression of massiveness that contrasts with the lovely, soft rose-lavender color and trumpet-shaped lip with its characteristic lipstick mark at the tip. *C. trianaei* is an important species in producing large-flowered hybrids of all colors. Its only drawback is a tendency to be a large, too-exuberant grower. Native to Colombia.

Cattleya walkeriana

■ *Cattleya walkeriana*: Bifoliate. Although technically a bifoliate cattleya, *C. walkeriana* often has only one leaf on its pseudobulbs that grows 4 to 6 inches tall. This is a popular species because of its compact plant habit coupled with its relatively large, often fragrant, shapely bright rose-lavender flowers. The long-lasting flowers are usually borne singly, although sometimes two or three appear on an abortive growth arising from the base of the most recently matured pseudobulbs.

Grow plants of *C. walkeriana* on cork slabs or in baskets, where their need for dryness during winter can be accommodated. *C. walkeriana* benefits from higher light than most cattleyas and may not flower if given too much fertilizer, particularly in winter. Native to Brazil.

Hybrids

■ *Cattleya* Chocolate Drop (*guttata* × *aurantiaca*): Bifoliate. One of the most popular hybrids of the mid-1960s, *C.* Chocolate Drop is making a resurgence as a parent of hybrids. *C.* Chocolate Drop is a husky plant that puts out clusters of up to 15 or more oxblood, maroon or orange star-shaped flowers. The flowers are about 3 inches across and of heavy substance. Bright light, a well-drained medium, and frequent applications of a dilute fertilizer during the growing season will transform an ordinary plant into a great show specimen.

■ *Cattleya* Porcia (Armstrongiae × *bowringiana*): Bifoliate. An older hybrid, registered in 1927 by H. G. Alexander, Ltd., of Great Britain, this lavender beauty is best known for the clone 'Cannizarro,' AM-FCC/AOS. *C.* Porcia grows into massive plants that can be up to 36 inches tall with 12-inch-long inflorescences of brilliant rose flowers with a darker lip. Showy *C.* Porcia is worth searching for, although it requires room and needs to be grown where there is space.

Cattleya Porcia

Cattleya Chocolate Drop

Cattleytonia **Why Not**

Cattleya *continued*

Intergeneric hybrids

■ *Cattleytonia* **Why Not (C. aurantiaca × Broughtonia sanguinea):** (Abbreviation: Ctna.) Perhaps no other cattleytonia has been so widely propagated by both seed and meristems as *Ctna.* Why Not. The dwarf plant is often no more than 8 inches tall, putting out branching inflorescences with bright red, circular 1½-inch-wide flowers. The flowers are long lasting and the plant is easy to grow in mild-winter areas where it can be a good garden plant.

■ *Potinara* **Twentyfour Carat (Pot. Lemon Tree × Blc. Yellow Imp):** (Abbreviation: Pot.) This eye-catching hybrid has been

Potinara **Twentyfour Carat**

widely propagated by meristems, particularly the clone 'Lea,' AM/AOS. This potinara is popular for its compact growth habit— it flowers when only 15 inches tall—and for its ease of growth. Another exciting feature is the production of bright golden yellow flowers that are highly perfumed with citrus and may appear more than once a year. This plant is an excellent choice for under lights, on windowsills, or anywhere else where it will receive sufficient light and have moderate room to grow.

Relatives

■ *Barkeria lindleyana:*
(Abbreviation: Bark.) The genus *Barkeria* (bar-CARE-ee-ah) is related to the genus *Epidendrum*. Fifteen species of *Barkeria* are native to Mexico, Guatemala, Cuba, and Panama, where they grow as epiphytes. *Bark. lindleyana* is one of the most popular and satisfactory of the genus. It is valued for its tall inflorescences that carry 12 or more 1-inch-wide rose-lavender, birdlike flowers. These reedlike plants are deciduous in winter and are best grown on mounts where they are most easily given the dry rest they require. Native to Mexico and Costa Rica.

Barkeria lindleyana

■ *Broughtonia sanguinea:*
(Abbreviation: Bro.) Six species and one natural hybrid comprise the genus *Broughtonia* (brow-TOH-nee-ah). *Bro. sanguinea* is an epiphyte with clusters of typically reddish-purple flowers, although forms with yellow and white flowers are known. Today, there are select sibling crosses, superior to the wild types, available to hobbyists who want to add this compact-growing plant to their collection along with hybrids it has parented. It is best grown on

Broughtonia sanguinea

mounts in relatively high light. *Bro. sanguinea* does well as a garden plant in South Florida. Native to Jamaica.

■ *Schomburgkia tibicinis*
(syn. *Myrmecophila tibicinis*):
(Abbreviation: Schom.) *Schomburgkia* (shom-BERG-kee-ah) is a genus of about 20 species native to the Caribbean, Mexico, Central America, and northern South America. Specimens of *Schom. tibicinis* are often seen rambling up sea grapes and cabbage palms. In nature, the tall cylindrical, hollow pseudobulbs are home to defensive stinging ants. These ants are rarely present in cultivated plants. The pseudobulbs can reach more than 30 inches tall with the inflorescences growing to more than 8 feet. This winter-flowering species puts forth wavy, 4-inch-wide rose flowers. The plants can attain prodigious size and are not well contained in a pot. They do better attached to a mount or, better still, secured to a live tree in a climate where frost does not threaten. Provide the necessary warmth and humidity for this tropical wonder. Native to Mexico, Honduras, Guatemala, and Belize.

Schomburgkia tibicinis

CYMBIDIUM

sim-BID-ee-um

Abbreviation: Cym.

Growth: Sympodial

Light: Bright (standards); medium to bright (miniatures)

Temperature: Cool (standards); cool to intermediate (miniatures)

Flowering: Variable; peak in early spring

Care: Beginner

Substantial, waxy, long-lasting cymbidium flowers are as common as cattleyas in flower shops in both corsages and cut sprays. Cymbidium flower colors, which include all but blue, are often combined in lovely patterns. Imagine, for example, a pistachio green flower with a scarlet-and-white lip. Individual flowers are popular for corsages or arrangements and, when left on the plant, last between 8 and 10 weeks.

Years of intense breeding have yielded hybrids that outshine the species in flower form, extraordinary colors, and longevity. Cymbidium hybrids are also usually easier to grow than the species, tolerating broader ranges of temperature and blooming more freely.

Culture

A most important lesson to learn about cymbidiums is that some are hemiepiphytes—partly of the earth but also of the air. They grow on the ground, but not in it. Their natural habit is in forest duff, the accumulated humus of the forest floor. Therefore, they require a turfy or otherwise humus-rich growing medium that constantly allows air to reach the roots but also nurtures them with some moisture at all times.

Cymbidiums also need sunlight, so much so that the leaves should appear slightly yellowish green. If they are dark green, then the light either is not strong enough or is not being received for a sufficient duration. If the leaves burn, there has been too much sun.

When potting, set the plant in a pot of sufficient size to balance the top, probably a clay one—although they do well in plastic. Then leave the plant to establish until the surface is nearly filled with pseudobulbs. Fertilize faithfully through spring and summer. Top dressing with 14-14-14 timed-release fertilizer pellets works well; some media benefit from a dose of 30-10-10 every other week.

Specimen cymbidiums purchased in bloom as house decorations are often set outdoors in the summer. Over much of the continental United States, they adapt and bloom again. The secret is to find a place outdoors where there is good air circulation but protection from strong winds; where the sunlight is strong enough to nurture the leaves and pseudobulbs, but not to scorch them; and where the hose will be handy to give them water when rainfall is not sufficient to maintain fairly evenly moist conditions. Cymbidiums will often bear flowers in winter to spring if they are fertilized regularly, left outdoors until the day before frost is predicted to set the flower buds, and then brought in to a cozy but not too warm sun porch.

Species

Although most people grow hybrids, *Cymbidium* species have a loyal following of enthusiast hobbyists eager to meet their cultural needs. Both the Japanese and the Chinese have long been fascinated with the species cymbidiums native to their countries, coveting their treasures and seeking out variations. Some hobbyists raise species cymbidiums in special tall clay containers, often embellished with glazes and carved decorations.

■ **Cymbidium devonianum:** This species is unusual among cultivated cymbidiums in that it benefits from more shade to protect its rather broad

Cymbidium devonianum

leaves. Seldom seen in collections, it is notable more for its contribution to the popular line of pendent, or cascading, types that have an almost cultlike following in Southern California. The first hybrids from this species were the production of Keith Andrew. Many others have followed since the mid-1960s. The colors of hybrids derived from *Cym. devonianum,* once regarded as slightly muddy, now come in a broad palette from red to pink to white and beyond, nearly all offset by a bright blood red, banded lip. *Cym. devonianum* and its hybrids make outstanding specimen plants, particularly well adapted to basket culture, where their flowing inflorescences can be most easily accommodated and viewed. Expect to pay a premium for these highly sought-after plants. Native to Northeast India and Northern Thailand.

■ **Cymbidium ensifolium:** This attractive plant features handsome, upright leaves with nearly inconspicuous pseudobulbs. The tall, narrow Asian pots suit this species. When the upright spikes of striped cream flowers appear in the autumn, the grower will be rewarded not only with a lovely floral display but also with an elegant, haunting fragrance. *Cym. ensifolium* will grow equally well with other cymbidiums or in warmer climates. Native to the Philippines, China, and India.

Cymbidium ensifolium

Hybrids

Cymbidium hybrids fall into two main groups, miniatures and standards.

MINIATURE HYBRIDS: The flowers of miniature cymbidiums are between 1 and 3 inches in diameter. Although some plants are still too large to be considered true miniature orchids (which are generally less than 6 inches tall), their 1- to 2-foot maximum height makes them more manageable.

Many miniatures will produce flowers in warmer temperatures than will standards. Their high light requirement still makes them greenhouse or outdoor plants.

It is unlikely they will prosper as year-round indoor or light-garden plants. If miniature cymbidiums can be summered outdoors, they will bloom beautifully indoors through the autumn and winter months.

Standards and miniatures are semiterrestrial plants. They need constant moisture and are potted in plastic or clay pots in mixes that retain large quantities of water while still allowing adequate aeration. As with other orchids, many mixes are suitable. Some growers use fine fir bark; others pot cymbidiums in a mixture of 20 percent peat moss, 45 percent medium-grade fir bark, and 35 percent redwood chips.

Miniatures bloom any time from late autumn to spring. Popular *Cym.* Golden Elf 'Sundust', HCC/AOS, flowers in summer. A variety of colors is available among the miniature cymbidiums, with hundreds of exceptional hybrids. The miniature cymbidium's success guarantees that more new hybrids will be developed. Today you will still see what are known as novelty or intermediate types, which are a complex combination of standards and miniatures.

STANDARD HYBRIDS: Standard cymbidiums bear flowers between 3 and 5 inches across and grow up to 3 feet tall. They require bright sunlight and cool night temperatures. Along the California coast, where these requirements are easily satisfied, standard cymbidiums are considered low-maintenance outdoor plants. In other areas, standard cymbidiums are considered rather difficult cool-greenhouse plants.

Most standard hybrids were originally produced for the cut-flower trade, where timing is critical. As a result, you can choose plants for bloom in any of three seasons. Early hybrids flower before January, midseason hybrids flower from January to April, and late-season hybrids from April to May. Award-winning hybrids are available for each blooming season. Currently, however, breeding is focused on potted plants. The compact stature and freedom of bloom are more important than before.

Cymbidium *continued*

■ *Cymbidium* Golden Elf (*ensifolium* × Enid Haupt):

Registered in 1978 by the Rod McLellan Company, this is one of the most often propagated cymbidiums because it is so widely adaptable to a variety of conditions. Brilliant yellow, highly perfumed flowers are borne above compact foliage. The clone 'Sundust,' HCC/AOS, will not only tolerate but prefers warmer conditions than most cymbidiums. It is quite at home in South Florida or in California. As with other

Cymbidium Golden Elf

warmth-tolerant cymbidiums, flower life is not as long as traditional types, usually two to three weeks.

■ *Cymbidium* Sweet Dreams (*sinense* × Nila):

This is another popular, though less widely distributed, warmth-tolerant cymbidium. Tall, upright spikes

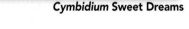

Cymbidium Sweet Dreams

of clear pale green, star-shaped blooms give a charming display. The decorative foliage is an attractive bonus, coming from the species parent, which is often grown solely for its foliage in China. It flowers in late winter.

WARMTH-TOLERANT HYBRIDS:

Florida's Milton Carpenter of Everglades Orchids is a focused breeder, striving for more than 30 years to create cymbidium hybrids that will grow and flower in warmer climates. One example of his success in this

line is *Cym.* Everglades, combining the known warmth-tolerance of the famous *Cym.* Peter Pan with the beautiful species *Cym. parishii*. A single spike may bear as many as 18 rose-flushed cream flowers of medium size offset by a boldly marked lip. With the expansion of the orchid pot-plant industry in South Florida, hobbyists can look forward to seeing more of this adaptable type in markets soon.

Relatives

■ *Ansellia africana:* (Abbreviation: Aslla.)

This robust epiphyte is named after an English gardener John Ansell, who collected the specimen on which botanists based

Ansellia africana

the official description. This variable species is widespread in its native habitat, south and tropical Africa. *Ansellia* (an-SELL-ee-ah) generally grows well with cattleyas, though it will make an excellent garden specimen in South Florida or Southern California. Commonly known as the leopard orchid for its 1½- to 2-inch bold yellow blooms heavily barred with mahogany, the plant displays a bounty of spikes from the top of the canelike pseudobulbs as well as from nodes along the canes. Some growers enjoy the musky fragrance, which other people may consider overpowering in an enclosed environment.

One of the more commonly seen cultivars is 'Garden Party,' HCC/AOS (an alba form), with clear yellow blooms on plants about half the size of many other examples of the species. Introduced by Cal-Orchid, Inc., it is now fairly widespread.

■ *Cyrtopodium andersonii*:
(Abbreviation: Cyrt.) *Cyrtopodium* (sir-toh-POH-dee-um) is a genus

native to the New World tropics and is easily recognized by its large pseudobulbs with sugarcane-like deciduous leaves. Husky branched inflorescences emerge from newly initiated growths and can swell to great size, giving a spectacular floral display. Cyrtopodiums are grown more often as large garden plants where conditions permit. These plants are hard to find but are worth searching out.

Cyrt. andersonii is one of the better-known members of this genus, notable for its brilliantly colored green and yellow blooms. Branching inflorescences can be in excess of 4 feet tall and may display 60 or more 1½-inch flowers. This species is best grown in bright light, like that provided for terete-leaved vandas, and will need a dry rest during winter months. As new growth emerges, watering and fertilizer should be gradually increased. Where conditions are right, as in South Florida and related climates, few other orchids will put on an incredibly spectacular display. Native from Brazil to the West Indies.

Cyrtopodium andersonii

DENDROBIUM

den-DROH-bee-um

Abbreviation: Den.

Growth: Sympodial

Light: Medium to bright

Temperature: Cool to warm

Flowering: Varies, depending on species

Care: Beginner to advanced, depending on species

The genus *Dendrobium* is extremely large. It contains as many as 1,500 species, found in a vast area stretching from Korea and Japan through Malaysia and from Indonesia to Australia and New Zealand. New Guinea alone is rich in dendrobium, home to more than 350 species, with some researchers pushing the total to above 500.

The plant and flower forms of dendrobiums vary considerably. To clarify this, experts have divided the genus into sections with similar characteristics. Most of the popular dendrobiums fall into one of the eight sections described on page 127. In many cases, plants in a section share common cultural needs, which can vary widely in this genus. You can decide how to best grow a dendrobium plant by determining the section to which it belongs.

Dendrobiums exhibit a tremendous range in size, from miniatures suitable for growing under lights to sprawling specimens with 10-foot-long canes or pseudobulbs better adapted to life in a greenhouse or outside in a tropical garden on a tree. Some are remarkably easy to grow, making them almost foolproof, while others challenge even a seasoned grower's skills. Some of the species produce fabulous fragrances, from the lemon-scented flowers of *Den. senile* to the delightful raspberry scent of *Den. parishii*. The diversity of dendrobiums makes members of this genus accessible to growers with varied environments in which to raise their plants, placing this group of Old World orchids within reach of every hobbyist.

Most dendrobium hybrids are offspring of *Den. nobile* or *Den. phalaenopsis,* although the antelope-type dendrobium hybrids are increasingly popular at nurseries and big-box stores. Of the *Den. nobile* hybrids, some of the most popular are the Yamamoto crosses that have been registered with the Royal Horticultural Society by Yamamoto Dendrobiums of Hawaii. These plants are now more commonly grown than the selections of *Den. nobile* species.

Culture

Dendrobiums grow in climates that vary from steamy tropical lowlands to frosty mountain forests. The flowering habits of the plants are often directly related to seasonal patterns. In order to flower, some species need cool conditions in the autumn, some require a dry spell after the new growths mature, and others need a cool dry spell.

Den. phalaenopsis will bloom in light at the low end of the medium range, alongside plants in the genus *Phalaenopsis*. Plants will produce sturdier growths and more flowers if given more light.

Many dendrobiums can be potted in containers, usually clay or plastic. Many also grow equally well when placed inside wood-slat baskets, attached to mounts, or placed directly on trees in tropical gardens.

Potted specimens are best kept potbound even though a plant will seem out of proportion to the size of the container. To keep top-heavy plants upright, stake them and place small containers inside larger ones with drain holes

Smaller containers packed with roots will need watering more frequently. During the growing season, copious amounts of diluted fertilizer will encourage strong healthy growth.

Dendrobium smilliae

Dendrobium loddigesii

Sections

CALLISTA: These are evergreen plants, and most have pseudobulbs. The flower spikes, produced in the spring, are usually pendent and carry flowers in shades of yellow, white, or lavender. Grow these types under intermediate conditions in summer. In winter, they need cool nights and dry conditions. The youngest pseudobulbs should shrivel slightly during this winter treatment, but water them enough to keep them from wasting away. Species in this section include *Den. chrysotoxum, Den. densiflorum, Den. farmeri, Den. lindleyi* (syn. *aggregatum*), and *Den. thyrsiflorum.*

SPATULATA: The species in this section are commonly called antelope dendrobiums because the flowers have paired upright, twisted petals that resemble the horns of an antelope. The plants are evergreen and have slender pseudobulbs. They need intermediate conditions throughout the year but tolerate cool winters if kept dry. Species in this section are easier to grow than some of the others because they flower without any special rest. This section includes the species *Den. antennatum, Den. canaliculatum,*

Den. discolor, Den. gouldii, Den. johannis, Den. lineale, Den. stratiotes, Den. strebloceras, and *Den. taurinum.*

DENDROBIUM: These species are deciduous, and most have drooping canes. Flowers are held near the ends of the mature, leafless canes. The plants need medium to bright light and intermediate to cool temperatures in summer. They must have a cool, dry winter to flower—between 40° and 50° F at night, little water, and no fertilizer.

Species in this large group include *Den. anosmum, Den. chrysanthum, Den. falconeri, Den. fimbriatum, Den. findlayanum, Den. friedricksianum, Den. heterocarpum, Den. loddigesii, Den. moniliforme, Den. nobile, Den. parishii, Den. primulinum, Den. transparens,* and *Den. wardianum.*

FORMOSAE: These plants have evergreen leaves and narrow, upright pseudobulbs with patches of black hair where the leaves join. Flowers are white, up to 4 inches across, and marked with yellow, orange, green, or violet. Plants in this section require cool to intermediate conditions all year and should dry out slightly in winter. Species include *Den. bellatulum, Den. draconis, Den. formosum, Den. infundibulum, Den. lowii, Den. lyonii* (syn. *Epigeneium lyonii*), *Den. margaritaceum,* and *Den. sanderae.*

LATOURIA: These plants are evergreen and have pseudobulbs. The flowers are usually yellow to green. A relatively easy group, these plants grow and flower well in cool to intermediate conditions. No special resting treatments are needed. Keep the plants on the dry side if the temperature drops into the cool range. Species in this group include *Den. atroviolaceum, Den. johnsoniae, Den. macrophyllum,* and *Den. spectabile.*

OXYGLOSSUM: These small-growing evergreen plants come primarily from middle to high elevations. The

long-lasting flowers are intensely colored. Cool night temperatures, sunny days, and high humidity are essential for success with these petite orchids. Keep them from drying out. Richard Warren of the Equatorial Plant Company in Edinburgh, Scotland, introduced several of these exciting species into wider cultivation through seed-grown plants. These artificially propagated plants provide hobbyists with a chance to try these gems without harm to the plants' native habitats. Species in this group include *Den. cuthbertsonii, Den. hellwigianum, Den. laevifolium,* and *Den. vexillarius.*

PEDILONUM: These medium-size plants have upright and pendent canes with leaves. Inflorescences with multiple flowers are borne on leafless canes. The flowers are often vivid—pink, purple, orange— although some are white and cream. The plants grow in cool to intermediate temperatures, some requiring a cool winter rest. Species in this group include *Den. amethystoglossum, Den. miyakei, Den. secundum, Den. smilliae,* and *Den. victoriae-reginae.*

PHALAENANTHE: These plants may be evergreen or deciduous, depending on conditions. Their pseudobulbs are tall and thin. The most popular species in this section, *Den. phalaenopsis,* bears flowers that are similar in many ways to those in the genus *Phalaenopsis.* They have a flattened shape and are arranged on the inflorescence in two parallel rows. The individual flowers last a long time—six to eight weeks— and a plant may remain in bloom for three to four months. New and old growths produce inflorescences, beginning in early spring. *Den. phalaenopsis* requires intermediate to warm temperatures all year. *Phalaenanthe* types need no special treatment, although overwatering will make a plant produce keikis, not flowers. Other species in this section include *Den. affine, Den. bigibbum, Den. dicuphum,* and *Den. williamsianum.*

Dendrobium *continued*

Species

■ *Dendrobium amethystoglossum:*
Section *Pedilonum*. This less
common winter-flowering species
produces showy, waxy, fragrant
flowers that last for up to a month.
Connoisseurs of dendrobiums
cherish the gracefully pendent
open clusters of white flowers
with a purple lip that are borne
several to a 20- to 40-inch tall cane.
Pot in an open mix with good
drainage, and provide cool to
intermediate temperatures. Native
to the Philippines.

Dendrobium
amethystoglossum

Dendrobium anosmum

Dendrobium antennatum

■ *Dendrobium anosmum (syn.
Den. aphyllum, Den. superbum):*
Section *Dendrobium*. A robust
epiphyte, this plant grows slender
but lanky canes with deciduous
leaves. Plants in cultivation typically
grow 2- to 5-foot-long canes,
although much longer ones are
found on plants in nature. Young
stems are upright to ascending but
later become pendent. In spring,
clusters of magenta-purple 4-inch
flowers cover the canes for several
weeks, creating a brilliant display,
especially on longer canes. The
sweet fragrance is reminiscent of
rhubarb. An album variety has
white flowers. A plant with several

long canes can be accommodated
in a 4-inch pot. It does better when
potbound or can be mounted on a
piece of wood or cork. In tropical
gardens, limbs of oak trees draped
with *Den. anosmum* create a
spectacle when in flower. Native to
the Philippines, Borneo, Thailand,
Vietnam, and New Guinea.

■ *Dendrobium
antennatum (syn.
Den. d'albertisii):*
Section *Spatulata*.
One of the antelope
dendrobiums, the
white flowers have
striking upright,
twisted green petals.
Several forms of this
species show various
amounts of twisting
in the petals. Some
plants reach
flowering size when
only 10 inches tall,
making this small- to medium-size
dendrobium with evergreen upright
canes suitable for windowsills as
well as the greenhouse. Pot in an
open mix, provide warm
temperatures, and water frequently
during the growing season. Native
to New Guinea, the Solomon Islands,
and Australia.

Dendrobium atroviolaceum

■ **Dendrobium atroviolaceum:**
Section *Latouria*. This free-flowering dendrobium comes from rainforests. Each of the 10- to 15-inch-tall pseudobulbs bears two to four purple-pigmented leaves. Each inflorescence holds 20 slightly nodding sinister-looking flowers colored a bizarre combination of creamy white, purple, and green. *Den. atroviolaceum* is easy to grow and a parent of several intriguing hybrids, *Den.* Andree Millar among them. Native to New Guinea.

■ **Dendrobium bigibbum:** Section *Phalaenanthe*. The evergreen canes, of this epiphyte can grow about

20 inches tall, although there are shorter plants. The inflorescences bear up to 20 long-lasting rose to purple 1½- to 2½-inch flowers that resemble a phalaenopsis or moth orchid. Mount this plant or pot in a small container with a well-drained mix. Repot when new roots show. Native to Australia.

■ **Dendrobium chrysotoxum:**
Section *Callista*. The closely spaced upright pseudobulbs on this sympodial orchid grow about 1 foot tall. The gracefully arching or pendent 18-inch-long inflorescences originate from near the top of the pseudobulbs. Fragrant golden yellow 2-inch flowers are openly spaced along the spray, and last several weeks. Plentiful light is recommended to nudge this dendrobium into flower. Native to Southeast Asia.

■ **Dendrobium cuthbertsonii (syn. Den. sophronites):** Section *Oxyglossum*. This miniature can prove a challenge even to seasoned growers, although those in the San Francisco Bay area have had considerable success. It is native to high elevations—6,500 feet—where it receives daily rain, cool nights, and sunny days. The petite dark green plants bear few leaves and form a small mound of tufted foliage. In spring, 1½-inch flowers appear. The

Dendrobium chrysotoxum

species shows considerable variation in flower color—red, orange, pink, purple, and yellow. The real attraction is that flowers can last for six or even eight months.

The cheery flowers of *Den. cuthbertsonii* are also unusual because the lip, which faces downward in most orchid flowers, points upward. These cool-growing orchids benefit from high humidity, plentiful fresh air, and cool nighttime temperatures. Pot in sphagnum moss. Native to New Guinea.

Dendrobium bigibbum var. compactum

Dendrobium cuthbertsonii

Dendrobium *continued*

■ *Dendrobium discolor:* Section *Spatulata*. Crinkled flowers with a spicy scent adorn this medium-to-tall evergreen epiphyte. Its canes can grow very tall in nature, although cultivated plants are often much shorter. Inflorescences 1 to 2 feet long bear long-lasting 2- to 2½-inch yellow or bronze flowers with twisted and crimped petals and sepals. Vigorous and easy to grow, this dependable dendrobium is a good choice for beginners wanting abundant flowers on arching inflorescences. The hot tropical conditions of its native habitat can be duplicated in a warm, humid greenhouse or on a patio or pool cage in a subtropical or tropical garden. Native to Australia and New Guinea.

Dendrobium discolor

flowers are short-lived, but they will remain fresh longer when kept on the cool side. After plants flower, repot if necessary. Keep plants in small pots so they are potbound.

An alternative is to mount the plant, making sure there is sufficient moisture during the growing season. *Den. farmeri* flowers best after a long dry period. Native to Nepal, India, Burma, Thailand, Laos, and Malaysia.

■ *Dendrobium formosum:* Section *Formosae*. Short inflorescences that bear 3- to 6-inch-wide flowers that are white with a glittering crystalline surface and a splash of bright yellow or orange on the lip emerge toward the end of each stem. The faintly scented flowers stay fresh for four to six weeks, creating a long-lasting display. Once the pseudobulbs have matured, reduce water and fertilizer. Resume watering in the spring when the plant begins growing again. Native to Nepal, Bhutan, and India.

Dendrobium farmeri

■ *Dendrobium farmeri (syn. Den. densiflorum var. farmeri):* Section *Callista*. This plant grows about 12 to 18 inches tall. Foot-long inflorescences bear 2-inch-wide flowers with pink sepals and petals and an orange-yellow lip. The

Dendrobium formosum

Dendrobium lindleyi

Dendrobium nobile

■ ***Dendrobium lindleyi (syn. Den. aggregatum):*** Section *Callista*. A popular species in this section of the genus, this is a 3- to 6-inch-tall plant with spindle-shaped pseudobulbs and oblong, leathery leaves. The plentiful orange-yellow flowers have a large, rounded lip, and are slightly more than 1 inch in diameter. A single pendent inflorescence may bear up to 30 flowers. While the display may be shorter-lived than that of other species, it is worth growing a plant of this dramatic species. Similar-looking *Den. jenkinsii* is a dwarf plant with only one to three flowers in an inflorescence. It is sometimes listed in catalogs as a variety of *Den. lindleyi,* or misidentified as that species. Grow *Den. lindleyi* in a pot or basket, or on a mount. Plants tucked into plastic mesh baskets or attached to a tree-fern ball eventually create an irresistible symmetrical specimen. Native to India, Burma, Thailand, Laos, Vietnam, and China.

■ ***Dendrobium nobile:*** Section *Dendrobium.* This upright species is one of the most popular dendrobiums. Its fragrant flowers are about 3 inches across and usually borne in groups of three The flower colors are variable. Popular forms have white petals with rose or mauve tips and a ruffled lip with a deep maroon throat, grading into yellow and white. The edge of the lip may be tinged to match the petals. *Den. nobile* plants need to be cool and dry in autumn to set the flower buds Many hybrids are available, with some easier to flower than the species. Native to India, Burma, Thailand, Laos, Vietnam, and China.

■ ***Dendrobium parishii:*** Section *Dendrobium.* Growing 1 or 2 feet tall, this epiphyte is deciduous. The short inflorescences hold 1½- to 2-inch-wide dark rose flowers that are white toward the center. Many growers are seduced by the delicious raspberry fragrance. Pot in a porous medium, or mount. Water during active growth. Reduce the frequency of watering once growths mature. Native to India, Burma, Thailand, Laos, Vietnam, Cambodia, and China.

Dendrobium parishii

Dendrobium *continued*

■ *Dendrobium phalaenopsis:*

Section *Phalaenanthe*. Some experts place *Den. phalaenopsis* with *Den. bigibbum*. However, *Den. phalaenopsis* is a robust plant, as tall as 1 to 3 feet, with 1½- to 3-inch-wide, long-lasting flowers that can be lilac, white, magenta, or purple. As the specific epithet *phalaenopsis* indicates, the flowers look like those of the genus *Phalaenopsis*, the moth orchid. Position plants where they will receive bright light and good air circulation. Pot or mount on a plaque, allowing the plants to dry slightly between waterings. Staking is often necessary for these top-heavy plants. Repot when new growths emerge. Native to Australia.

Dendrobium phalaenopsis

■ *Dendrobium secundum:*

Section *Pedilonum*. Growing up to 30 inches tall, this orchid puts forth 3- to 6-inch-long inflorescences packed with many light pink, reddish, or purple flowers. The flowers are arranged in a peculiar way, all aiming in the same direction. *Dendrobium secundum* originates where there is an obvious dry season, indicating plants in cultivation need a rest to flower best. Provide bright light and mount plants so they can dry between waterings. Native to Thailand, Burma, Cambodia, Laos, and Vietnam.

■ *Dendrobium senile:*

Section *Dendrobium*. This compact low-growing epiphyte always has a few leaves on the 1- to 3-inch-tall psuedobulbs, which are decorated with white hairs. Short inflorescences bear one to three waxy 1½- to 2½-inch-wide bright yellow flowers. A lemon scent adds to the allure. Providing adequate ventilation and growing this plant on a mount coax it into flower after its rest period. Native to Laos, Burma, and Thailand.

Dendrobium senile

■ *Dendrobium thyrsiflorum:*

Section *Callista*. The pseudobulbs grow 1 or 1½ feet tall, bearing smooth evergreen leaves. Drooping inflorescences that carry 1- to 2-inch white flowers with an orange to yellow-orange lip grow from near the top of the pseudobulbs. Although short-lived, a cluster of *Den. thyrsiflorum* flowers is a spectacular sight and worth the annual wait for this remarkable orchid to burst into bloom. A dry period is necessary for a strong

Dendrobium thyrsiflorum

Dendrobium secundum

Dendrobium **Andree Millar**

flowering. Pot in a well-drained mix. Water and fertilize regularly during active growth. Native from India to Vietnam.

Hybrids

■*Dendrobium* Andree Millar (*atroviolaceum* × *convolutum*):

A well-grown plant can be a show-stopper, covered in long-lasting, exotic nodding flowers that last for months. This hybrid honors the former director of the National Capital Botanic Gardens in Port Moresby, Papua New Guinea, and author of *Orchids of New Guinea*, printed in 1978 and revised in 1999. Andreé Millar spent her life studying the orchids of New Guinea. Her work is still well respected in the orchid world.

■*Dendrobium* Blue Twinkle (Betty Goto × *canaliculatum*):

Several clones of this dainty dendrobium are available, including 'Carmela', which gets its name from a highly esteemed Hawaiian orchid nursery, Carmela

Orchids. Staking this orchid's inflorescence displays its flowers to best advantage. The time to stake is when the flower buds are still developing, before they have opened. The lovely lavender-blue

flowers of *Den.* Blue Twinkle are borne on a petite plant that will do well mounted if given good humidity. Grown in a small pot with excellent drainage, it is ideal for windowsills and even under lights.

Dendrobium **Blue Twinkle 'Carmela'**

Dendrobium Burana Stripe

Dendrobium *continued*

■ *Dendrobium* **Burana Stripe (Thanaid Stripes × Chorthip Ohashi):** Most nurseries or big-box stores have *Phalaenopsis*-type dendrobiums for sale. They are commonly referred to as den-phals, because the flower shape, colors, and inflorescences resemble those of the moth orchid, *Phalaenopsis*. A good example is *Den.* Burana Stripe, a well-shaped hybrid with long-lasting pink flowers striped magenta with white in the lip and toward the center of the flower. However, several color forms of *Den.* Burana Stripe have been selected and mericloned, so under this single hybrid name consumers may encounter floral variation. *Den.* Burana Stripe is part of a series of more than 25 *Dendrobium* hybrids registered by Nopporn Buranaraktham in Bangkok, Thailand. Each hybrid name begins with the word Burana, such as *Den.* Burana Jade (Bangkok Green × Burana Fancy), *Den.* Burana Red-Stripes (Youppadeewan × Thanaid Stripes), and *Den.* Burana White (Adisakdi White × Hirota White). Like other den-phals, *Den.* Burana Stripe is a good choice for beginners because it's easy to grow. For best flowering, pot a den-phal orchid in a porous, free-draining medium, to which you add a diluted balanced fertilizer when the plants are actively growing. Set them where they will receive bright light, in an eastern, western or shaded southern exposure. Warm temperatures and 50 percent humidity round out the cultural regime for the den-phals that provide colorful variety in exchange for minimal care.

■ *Dendrobium* **Frosty Dawn (Dawn Maree × Lime Frost):** This delightful hybrid, first introduced by H&R Nurseries of Hawaii in 1997, is still popular. Clones of *Den.* Frosty Dawn, a variable hybrid, bear clusters of large fragrant white flowers with shades of golden yellow, orange, or even deep red in their throats. Tiny black hairs grow along its canes. Grow this orchid in bright light and intermediate to warm temperatures.

Dendrobium Frosty Dawn

■ *Dendrobium* **Mini Diamond (Little Diamond × Pinky):** Miniature dendrobium hybrids are an under-lights and windowsill grower's delight. The plants are petite, with many of them staying less than 1 foot tall, including the height of the inflorescence. The numerous flowers are large in proportion to the plant and flower more than once a year. *Den.* Mini Diamond flowers in a 3-inch pot. The 4-inch-tall evergreen canes bear short inflorescences lined with full-bodied flowers that remain fresh for weeks. Many of the miniature dendrobium hybrids are sold in clay pots and held in place with pieces of coconut husk, bark, horticultural charcoal, or tree fern. Bright indirect light, 50 percent humidity, a small pot, and well-drained medium satisfy these compact orchids.

■ *Dendrobium* **Quique Ramirez (Burmese Ruby × Odom's Smoky Topaz):** *Den.* Jaquelyn Thomas (*gouldii × phalaenopsis*), which was registered in 1949, played a role in the development of new dendrobium hybrids in the Hawaiian Islands. Leading the way among the hybridizers is Haruyuki Kamemoto, who began research on dendrobiums at the University of Hawaii in 1950 and continued for more than five decades to develop and release new hybrids. Today, *Den.* Jaquelyn Thomas is still used in hybrids, as hybridizers develop new introductions for the cut-flower market and the pot-plant trade. Hybrids with *Den.* Jaquelyn Thomas in their parentage may be seed-grown, which allows for

Dendrobium Mini Diamond

variation, or propagated through mericlones, which guarantees the plants will bear identical flowers. These orchids can flower several times a year, grow to medium height, produce many flowers on each inflorescence, and last as well as cut flowers. One choice is the dramatic *Den.* Quique Ramirez 'Karen's Delight', AM/AOS, which is an almost black *Den.*

Dendrobium Roy Tokunaga

Dendrobium Quique Ramirez

Jaquelyn Thomas-type hybrid. It was registered in 2000 by Orchids of Waianae in Waianae, Hawaii. Like other dendrobium hybrids, it is a robust grower when given bright light, plentiful water and dilute fertilizer, a well-drained mix, and warm temperatures. In warm frost-free climates, such as South Florida, these dendrobiums can be grown outdoors in pool cages. They make impressive garden plants in the tropical landscape, where they can be grouped into masses or attached to trees.

■ *Dendrobium* Roy Tokunaga (*atroviolaceum* × *johnsoniae*): The name of this hybrid honors Roy Tokunaga, one of the founding partners of Hawaii's H&R Nurseries and a pioneer in the field of hybridizing dendrobiums. The showy, long-lasting flowers often appear in clusters, reminiscent of an open, shaggy hydrangea head. It flowers from spring into summer. This hybrid remains compact, suitable for growing under lights or on a windowsill. A well-grown plant given high light and steady fertilization during active growth will reward its owner with masses of flowers.

■ *Dendrobium* Second Love (**Peace** × **Awayuki**): Hybrids with *Den. nobile* in their parentage display a distinct and beautiful growth habit and flower, and often a delightful fragrance as well. *Den.* Second Love is no exception, exhibiting the classic *nobile*-type clusters of blooms close to the plant's canes. This hybrid will benefit from bright light and cool nights. It flowers more prolifically when grown with nighttime lows of about 55° F during the winter.

Dendrobium Wonder Nishii

■ *Dendrobium* Wonder Nishii (*atroviolaceum* × *alexandrae*): The exotic, long-lasting flowers on this member of the *Latouria* section of the genus *Dendrobium* are pale chartreuse green, with a contrasting violet lip and violet speckling on the reverse of the petals and sepals. This is an optimal plant for windowsill growers with some vertical space. Although it is a taller hybrid, reaching up to 20 inches, it does not require higher light to produce impressive flowering as many dendrobiums do.

Dendrobium Second Love

DORITAENOPSIS

doh-rye-tee-NOP-sis

Abbreviation: Dtps.

Growth: Monopodial

Light: Low to medium

Temperature: Intermediate to warm

Flowering: Winter and spring

Care: Beginner

Doritaenopsis is an intergeneric hybrid genus between *Phalaenopsis* and *Doritis* (doh-RYE-tis). While *Phalaenopsis* is a large genus boasting many species, the genus *Doritis* has few. *Doritis pulcherrima* is a lovely and variable species. It hybridizes readily when crossed with *Phalaenopsis* species and hybrids, and often imparts its brilliant fuchsia coloration to its progeny. The genus *Doritis* was described by Lindley in 1833 and named for Doritis, one of the names of the goddess Aphrodite—Aphrodite Doritis, the goddess of bountiful love.

Culture

Doritaenopsis, like phalaenopsis, are excellent beginner's orchids, offering vibrant displays of long-lasting color in exchange for minimal care. When you bring a new plant home, place it in a well-lit area, keeping it out of direct sun. Water it once or twice a week, taking the plant to a sink and running water through the medium so it is thoroughly drenched. Fertilize with a weak solution on a regular basis, and remove the flowers as they fade. When the spike has ceased flowering, use a sterilized single-edge razor blade or other sterilized cutting tool and sever the spike from the plant. Move the plant to where it will receive adequate light and warm temperatures—highs in the mid to upper 80s and lows in the 60s.

Hybrids

Hundreds of doritaenopsis hybrids are available, many of them offering the same colors and patterns seen in phalaenopsis. New hybrids are introduced each year. Visitors to nurseries as well as orchid shows and sales are likely to see fresh color combinations and improvements on traditional types for sale.

Doritaenopsis grown from seed flower in two or three years. Growers with sufficient room may want to buy seedlings or a community pot. First-bloom seedlings have shorter inflorescences, often with smaller flowers. In successive years, the inflorescences will be longer and the flowers more plentiful.

■ *Doritaenopsis* **Brother Pungoteague Creek (*Dtps.* King Shiang's Beauty × *Phal.* Brother Pirate King):** Its vivid, saturated fuchsia coloration makes this handsome hybrid a jewel in any orchid collection. Grex names can indicate the origin of a cross. In the genera *Doritaenopsis* and *Phalaenopsis*, "Brother" often indicates a hybrid registered by Brother Orchid Nursery in Taichung, Taiwan. Established in 1971, this nursery is a leader in breeding new moth orchids. Since the 1990s it has registered more than 350 *Phalaenopsis* and *Doritaenopsis* crosses.

Doritaenopsis Brother Pungoteague Creek

■ *Doritaenopsis* **Mythic Beauty (*Phal.* Chamonix × *Dtps.* Orglade's Puff):** The strong influence of its phalaenopsis ancestry is evident in this hybrid that could easily be mistaken for a traditional moth orchid. Lovely in its own right, *Dtps.* Mythic Beauty, which was registered in 1992, bears 5-inch-wide pure white flowers with delicate yellow and red markings in the center. An inspection of the overlapping petals and sepals reveals a full-formed flower, as expressed in the clone shown here, 'Prince Mulligan', HCC/AOS.

Doritaenopsis Mythic Beauty

■ **Doritaenopsis Sogo Vivien
(*Dtps.* Sogo Alice × *Phal.* Zuma's
Pixie):** This charming small-growing
hybrid flowers on a plant with an
8-inch leafspan and fits comfortably
into a 4-inch pot. The clone name
'Sweetheart', AM/AOS, refers
to its being a sweetheart-type
phalaenopsis, a multifloral plant
that stays small. Given proper
care, it will produce a profusion
of petite, colorful blooms, usually
on branched spikes. The arching
inflorescence, which grows about
10 to 15 inches tall, is covered
with 1½-inch white flowers that
are flushed with pale lavender
on sepals and petals with magenta
stripes. Its compact size makes
it ideal for growing under lights
and on windowsills. Decorators
will find it useful when creating
living centerpieces.

■ **Doritaenopsis Taisuco Melody
(*Dtps.* Taisuco Candystripe × *Phal.*
Chih Shang's Stripes):** These eye-
catching 3½-inch-wide flowers show
fuchsia spots and veins against a
fuchsia background, while a bit of
white in the center of the flower
imparts contrast. This is another case
where the grex name indicates the

Doritaenopsis **Taisuco Melody**

originator. "Taisuco" is the name
of the Taiwan Sugar Corporation,
a Taiwan-based nursery and a major
hybridizer of phalaenopsis.

Relative

■ **Doritis pulcherrima (syn.
Phalaenopsis pulcherrima):** Since

the genus *Doritis* was established
in 1833, botanists have continued
to recognize it as a separate entity
while others put it in the genus
Phalaenopsis. Recent studies
based on analysis of the plants'
DNA, however, suggest *Doritis*
belongs in *Phalaenopsis.* When
recognized on its own, the genus
Doritis contains three species,
the most common being *Dor.
pulcherrima*, a terrestrial or
lithophyte with summer-flowering
upright spikes reaching 24 inches
tall. The specific epithet
pulcherrima means "most
beautiful," in reference to the
multitude of 1-inch-wide flowers,
which are most commonly bright
cerise. Varieties that are white,
white with a rose lip, and blue-
violet also exist.

For the most part, doritis
thrive under phalaenopsis-type
conditions: warm temperatures,
frequent watering, and 50 percent
or more humidity. Doritis needs
higher light conditions than
phalaenopsis; an eastern exposure
or well-shaded southern or western
exposure should suit these orchids.
Native to northwest India and
southern China to Borneo.

Doritaenopsis **Sogo Vivien**

Doritis **pulcherrima**

ENCYCLIA

en-SIK-lee-ah

Abbreviation: Encycl.

Growth: Sympodial

Light: Medium to bright

Temperature: Cool to warm

Flowering: All seasons, primarily spring to summer

Care: Beginner

Native to the New World tropics, encyclias generally have compact growth habits and freely produce their fragrant flowers while growing under home conditions. The shell-type encyclias, such as *Encycl. cochleata* and *Encycl. fragrans,* are particularly interesting because their delightfully fragrant flowers, which appear to be upside down, look like squid or octopuses. *Encyclia* was once included in a broadly defined genus *Epidendrum,* as nearly all epiphytic orchids were at one time. Recent studies of plants, flowers, and their DNA suggest dividing *Encyclia* into three groups: *Encyclia* (about 100 species, with onion-shaped pseudobulbs), *Prosthechea* (more than 100 species, with variable but usually somewhat flattened pseudobulbs), and *Euchile* (a few species with onion-shaped pseudobulbs and gray-white leaves). Some *Encyclia* species are also available in the trade under the genus names *Epidendrum* and *Prosthechea.*

Encyclias require the same easy-to-provide care as their close relatives, the cattleyas. Give medium to bright light and allow the potting mix to dry slightly between waterings. During the active growing season, fertilize often with a weak solution to develop robust plants that flower reliably. Pot encyclias in a porous medium or attach them to a mount. An alternative is to grow them in wood-slat baskets or plastic mesh baskets, which allow them to develop into impressive specimens. Like cattleyas and other epiphytic orchids, encyclias can be grown outdoors mounted directly onto trees in subtropical and tropical gardens.

Species

■ **Encyclia adenocaula (syn. Epidendrum adenocaulum):** Strap-like leaves arch from the pseudobulbs on this spring-flowering plant that can grow 1 foot tall. The flower spikes hold many pink to rose-pink blooms with narrow petals. The long, pointed lip has dark pink markings and an interesting winged column. Native to Mexico.

■ **Encyclia alata (syn. Epidendrum alatum):** The arching, branched inflorescences can grow to 6 feet and bear abundant fragrant greenish-yellow and brown flowers. The lip is cream-white with maroon lines toward the tip. It flowers May to August. Native from Mexico to Costa Rica.

Encyclia adenocaula

Encyclia alata

■ **Encyclia cochleata (syn. Epidendrum cochleatum, Prosthechea cochleata):** Of all the shell- or squid-type encyclias, this one looks the most like an octopus. The plant is about 1 foot high and fits neatly under lights. The shell-shaped lip is mostly green with purple and black stripes. The petals and sepals are yellow-green. The plant blooms from autumn to spring, often more than once a year, and can remain in bloom for six months. Because it flowers consecutively for several months on the same spike, *Encycl. cochleata* is an worthy orchid to grow in a window or fluorescent-light garden. A mature

Encyclia cochleata

plant may bloom almost continuously. Provide bright light and average temperatures. Native from Mexico to Venezuela and Cuba.

■ **Encyclia cordigera (syn. Epidendrum atropurpureum):** A heavy plant with conical pseudobulbs and leathery straplike leaves, it grows up to 2 feet tall. The fragrant flowers have brown to purple petals that curve forward at the tips. The lip is creamy white

Encyclia cordigera

with three bright pink splotches. In some forms, the entire lip is rose-red. The flowers appear in spring and summer. Many varieties are available. Native from Mexico to Central America.

Encyclia fragrans

■ **Encyclia fragrans (syn. Epidendrum fragrans, Prosthechea fragrans):** This is a stout species with erect growths between 10 and 15 inches tall. It has shell-type flowers with a spicy fragrance. The petals and sepals are cream to yellow. The lip is the same color, candy-striped with red. *Encycl. fragrans* blooms from May to June. Native from Mexico and the West Indies to Ecuador, Peru, and Brazil.

summer and is often grown on a bark mount. Native to South Florida and the Bahamas.

■ *Encyclia vitellina* (syn. *Epidendrum vitellinum, Prosthechea vitellina*): A small plant, this epiphyte grows only 5 to 10 inches tall, making it suitable for growers with limited space. The 2-inch-wide flowers are comprised of relatively broad orange-red petals and sepals and a narrow yellow and orange lip.

Encyclia vitellina

Encyclia mariae

Encyclia *continued*

■ *Encyclia mariae* (syn. *Epidendrum mariae, Euchile mariae*): A glaucous coating gives this plant an easily recognized gray-green appearance. Each inflorescence bears two to four flowers with green sepals and petals. The base of the white lip folds around the column, while the tip of the lip flares out into a showy display. Like *Encycl. vitellina*, this species grows at cooler temperatures than most encyclias. It flowers in the summer. Native to dry oak forests in northeastern Mexico.

■ *Encyclia tampensis* (syn. *Epidendrum tampense*): Commonly called the butterfly orchid, this plant has pseudobulbs that cluster to form mats supporting leathery

leaves up to 15 inches long. The 1-inch-wide flowers are fragrant and pretty. The sepals and petals are brownish green to apple green. The lip is white with some magenta. *Encycl. tampensis* usually flowers in spring or

Encyclia tampensis

Originally from high elevations, it is a cool-growing species. Native to Guatemala and Mexico.

Hybrids

■ *Encyclia* Atropine (*tampensis* × *cordigera*): Originally registered in 1962, this same cross was registered again in 1986 under the name *Encycl.* Green Glades with the parentage listed as *Encycl. tampensis* and *Encycl. atropurpurea*. Because *Encycl. atropurpurea* is a synonym of *Encycl. cordigera,* the earlier hybrid name—*Encycl.* Atropine— is preferred. This 12-inch-tall plant is an epiphyte bearing branched inflorescences 24 to 30 inches long in May and June. Variable in color, the fragrant flowers range from olive green to green with chocolate brown. A white lip sometimes has purple striations. This perky hybrid can be grown in a well-drained medium in a clay or plastic pot, or it can be attached to a mount such as a piece of cork. Allow to dry between waterings, fertilize often during the growing season, and place in intermediate light.

Encyclia **Atropine**

■ *Encyclia* Green Hornet (*cochleata* × *lancifolia*): With its compact growth habit and squid-shaped flowers, this hybrid takes after its *Encycl. cochleata* parent. The inverted dark purple lip with its purple veins appears almost black on these flowers that last for months and appear in autumn and winter. Other parts of the flower are light green.

Encyclia **Orchid Jungle**

■ *Encyclia* Orchid Jungle (*alata* × *phoenicea*): Here is a robust plant that can quickly fill a clay or plastic pot or be easily grown in a wood-slat basket or on a cork slab in the greenhouse. Flowering in late spring or early summer, it puts forth 3-foot-long branching inflorescences lined with fragrant, 2-inch-wide star-shaped flowers. The deep mahogany brown and chartreuse sepals and petals contrast with the white or cream-colored lip.

Encyclia **Green Hornet**

EPIDENDRUM

eb-pee-DEN-drum

Abbreviation: Epi.

Growth: Sympodial

Light: Medium

Temperature: Cool to warm

Flowering: All seasons, primarily spring to summer

Care: Beginner

The New World genus *Epidendrum* is large. More than 1,000 species are distributed in South America, Central America, Mexico, Florida, and the Caribbean, where they are found in various habitats from sea level to high elevations, including the Andes. New species continue to be discovered and described.

There are two main types of *Epidendrum* species: Those with reedlike stems and those with pseudobulbs. There are also some in-between forms. Some of the pseudobulbous epidendrums have been renamed by botanists and are now properly placed in the genera *Encyclia* or *Prosthechea,* though they may still be referred to as epidendrums in books and catalogs.

Reed-stem epidendrums are important cut-flower orchids in Hawaii, but most grow too tall and need too much light for indoor culture. They make wonderful garden plants in areas where frost is rare. Epidendrums naturalize readily. Hybridizers are registering more compact, floriferous types.

Culture

Epidendrums are remarkably tolerant of the potting mixes in which they can be grown, provided the medium drains well and is allowed to dry slightly between waterings. Potting mixes can include medium- to fine-grade fir bark, tree fern, or a blend of charcoal, peat, perlite, or coconut fiber. Use 30-10-10 fertilizer in a bark mix. Epidendrums can be grown in plastic or clay pots. Some with scrambling-type stems adapt well to urns or raised beds in subtropical and tropical gardens.

Provide sun in morning or afternoon but some shade at midday. Epidendrums benefit from daytime temperatures of 60 to 90° F with a drop at night and plentiful fertilizer when the plants are actively growing. Epidendrums can grow year-round without going dormant but they may require less frequent applications of water and fertilizer during the winter.

The tall nature of the species makes them ideal for gardens and greenhouses rather than windows or lights, although new hybrids are more compact and suitable for growing in the home in bright light. When making a purchase, look for plants that are firmly rooted in the container and have blemish-free foliage. Epidendrums can be propagated by cuttings and from the keikis that may develop along the stems.

Species

■ *Epidendrum ciliare:* Upright pseudobulbs arising from a creeping rhizome make this plant look much like a cattleya. It usually grows to about 1 foot tall. The fragrant flowers are about 5 inches across and have yellowish-green petals and sepals. The lip is white and split into three lobes. The side lobes are fringed; the center lobe is narrow and straight. *Epi. ciliare* blooms in winter and is easy to grow. Native to Mexico, the West Indies to Colombia, and Brazil.

Epidendrum ciliare

■ *Epidendrum ilense:* This epiphyte was found in the latter half of the 20th century and has been meristemmed at the Marie Selby Botanical Gardens, Sarasota, Florida. A reed-stem type, it continues to bloom on old and new stems, the flowers being white with narrow-fringed green sepals and petals in nonstop, nodding clusters of five to 10. It has been used to create

Epidendrum ilense

Epidendrum pseudepidendrum

Epidendrum Costa Rica

■ *Epidendrum* **Plastic Doll** (*pseudepidendrum* × *ilense*): Registered in 1989, this hybrid includes the Ecuadorian native *Epi. ilense* in its parentage, which gives some fringe to the lip. This tall-growing hybrid bears its 1½- to 2-inch-wide flowers in three to five open pendent clusters that are yellow with pink and green.

Epidendrum **Plastic Doll**

some hybrids that offer an expanded color range, among them *Epi*. Plastic Doll. Native to Ecuador.

■ *Epidendrum pseudepidendrum* (syn. *Pseudepidendrum spectabile*): Originally described in 1852, this species was transferred to the genus *Epidendrum* in 1856. It is a tall epiphyte with tufted stems, growing to 3 feet. The medium-sized showy flowers have green sepals and petals, while the large lip is golden yellow with orange in the throat and a white-marked purple column. Native to Costa Rica and Panama.

Hybrids

■ *Epidendrum* **Costa Rica** (*pseudowallisii* × *schumannianum*; syn. *Oerstedella*): A robust hybrid, this eye-catching beauty features 1½–inch-wide flowers with a purple lip that contrasts with orange-spotted sepals and petals. The flower spike grows 2 to 3 feet tall, with flowers covering the top third. Bright light, a well-drained medium, and good air circulation are suggested.

■ *Epidendrum* **Hokulea** (Joseph Lii × *cinnabarinum*): The bright orange to brilliant red 1½-inch-wide flowers of this vigorous hybrid have been recognized by judges of the American Orchid Society, who have awarded several clones. The slender upright stems are topped with round or oval clusters of brightly colored flowers, with new buds opening over a period of several months. Some clones show color variation, including one that features more orange to contrast with the yellow-orange lip. Plants of *Epi*. Hokulea can start flowering when only 1 foot tall, although they will grow taller. This hybrid is remarkably temperature tolerant.

■ *Epidendrum* **Joseph Lii** (Orange Glow × *cinnabarinum*): The upright-growing stems put forth erect spikes that terminate in an umbel-like cluster of many intense red flowers that offer weeks-long color. There is yellow in the fringed lip, which, unlike most orchids, points upward. Bright light, a well-drained medium, and plenty of fertilizer coax this orchid to flower reliably.

Epidendrum **Hokulea**

Epidendrum **Joseph Lii**

LAELIA

LAY-lee-ah

Abbreviation: L.	
Growth: Sympodial	
Light: Medium to high	
Temperature: Intermediate	
Flowering: Varies	
Care: Beginner to intermediate	

Laelias are so closely related to cattleyas that sometimes it is difficult to discern the difference. Botanists distinguish them by the number of pollinia: laelias have eight pollinia while cattleyas have four. While recent DNA studies have caused scientists to shuffle some species in the *Cattleya* Alliance, orchid fans continue to recognize certain species as laelias. These dynamic orchids with showy flowers perk up any collection when they burst into flower. Some also offer delightful fragrances.

Culture

As a rule, laelias and cattleyas may be grown together. Like cattleyas, laelias need to be grown in a potting medium that drains perfectly and is allowed to dry slightly between waterings. Watering should be done when plants are approaching dryness, which can be tested by inserting a bamboo skewer into the medium. Most species require bright light to flower reliably, but many are adaptable to flowering on windowsills or under lights.

Some species come from higher elevations and require cooler temperatures. Choose species to match your growing conditions. The plants thrive outdoors in summer and on a regimen of light weekly fertilizing in spring and summer, reduced to every other week in autumn and none in winter.

Species

■ *Laelia anceps:* Each 4- to 6-inch-tall pseudobulb bears one leathery leaf up to 8 inches long. The flowers, to 4 inches across, are on long stems. Typical flowers are pale rose-purple. The outside of the three-lobed lip matches the petals, but the mid-lobe is bright crimson-purple with yellow. The throat is rich yellow overlaid with red stripes. Other forms are white or blue. Some cultivars show strong flaring on the petals. The species has been in cultivation since 1835, and breeding has produced cultivars of superior form. *L. anceps* is part of a group of *Laelia* species known for bearing their flowers on tall inflorescences. It has also been used to create attractive intergeneric *Cattleya*-type hybrids that produce well-shaped flowers on tall, erect inflorescences. The plants flower most often in winter, but flowers can appear during other seasons. *L. anceps* is renowned for its tolerance of high and low temperatures, withstanding spells as hot as 100° F and cold snaps as low as 30° F. In cool temperatures, flowers last about two months on the plant. Flowers fade fast when cut, however. Native to Mexico.

■ *Laelia dayana:* Three-inch-wide flowers top this charming miniature. Although typical flowers have petals and sepals that are bent backward (reflexed), select forms such as the clone pictured above possess flat flowers. The flowering season is usually summer, but flowers can

Laelia dayana var. coerulea

appear anytime or several times a year. The orchid-lavender flowers have a deep, intense lavender lip with fine dark veins in the throat. There are also bluish and white forms. Because it's a forest dweller, *L. dayana* does well on windowsills or under lights with intermediate temperatures. It benefits from a drop in temperature at night, as does *L. pumila.* Grow in small pots of sphagnum moss or fine fir bark, and keep medium from completely drying out. Native to the Organ Mountains of Rio de Janeiro state, Brazil, where it grows on trees at low elevations.

Laelia anceps

Laelia milleri

with a rich purple-lavender lip. Overall form of cultivars is full and flat, making it a valuable parent to create popular miniature cattleya hybrids such as *Laeliocattleya* Mini Purple (*L. pumila* × *C. walkeriana*) and *Lc.* Zuki Josemila (*L. pumila* × *Lc.* Jose Dias Castro). As a rule, plants are less than 6 inches tall, while the flowers can be up to 4 inches wide. *L. pumila* is suitable for either windowsill or under-lights culture with intermediate temperatures. Grow *L. pumila* in small pots of sphagnum or fir bark and provide 65 to 70 percent humidity. Native to Brazil.

Laelia pumila

■ **Laelia purpurata:** The national flower of Brazil, *L. purpurata* is an elegant, impressive orchid. Plants can reach 30 inches tall and carry heads of five flowers, each 7 inches across. Because the plant has a decidedly vertical habit and short rhizomes, an 8-inch pot can easily hold a plant with three to four flowering growths. A coastal species, it has many beautiful named color varieties. This characteristic has made it a favorite among orchid collectors. In Santa Catarina, Brazil, there are orchid shows that feature only this species.

Some color varieties are var. *purpurata* (the type, white with red-violet lip), var. *carnea* (white with pink lip), var. *flammea* (flared petals), var. *werkbaeuserii* (white with blue lip), and var. *virginalis* (pure white). Most varieties have a yellow throat with darker veining. The diversity of the many color forms has been recorded by Brazilian forestry engineer L.C. Menezes in her book *Laelia Purpurata*. These large orchids do better when grown on the slightly dry side, especially in winter. Keep mature plants in intermediate to warm temperatures. Use large pots of coarse, well-drained medium, and allow it to dry between waterings. Bright light will ensure reliable flower production. *L. purpurata* has been used to create thousands of hybrids with cattleyas and other genera to which it lends its richly colored, full lip, good flower count, and impressive size. Native to Brazil.

Laelia purpurata

■ **Laelia milleri:** This brightly colored species is part of a group of lithophytes called rupicolous laelias. The first plants of *L. milleri* seen in the United States were part of a shipment of *L. flava* sent to the Rod McLellan Co. in the early 1960s. These bright red orchids, which were mixed in among the yellow-flowered *L. flava,* created excitement and were first called *L. flava* var. *aurantiaca.* Later it was learned that the species *L. milleri* had been described in Brazil in 1960. Plants of *L. milleri* average 5 inches tall. In the spring, three to six bright red flowers, 1½- to 2-inches wide, are borne at the end of a 12-inch-tall inflorescence. Grow *L. milleri* in clay pots of inorganic media such as lava rock or Aliflor under bright light and intermediate temperatures. Extensive iron-ore mining has made *L. milleri* nearly extinct in its natural habitat. Native to Brazil.

■ **Laelia pumila:** A miniature species, *L. pumila* produces one, rarely two, flowers from the developing leaves of a new growth during summer and autumn. Flower color can approach fluorescent cerise

Laelia tenebrosa

■ **Laelia tenebrosa:** This plant is similar in appearance to, but generally smaller than, *L. purpurata,* to which it is related. *L. tenebrosa* produces heads of three or four flowers with colors ranging from coppery brown to clear yellow. All forms have deep lavender lips with a white margin of varying width. The throat is yellow with fine, dark veins. *L. tenebrosa* can be grown like *L. purpurata,* although it does not need as bright light.

Intergeneric hybrids

Among the intergeneric hybrid genera are *Laeliocattleya* (*Laelia* × *Cattleya*), *Brassolaelia* (*Brassavola* × *Laelia*), and the trigeneric *Brassolaeliocattleya* (*Brassavola* × *Laelia* × *Cattleya*), of which there are hundreds known under the abbreviation *Blc.*

■ **Dialaelia Snowflake (Caularthron bicornutum × L. albida):** (Abbreviation: Dial.) his hybrid was registered by Stewart Orchids,a firm originally based in Santa Barbara, California, and well-known for its cattleya hybrids. *Caularthron* (kawl-AR-thron) is horticulturally known as *Diacrium* (dy-a-KREE-uhm), the name that is also used by the awards registrar for its hybrids. *Caularthron bicornutum* is a species from Central and South America that produces tall inflorescences of sequentially opening 2-inch-wide sweet-scented white flowers. This hybrid is easy to grow and adapts to most intermediate growing conditions. It has produced a number of attractive hybrids of its own, most notably *Iwanagara* Appleblossom (*Dial.* Snowflake × *Blc.* Orange Nugget).

■ **Laeliocattleya Atticus (Lc. Love Knot × C. walkeriana):** (Abbreviation: Lc.) This hybrid, registered in 1996 by Krull-Smith, improved upon the already popular *Lc.* Love Knot, adding fuller form by backcrossing to *C. walkeriana.* Small-growing plants produce large, round lavender flowers in early spring. Grow *Lc. Atticus* alongside other cattleya hybrids under intermediate temperatures in a well-drained potting medium.

Laeliocattleya Atticus

■ **Laeliocattleya Canhamiana (C. mossiae × L. purpurata):** Registered in 1885 by Veitch, this hybrid was once popular in the cut-flower industry. Although the cross has been made with typically colored forms of the parents, today the blue-colored forms made with var. *coerulea* parents are by far the most popular. The pictured clone—'Azure Skies', AM/AOS—represents the best qualities of both parents: broad petals and

Dialaelia Snowflake

Laeliocattleya Canhamiana

a full lip from the cattleya parent and intense color from the lael a parent. This hybrid adapts to a wider range of light conditions than *L. purpurata*. Provide these plants with intermediate temperatures and a well-drained potting medium.

■ *Laeliocattleya* Lasseter's Gold (C. Chocolate Drop × Lc. Chine): The rich foliage colors of the flowers of *Lc.* Lasseter's Gold are suited to its autumn blooming season. The 3-inch flowers are well spaced on the strong inflorescence with a rich, sweet fragrance as a bonus. One parent of this hybrid—*C.* Chocolate Drop—has been frequently used for breeding. Occasionally, it will produce offspring, such as *Lc.* Lasseter's Gold, with flared flowers. Pot this sometimes slow-growing hybrid in a medium bark mix and place it in bright filtered light. Water and fertilize as for other cattleya hybrids.

■ *Laeliocattleya* Red Gold (C. aurantiaca × Lc. Charlesworthii): Here is a colorful multifloral hybrid that produces inflorescences of eight or more flowers around Christmas. The slightly cupped 2-inch flowers are brilliant red-orange with a crimson lip. Alberts & Merkel, a Florida nursery well known for its orchids and other exotic plants, registered this hybrid in 1964. It will tolerate slightly less light than other cattleya hybrids.

Laeliocattleya Red Gold

■ *Laeliocattleya* Rojo (C. aurantiaca × L. milleri): This small-growing orchid produces 10 or more bright red 2-inch flowers on a moderately tall inflorescence that varies in height from plant to plant. This was one of the first *L. milleri* hybrids created by Rod McLellan Co., a major orchid nursery based in San Francisco. Grow under intermediate temperatures in a well-drained medium and place in bright light for the best flowering.

■ *Laeliocattleya* Summerland Girl (C. guttata × Lc. Grandee): Legendary, especially in South Florida, this hybrid was registered by Jones & Scully in 1967. Tall plants produce heads of 4- to 5-inch lacquer red flowers with a bright fuchsia lip. This is a sizable orchid that requires a large pot of coarse medium, intermediate to warm temperatures, and bright light to reach its full potential.

Laeliocattleya Rojo

Laeliocattleya Lasseter's Gold

Laeliocattleya Summerland Girl

LUDISIA

loo-DEE-see-ab

Abbreviation: Lus.

Growth: Terrestrial

Light: Low to medium

Temperature: Intermediate to warm

Flowering: Winter to spring

Care: Beginner to intermediate

Ludisias are the most popular of the jewel orchids, a group of spreading, ground-dwelling plants prized for their colorful leaves. Most jewel orchids have spikes of small white flowers in season, most often winter to spring, but they are grown for their foliage.

When this orchid was first described in 1818 and given the name *Goodyera discolor*, it was mistakenly thought to have originated in Brazil. In fact, the genus is from China and Southeast Asia. The genus name *Ludisia* was established in 1825. Later in the same year, another botanist named it *Haemaria,* the name by which it was known until a correction was published in the *Kew Bulletin* in 1970.

Culture

Ludisias need higher humidity and warmer temperatures than most other orchids. Consequently, they make superb plants for growing in terrariums and growing cases (see Aquariums, page 54).

A terrarium with a glass top is ideal. To provide a balance between high humidity and air circulation, leave the top partially open; a 2-inch gap is about right. Use a well-drained, humus-rich medium, such as a commercial terrestrial orchid mix or a mixture of equal parts peat moss, perlite, and potting soil.

The plants may be grown in pots within the terrarium or planted directly in its bottom. If you grow the plants in pots, surround them with moist peat moss or sphagnum moss to maintain the humidity. Ludisia grows best in temperatures between 75° and 85° F. If the plants refuse to grow, raise the temperature inside the terrarium by adding bottom heat (see Adding Bottom Heat, page 51), which will also increase the level of humidity.

Ludisias are easy to propagate from cuttings of the stem, which may be broken into pieces with several nodes where leaves have grown. Lay these on moist sphagnum moss (see page 69).

It is also possible to root tip cuttings if there are several healthy leaves at the growing tip. Propagate in late winter or spring or when constant warmth and high humidity can be readily provided.

Species

■*Ludisia discolor (syn. Haemaria discolor):* The only species in the genus, this is a low, spreading plant with 2- to 3-inch-long velvety maroon leaves that have contrasting metallic red or gold veins. The trait is more pronounced in the variety *dawsoniana.* The flowers are white with twisted yellow columns, measure about ¾-inch across, and are held on an upright stalk.

Relatives

Cultivars and hybrids of *Lus. discolor* are rare. Several other jewel orchids have beautiful foliage and will thrive in similar growing conditions. They include *Anoetochilus roxburghii* and *Anoetochilus sikkimensis* (creepers with bronze-green leaves netted gold) and *Goodyera pubescens* (rattlesnake plantain, with pointed leaves variegated white and green requiring coolness, 50°–70° F). *Macodes petola* and the variety *javanica, Macodes sanderiana* have dark green leaves with gold or silver veins in prominent patterns.

Ludisia discolor

LYCASTE

lye-KASS-tee

Abbreviation: Lyc.
Growth: Sympodial
Light: Medium
Temperature: Cool to intermediate
Flowering: Mostly spring to summer
Care: Beginner to advanced

The New World tropics are home to 35 species of *Lycaste*, with their pseudobulbs topped by large fan-folded leaves. The waxy flowers are borne singly on top of erect inflorescences on plants that may be evergreen or deciduous. One—*Lyc. skinneri*—is the national flower of Guatemala.

Lovely lycaste hybrids are available on the market. Intergeneric crosses with related genera further increase the number of choices. Among these are *Angulocaste* (*Anguloa* × *Lycaste*) and *Zygocaste* (*Zygopetalum* × *Lycaste*).

Lycaste deppei

Culture

Lycaste species are distributed from the lowlands to 6,000 feet. Knowing the elevation from which a species originates is helpful in determining what temperature it needs in cultivation. Those from lower elevations require more warmth, up to 80° F in the day if possible, while those from high in the mountains benefit from cooler conditions. Grow in light shade in the summer.

When autumn arrives, deciduous species shed their leaves and enter

a dormant phase during which time they should receive minimal water. With the return of spring, growth resumes, making it necessary to increase the frequency of watering and to fertilize again.

Species

■ *Lycaste aromatica*:

A deciduous epiphytic species, *Lyc. aromatica* lives up to its name, with 3-inch-wide waxy orange-yellow flowers that perfume the air with a cinnamon scent. It produces up to 20 flowers per pseudobulb in a single flowering between late spring and early summer. This compact plant grows 12 inches and is a good choice for the windowsill and under lights. Native to Mexico, Guatemala, and Nicaragua.

■ *Lycaste deppei*:

As many as seven to nine fragrant 4-inch-wide flowers are carried by this species that may flower throughout the year but blooms mostly in spring and autumn. A light peppering of red spots decorates the green sepals, which contrast with the white petals and spotted yellow lip. Like *Lyc. aromatica*, the plant requires a winter rest once it finishes its summer growing period. Native to Mexico, Nicaragua, Honduras, El Salvador, Belize, and Guatemala.

Anguloa clowesii

Lycaste aromatica

Relatives

■ *Anguloa clowesii*:

(Abbreviation: Ang.) The common name tulip orchid conveys the appearance of the flowers of the New World genus *Anguloa* (an-gew-LOW-ah), comprised of nine species that may be terrestrial or epiphytic. These orchids bear one flower per inflorescence in the spring but make up for it by putting up several spikes at a time. *Ang. clowesii* bears 3-inch-wide bright yellow flowers that look like tulips. Native to Colombia and Venezuela.

■ *Ida locusta* (syn. *Lyc. locusta*):

(Abbreviation: I.) There are 37 species of *Ida* (EYE-duh), which until recently were regarded as lycastes, originating in northern

Ida locusta

South America. They are mostly found between 6,000 and 9,000 feet, as terrestrials or lithophytes—often in full sun—or as epiphytes in light shade. Flowers tend to hang their heads, opening incompletely, but have dramatic colors. Dark green *Ida locusta*, with its white-edged lip, usually flowers in midsummer in cultivation. It is fragrant at night. Grow in intermediate conditions, with light shade, forgoing winter rest. Native to Peru.

MASDEVALLIA

maz-de-VAL-lee-ah

Abbreviation: Masd.

Growth: Sympodial

Light: Low to medium

Temperature: Most grow best under cool, some intermediate

Flowering: Varies, most spring to summer

Care: Beginner to advanced

The showiest parts of a masdevallia flower are the sepals. In this genus, the petals are tiny structures nestled in the center of the flower. The sepals join at the base to form a tube, narrowing toward its tip, often forming long tails, making the flowers of some species resemble kites. Most forms have distinctly triangular or tubular flowers. Flower colors include pure white, green, and brownish black. The most popular species are orange to red. Flower sizes range from about 1 to 10 inches wide. Some are pendent, others are erect.

Masdevallias were the rage in England in the late 1800s. Many growers crossed the species sent to them by New World plant explorers. Around the turn of the 20th century, interest in masdevallia waned and few hybrids were bred for more than 50 years.

In the last few decades, however, several orchid firms in the United States have produced some exquisite new hybrids. These breeders are combining the large flower size and bright colors of the cool-growing species with the vigorous growth and abundant blooming of the intermediate species to create stunning hybrids that are easier to grow than their parents.

One of the first of these new hybrids was *Masdevallia* Marguerite (*veitchiana* × *infracta*). According to growers, *Masd. infracta* gives the plants vigor and the ability to tolerate intermediate temperatures. The flowers look like those of *Masd. veitchiana*—orange with a purplish red band of tiny hairs down the centers of the sepals. *Masd. veitchiana* was first collected for Messrs. Veitch & Sons of England in 1867 near Cuzco, Peru, where it was found growing amid the ruins of Machu Picchu.

Today there are myriad hybrids from which to choose, including those with scented flowers. Among the top choices is *Masd.* Confetti (*strobelii* × *glandulosa*) with delightfully fragrant flowers. It was registered in 1988 by J&L Orchids of Easton, Connecticut. *Masdevallia* has also been crossed with its relative *Dracula* to create the intergeneric hybrid *Dracuvallia* (Abbreviation: Drvla.).

Botanically speaking, masdevallias are part of the Pleurothallid Alliance that includes other miniatures ideally tailored to light-garden and grow-case environments. In recent years, Carlyle A. Luer of Florida, has studied these New World miniatures extensively, describing and illustrating hundreds of new species and clarifying name problems. His contributions to understanding and cataloging the diversity found within this group have revived interest in these charming miniatures, to the point where some hobbyists have formed a group devoted exclusively to them called The Pleurothallid Alliance.

Culture

Hobbyists who reside in areas with cool summers and high humidity can grow masdevallias. True cloud-forest orchids such as masdevallias require constant moisture because they have no pseudobulbs. The fleshy leaves are borne on tiny stems sprouting from small rhizomes. Most are from high elevations (between 6,000 and 12,000 feet) and need cool conditions. A few species will grow in intermediate temperatures.

Even in areas with hot, muggy summers, small masdevallias can be accommodated by growing them under lights in an air-conditioned home or in a home greenhouse that is adequately shaded and cooled by means of an aspen-pad (swamp) cooler, which pulls air across moistened pads.

Although masdevallias need high humidity, excess water on the plants encourages a fungal infection that rots the leaves where they join the stem. Avoid trying to compensate for low humidity with frequent misting or watering. If your plants succumb to the fungus, treat them with a fungicide and give them adequate ventilation.

Because of the need for constant high humidity, masdevallias are difficult to grow in the house except in a fluorescent-light garden contained within a space where a humidifier can be operated at all times and where the air can be kept gently moving with an oscillating fan. They also thrive inside terrariums and grow cases where the humidity can be maintained and the correct amount of light is available.

Species

■ *Masdevallia floribunda:* This small, tufted plant grows to about 4 inches tall. Named for its abundant flowers, it blooms from early summer to early autumn. The pale yellow flowers are about 1 inch across and are spotted with brown or purple. The tips of the sepals have a reddish tinge. *Masd. floribunda* was discovered by Henri Galeotii, a French botanist, near Veracruz, Mexico, in 1840. One of

Masdevallia floribunda

the more warmth-tolerant masdevallias, *Masd. floribunda* thrives between 60° and 85° F, with plentiful humidity and air movement. This species is best grown evenly moist in low light with a well-drained but moisture-retentive medium. Native to Mexico, Guatemala, Honduras, and Belize.

■ *Masdevallia infracta:* This plant's tufts of leaves reach up to 8 inches. The sepals are joined at their bases to form a bell, then narrow into

Masdevallia infracta

three outwardly curving tails. The flower colors vary, but most are pale yellow with deep red to purple markings. *Masd. infracta* blooms from spring to summer. Discovered by the French botanist M. E. Descourtilz near Rio de Janeiro in the 1830s, it is still a popular species. Grow warmth-tolerant *Masd. infracta* between 60° and 85° F. Keep this species evenly moist, pot in a well-drained, moisture-retentive medium, and grow on the shady side with high humidity and good air circulation. Native to Brazil and Peru.

■ *Masdevallia tovarensis (syn. Masd. candida):* One of the most popular masdevallias, *Masd. tovarensis* is noted for its showy kitelike flowers. The plant grows in clumps reaching 4 to 7 inches tall. Each long stem bears several translucent white flowers with greenish tails. The lower sepals are wide and joined for most of their length. The upper sepal consists of little other than a narrow, upright spur. It was discovered near Tovar, Venezuela, by Jean Linden in 1842. Collectors consider this winter-flowering species essential. Like many orchids native to high elevations, *Masd. tovarensis* needs cool to intermediate temperatures (50°–75° F) to flourish. This miniature will do best with moist, humid, and shaded conditions year-round. Do not cut inflorescences after the flowers fade; they rebloom each year. Native to Venezuela.

Masdevallia tovarensis

Masdevallia Copper Angel

Hybrids

■ *Masdevallia Copper Angel (triangularis × veitchiana):* One of the leading hybridizers of masdevallias, J&L Orchids, created this enchanting miniature in 1982. It is the recipient of numerous awards and a parent to several awarded progeny as well. Many clones are available. Their upright inflorescences bear flowers ranging from golden to brilliant deep orange and a floral shape that may favor either parent or draw evenly from both. Keep this orchid on the cool side—between 55° and 65° F—and protect it from direct sunlight. Given ideal conditions, this masdevallia tends to fill a pot quickly.

Masdevallia *continued*

■ *Masdevallia* Pink Rainbow
(asterotricha × glandulosa): Leon Glicenstein at Hoosier Orchid Company in Indianapolis created this excellent miniature hybrid, ideal for growing under lights or in a Wardian case. *Masd.* Pink Rainbow needs only bright indirect light to grow and bloom well. It can take some weak morning sun but should be protected from strong sunlight. It requires cool to intermediate temperatures, ideally ranging between 60° and 70° F. Perhaps the most critical factors in the care of this charming hybrid are constant moisture and humidity. Avoid allowing the plant to dry out completely; it requires 60 to 80 percent humidity for optimal health.

from direct sunlight. Although its ideal temperatures drop into the intermediate range, this plant will tolerate some warmer conditions. This plant is also floriferous, and one of the easier masdevallias to cultivate successfully.

Relatives

■ ***Dracula vampira:*** (Abbreviation: Drac.) The genus *Dracula* (DRACK-yew-lah) contains approximately 100 species, native to Central America and the Andes.

Drac. vampira is an unusual species that is breathtaking when in flower. Its name refers to the flowers' batlike appearance. The flowers, up to 8 inches long, open successively from pendent inflorescences that may reach more than 12 inches tall. As the flowers hang below the plant and face downward, draculas are best grown in baskets or pots suspended high enough to set off those blooms. *Drac. vampira is* native to Ecuador.

■ ***Lepanthes calodictyon:*** (Abbreviation: Lths.) The genus *Lepanthes* (leh-PAN-theez) offers more than 800 small-growing species with a range of striking flower shapes, sizes, and colors. While the flowers of *Lths. calodictyon*—a warmth-

Dracula vampira

tolerant species—are attractive, the plant is most highly prized for its foliage. The species epithet *calodictyon* means "beautiful net" in Greek and refers to the netlike pattern of deep purple on the front and back of each leaf. The tiny ⅙-inch-wide flowers bloom successively from the center of the leaves. Native to Colombia and Ecuador.

Masdevallia Pink Rainbow

■ *Masdevallia* Sunspot
(sanctae-inesae × tonduzii): The sunny golden yellow flowers of this aptly named cross have received a number of awards. Another Hoosier Orchid Company hybrid ideally suited to life in a light garden, this cheery miniature grows well in the shade and should be protected

Masdevallia Sunspot

Lepanthes calodictyon

Pleurothallis grobyi

■ *Pleurothallis grobyi:*
(Abbreviation: Pths.) One of the largest genera in the orchid family, *Pleurothallis* (plur-oh-THAL-liss) boasts more than 1,000 species native to the subtropical and tropical Americas. *Pths. grobyi* is one of the miniatures in the genus, which has members that reach several feet tall. The flowers may range from bright sunny yellow through gold tones and into orange shades. All benefit from intermediate to warm temperatures and low light. These plants grow best mounted, as long as humidity is high. Native to Mexico, the West Indies, and Central and South America.

■ *Restrepia:* (Abbreviation Rstp.) The genus *Restrepia* (res-trep-EE-ah) consists of compact orchids native from Central America to the Andes of Peru, Venezuela, Ecuador, Bolivia, and Colombia. There are approximately 48 species in the genus. Their otherworldly flowers are attractively spotted or striped, many with beautiful hues of rose and purple. Some of the larger-flowered restrepias include *Rstp. antennifera* and *Rstp. guttulata.* Beautifully striped *Rstp. striata* flowers are smaller at 1½ inches long. Restrepias are some of the hardier members of the Pleurothallid Alliance. They are easy to flower and can withstand some drying between waterings, although this is best avoided. These plants benefit from shade, a moist medium, high humidity, and good air circulation.

Most require cool to intermediate temperatures with an optimal range of 60° to 75° F. Many restrepias produce keikis at the base of older leaves, which may be removed and potted separately as soon as the plantlets have developed a few growths with roots.

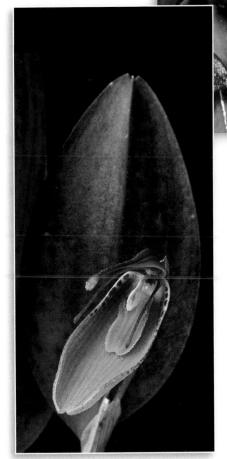

Restrepia striata

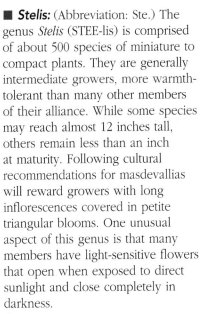

Stelis

■ *Stelis:* (Abbreviation: Ste.) The genus *Stelis* (STEE-lis) is comprised of about 500 species of miniature to compact plants. They are generally intermediate growers, more warmth-tolerant than many other members of their alliance. While some species may reach almost 12 inches tall, others remain less than an inch at maturity. Following cultural recommendations for masdevallias will reward growers with long inflorescences covered in petite triangular blooms. One unusual aspect of this genus is that many members have light-sensitive flowers that open when exposed to direct sunlight and close completely in darkness.

MILTONIA

mil-TOH-nee-ah

Abbreviation: Milt.

Growth: Sympodial

Light: Low to medium

Temperature: Intermediate

Flowering: Most summer to autumn

Care: Intermediate to advanced

Until recently, the genus *Miltonia* embraced two orchid groups that differ in their appearance as well as their cultural needs: warm-growing plants native to Brazil and cool growers from higher elevations ranging from Costa Rica to Peru. Experts who analyzed the DNA of these species separated them into two genera that reflect both their lineage and cultural needs. The Brazilian beauties remain in *Miltonia*, while the cool growers have been moved to *Miltoniopsis*.

The flowers of the Brazilian miltonias look more like odontoglossums. Although miltonias and miltoniopsis are closely related and confusingly similar in name, growers may distinguish the two by the number of leaves they carry on their pseudobulbs: miltonias bear two leaves per pseudobulb, while miltoniopsis hold only one.

Nurseries and orchid catalogs sell hybrids under either genus. The Royal Horticultural Society registers the hybrids under the name *Miltonia*. Any plant labeled as a miltonia but not from Brazil or adjacent Venezuela is either a miltoniopsis or from another genus.

Culture

Miltonia species and hybrids do best in medium light intensities and slightly warmer temperatures than those suggested for miltoniopsis, which are native to the highlands of Colombia. The foliage will sunburn if the plants receive too much light. If the plants have sufficient light, the leaves will be light green compared to other plants. A slight tinge of pink indicates that the plants are receiving as much light as they will tolerate. To prevent sunburn, shade the plants or move them away from windows during hot spells.

Despite the presence of their water-storing pseudobulbs, miltonias cannot withstand periods of dryness. Water them like cymbidiums, keeping the medium moist but not soggy at all times. A potting mix of fine fir bark amended with sphagnum moss, perlite, and a little charcoal provides a good balance for these moisture-sensitive plants.

If the new leaves emerge pleated, the plant is not receiving enough water. Increased watering will not flatten them out, but the next leaves should be smooth.

The flowers of the Brazilian miltonias are good for cutting and arranging.

Miltonia regnellii

Miltonia clowesii

Species

■ *Miltonia clowesii (syn. Oncidium clowesii):* The sepals and petals of these 2- to 3-inch-wide fragrant flowers are chestnut brown with yellow markings. Shaped like an inverted spade, the lip is white at the bottom and violet to purple with yellow markings at the top. The plants grow between 1 and 1½ feet tall and bloom from summer to autumn on 2-foot-tall spikes. Each spike holds 7 to 10 flowers. Native to Brazil.

■ *Miltonia regnellii:* The white sepals and petals of this species are sometimes tinted with rose. The broad, slightly undulating lip is light pink streaked with deeper pink. At the center of the lip is a prominent yellow callus. The flowers are generally between 2 and 3 inches across. Each 2-foot-tall inflorescence bears three to five flowers. The plant, which reaches

1 to 1½ feet tall, flowers from summer to autumn. Native to Brazil.

■ **Miltonia spectabilis:** The growth habit of this 10-inch miltonia is unruly. The pseudobulbs are spaced about an inch apart and are quickly forced over the edges of the pot by the rapid growth of the rhizome. The 3-inch flowers, however, are splendid. Borne one to a stem, they have white sepals and petals, sometimes with a rosy tinge toward the base. The white lip is large and spreading, with reddish-purple lines radiating from the yellow callus. In the variety *moreliana,* sepals

Miltonia spectabilis

and petals match the reddish-purple markings in the lip. Plants put on a wonderful show in late summer. Native to Brazil.

Hybrids

■ **Miltonia Anne Warne (Bluntii × spectabilis var. moreliana):** This is the first registered Brazilian miltonia hybrid, the result of a cross originally made in 1949. Its 4-inch flowers are a deep purple and are held singly above the foliage. Brazilian miltonias easily form natural hybrids. One of the most important, *Milt.* ×*bluntii (clowesii × spectabilis),* has also been made in cultivation—in which case the name is written as *Milt.* Bluntii. The foliage of *Milt.* Bluntii closely resembles that of *Milt. spectabilis.* The fragrant, light yellow flowers have reddish brown blotches. The lip is similar to that of *Milt. spectabilis* but does not come to a point. This 12-inch plant flowers summer to fall.

■ **Miltonia Hurricane Ridge (Herrenhausen × Woodlands; syn: Miltoniopsis):** If their cultural needs are met, expect three to six large, 5-inch, crystalline-white flowers accented with shades of crimson, gold, and violet from this orchid hybrid. Its flowers are usually of good form and appear on multiple spikes from late winter into spring.

Intergeneric hybrids

■ **Miltonidium Panama (Mtdm. Royal Monarch × Oncidium fuscatum):** (Abbreviation: Mtdm.) Given proper culture, this grex will flower more than once a year, producing many long-lasting flowers more than 3 inches across in romantic shades of goldenrod and red-mahogany with splashes of rosy pinks

Miltonia Anne Warne

and a deep velvety orange in the callus. Miltonidiums are among the easier orchids to grow and flower. They thrive for the indoor grower in an eastern or shaded western exposure or under lights. They are intermediate growers and will do well in minimum temperatures of 55° to 60° F on winter nights and maximum temperatures of 85° F on summer days. A period of cool evenings will help this hybrid set buds.

Miltonidium Panama

Miltonia Hurricane Ridge

MILTONIOPSIS

mill-toh-nee-OP-sis

Abbreviation: Mps.
Growth: Sympodial
Light: Low to medium
Temperature: Cool to intermediate
Flowering: Most spring
Care: Intermediate to advanced

Miltoniopsis flowers resemble pansies, hence the common name of pansy orchid. Miltoniopsis have beautiful rounded shapes and bright combinations of red, pink, white, and yellow. The markings at the base of the lip, called the mask, are intricate and striking. In some hybrids, such as *Mps.* Celle (Lydia × Lingwood), the mask is a splash of colors in what are called waterfall patterns.

Previously included in *Miltonia*, the genus *Miltoniopsis* represents six species native to the New World tropics that grow in cool temperatures and low to medium light, making them especially popular among growers in the Pacific Northwest. Although they will not grow well in warmer climates, miltoniopsis are occasionally sold as flowering plants meant to be enjoyed while in bloom and then discarded.

Among the many hybrids registered with the Royal Horticultural Society are exquisite grexes created by the Eric Young Orchid Foundation on England's Isle of Jersey.

Founded by a successful jeweler, the foundation continues to develop hybrids in *Calanthe, Cymbidium, Miltoniopsis, Paphiopedilum,* and *Phragmipedium.*

Combining the keen eye of former curator Alan Moon with the botanical genius of the late Donald Wimber, the foundation brought forth remarkable hybrids in all of these genera, many of them winning awards from the Royal Horticultural Society and influencing the future of orchid hybridizing.

Several clones of one of the foundation's most popular grexes—*Miltoniopsis* Saint Helier (Orkney × Alger)—are available.

Culture

The pansy orchids grow naturally in the high, cool areas of Colombia and countries from Costa Rica to Peru In cultivation, they do best in light intensities in the 1,000 to 1,500 foot-candle range, which is about the same as that prescribed for phalaenopsis. Miltoniopsis, however, need cool night temperatures and are sensitive to daytime highs above 80° F. Keep temperatures below 80° F to ensure the plants flower, but avoid letting them fall below 50° or 55° F.

Water regularly to keep well-drained medium slightly moist. If you allow the plant to dry out, the new leaves may emerge folded in an accordion pattern, similar to what happens when miltonias are watered insufficiently.

To avoid a buildup of fertilizer salts, water plants at least once a month with plain water to flush any accumulation out of the medium.

Fertilize plants every week with a quarter-strength solution or every other week with a half-strength solution, applying fertilizer less often during cloudy weather.

Repot miltoniopsis when flowering comes to an end and the new growths are emerging. Some hobbyists repot their miltoniopsis every year, placing the rootballs into fresh medium to avoid the roots touching a potting mix with accumulated salts.

Species

■ **Miltoniopsis phalaenopsis (syn. *Miltonia phalaenopsis*):** The flowers may be smaller than the other species—2 to 2½ inches wide—but what they lack in size they make up for in quantity, covering a plant with a profusion of pretty flowers. Each one is white with a bold or pale reddish mask on the lip that has the boxy or squarish contour reminiscent of a pansy. Cool to intermediate conditions suit thismiltoniopsis species, which will flower reliably on inflorescences that are shorter than the leaves. Native to Colombia.

Miltoniopsis phalaenopsis

■ **Miltoniopsis roezlii (syn. *Miltonia roezlii*):** A player in the development of modern miltoniopsis hybrids, *Mps. roezlii* bears 3- to 4-inch-wide flowers tucked among soft light green leaves. Each of the white flowers is decorated with a prominent purple blotch at the base of each petal and a splash of orange-yellow at the base of the broad wavy lip.

Although miltoniopsis typically are found at higher elevations, *Mps. roezlii* is also found at lower altitudes, even at sea level, making it naturally more tolerant of warmer conditions. One common name is Queen of Dagua, which refers to where it was first collected—Dagua, Colombia, at an elevation of 4,880 feet. Native to Panama and Colombia.

■ **Miltoniopsis vexillaria (syn. *Miltonia vexillaria*):** This is the most popular of the Colombian species and appears in the pedigree of many hybrids. The large dazzling flowers—sometimes more than 4 inches

Miltoniopsis roezlii

■ *Miltoniopsis* Dainty Miss (Dainty Lady × *phalaenopsis*): The large percentage of the miniature species *Mps. phalaenopsis* in the background of this cross provides its petite stature and its tendency to flower frequently, especially in the spring and early summer months. Cascades of white flowers heavily blushed pink, with a flush of gold and a rose waterfall pattern in the lip, make it a good choice for growing on windowsills or under lights in intermediate temperatures. This grex is one of many created by Oregon's Marie Riopelle and her late husband James, pioneers in the field of growing and hybridizing miltoniopsis. Their contributions to growing and hybridizing miltoniopsis were recognized when the American Orchid Society established the James and Marie Riopelle Award, which is given annually by the Society's trustees to the best-grown miltonia or miltoniopsis hybrid or species.

Miltoniopsis Dainty Miss

in shades of scarlet to rich, saturated red, with a crimson to deep cherry-burgundy waterfall pattern in the lip and a touch of golden yellow below the column. The flowers are large, vibrant, and colorful on vigorous, early blooming plants. This cross was named in honor of Hawaiian orchid grower Hajime Ono, recipient of the first James and Marie Riopelle Award.

■ *Miltoniopsis* Memoria Maurice Powers (Red Knight × Jim Riopelle): Another hybrid created by the Riopelles, this orchid has also received its share of flower-quality awards from the American Orchid Society. Expect multiple flowers on each inflorescence and more than one inflorescence at each blooming on a mature, well-grown 12-inch tall. plant. The 4½ inch flowers are usually deep velvety shades of cherry red with white tips on the petals and sepals, and a wine-red mask and light yellow flushing in the lip. They are large, flat, and heavy with a good round shape.

Miltoniopsis vexillaria

across—are borne on 1-foot-tall plants. The bright rose and white sepals and petals are small in relation to the richly colored lip, which spreads out magnificently and splits into two fat lobes. The lip is mostly white, variously streaked with red and yellow. *Mps. vexillaria* flowers in the spring and summer. Native to Colombia, Ecuador, and Peru.

Hybrids

■ *Miltoniopsis* Jeannette Brashear (Saint Brelades Bay × Emotion): This highly awarded hybrid boasts large, fragrant flowers with a good round form on long, strong inflorescences that display the flowers to their best advantage. The colors for this cross range from violet purples to lavenders and even crystalline white. The husky plants stay fairly compact for the genus.

Miltoniopsis Hajime Ono

■ *Miltoniopsis* Hajime Ono (Martin Orenstein × Pearl Ono): There is a seemingly endless variety of beautiful *Mps.* Hajime Ono clones from which to choose. Although this hybrid exhibits some variation among mericlones, the predominant color scheme for the grex starts with white petals and sepals. They are overlaid faintly to almost completely

Miltoniopsis Jeannette Brashear

Miltoniopsis Memoria Maurice Powers

NEOFINETIA

nee-oh-fin-AY-tee-ah

Abbreviation: Neof.

Growth: Monopodial

Light: Medium

Temperature: Cool to intermediate

Flowering: Summer

Care: Intermediate to advanced

Neofinetia is a genus with a single species. This lone orchid has attracted a loyal following over the centuries in Japan, where devotees search out clones with minute differences to add to their collections. Historically, *Neofinetia* was rendered in woodblock prints and given the name *fuuran* (wind orchid). The enthusiasm continues today, as collectors covet forms showing even the tiniest variation, perhaps a flower with a pink blush or a form with variegated leaves or with light red or light green coloration.

A member of the *Vanda* Alliance, *Neof. falcata* crosses readily with its

Neofinetia falcata

cousins, infusing new colors, shapes, fragrances, and plant sizes into progeny that are often more warmth tolerant than the neofinetia parent. More than two dozen intergeneric hybrid genera involving *Neof. falcata* have been registered with the Royal Horticultural Society. Many are good choices for growing on the windowsill or under lights.

Culture

Grow neofinetia on a mount or in a container. On a mount, ensure there is ample humidity and moisture at the roots, providing the water they require while keeping them from being constantly wet. In a container, pot the orchid in a porous, well-drained mix or in sphagnum moss. During the growing season, fertilize regularly, periodically flushing the potting medium with plain water to rinse away any salts. Neofinetia benefits from 80 percent humidity and cool temperatures. In Japan, collectors pot their prized possessions in lovely ceramic containers, some of which are finely decorated. *Neof. falcata* does equally well even in a plain clay or plastic pot.

Species

■ **Neofinetia falcata:** Pristine white flowers with a delightful evening fragrance are a trademark of this diminutive orchid that grows 2 to 6 inches tall. A monopodial, it bears tiny leaves alternately arranged along the upright stems. Each short inflorescence carries a few flowers, bearing a 2-inch-long curved spur that imparts a dramatic look to the presentation. Besides the traditional white, some clones offer slight variations, perhaps with a pale pink blush. Although rare, these unusual colors are worth the search. Native to Korea and Japan.

Intergeneric hybrids

■ *Ascofinetia* **Peaches (Neof. falcata × Ascocentrum curvifolium):** (Abbreviation: Ascf.) In this primary hybrid, the neofinetia parent imparts its tolerance of cold temperatures while the ascocentrum lends its brilliant, sparkling color to the cheery flowers. The plants stay nearly miniature, start blooming while they are still small, and bear a profusion of flowers on upright inflorescences more than once each year, with peak bloom in the spring and summer. They require strong light

Ascofinetia **Peaches**

for optimal growth and flowering. They can even take full sun if they are exposed to it in gradually increasing intervals. The flowers are a lovely deep peach color, as the grex name suggests, and are deliciously fragrant as well.

A related cross, *Ascofinetia* Cherry Blossom (*Neof. falcata* × *Ascocentrum ampullaceum*) is similar in every respect except for flower color—this hybrid bears bright, crystalline cherry pink flowers.

■ *Darwinara* **Charm (Neof. falcata × Vascostylis Tham Yuen Hae):** (Abbreviation: Dar.) The violet-blue to fuchsia pink flowers—up to 1½ inches wide—are large for the compact plant size. They are long-lasting and sweetly fragrant day and night. *Dar.* Charm's small stature and adaptability make it easy to grow and flower, even in limited space. Its requirements are fairly basic.

Darwinara **Charm**

Placed where it receives the intermediate light of an east-, south- or shaded west-facing window, or filtered outdoor sun, it will produce flowers throughout the year. It needs intermediate to warm temperatures—60° to 80° F is ideal—and requires a minimum of 40 percent humidity, less than most vandaceous orchids require for optimum health.

■ Dorifinetia Pilialoha (Neof. falcata × Doritis pulcherrima):

(Abbreviation: Dfta.) A rare and unusual primary hybrid, *Dtfa. Pilialoha* remains diminutive in

Dorifinetia Pilialoha

stature even at maturity, making it an excellent candidate for windowsill or under-lights culture where fairly bright light is available. Long inflorescences are full of lovely white blossoms richly blushed in shades of magenta to purple. The flowers are intermediate in shape between those of its parents. As with many of its progeny, the neofinetia parent imparts some cold tolerance that balances the warmth-loving doritis ancestry. Although this pretty hybrid can be difficult to find, it is well worth the hunt.

■ Neostylis Lou Sneary (Neof. falcata × Rhynchostylis coelestis):

(Abbreviation: Neost.) This floriferous primary hybrid is an all-around winner, starting with its delicious cotton-candy fragrance that can perfume an entire room. The shapeof its flowers favors the neofinetia parent, and clones are available with white flowers blushed in shades of fresh raspberry

pink through cool lilac blues. It flowers easily and frequently if given plenty of light. An adaptable miniature to compact-growing plant, it will thrive in a warm or cool environment. It will do equally well on a windowsill or in a greenhouse as long as it has ample humidity and is potted in a growing medium that allows excellent drainage.

Vandofinetia Virgil

Neostylis Lou Sneary

■ Vandofinetia Virgil (Neof. falcata × Vanda cristata):

(Abbreviation: Vf.) This is an excellent choice for those who love vandaceous orchids but cannot accommodate their need for space. With fragrant flowers that bear a strong resemblance to its *V. cristata* parent, tiny *Vf.* Virgil is a good candidate for culture in a slatted wooden basket, either empty or filled with a few pieces of coarse horticultural charcoal around its base—it benefits from plentiful air circulation around its roots. Provide intermediate to warm temperatures, with high humidity and lots of light.

ODONTOGLOSSUM

oh-don-toh-GLOSS-um

Abbreviation: Odm.

Growth: Sympodial

Light: Medium

Temperature: Cool to intermediate

Flowering: Varies with species

Care: Intermediate to advanced

The genus *Odontoglossum* contains about 60 species. Botanists have moved some of the species to the genus *Rossioglossum,* but these orchids are still commonly called odontoglossums.

Their exquisite inflorescences are produced from the bases of the flattened pseudobulbs and are usually erect and arching. The flowers are often large and showy, in shades of white, yellow, or green, marked with purple or brown blotches. They are long-lasting on the plant or as cut flowers.

Hybrids created by crossing odontoglossums with relatives such as oncidiums and miltonias are more adaptable to intermediate temperatures than are the *Odontoglossum* species and their hybrids. In addition to growing well in a wide range of temperatures, the intergeneric hybrids have large flowers with interesting shapes and unusual colors.

The hybrids in the following artificial genera adapt to intermediate conditions. Some of these hybrids do not have genes from the genus *Odontoglossum,* but are listed for easy comparison: *Adaglossum (Ada × Odontoglossum), Aliceara (Brassia × Oncidium × Miltonia), Brassidium (Brassia × Oncidium), Colmanara (Miltonia × Odontoglossum × Oncidium), Miltassia (Miltonia × Brassia), Miltonidium (Miltonia × Oncidium), Odontocidium (Odontoglossum × Oncidium), Sanderara (Brassia × Cochlioda × Odontoglossum), Symphodontoglossum (Symphyglossum × Odontoglossum), Wilsonara (Odontoglossum × Cochlioda × Oncidium),* and *Wingfieldara*

(Aspasia × Brassia × Odontoglossum). Of these, the alicearas, brassidiums, miltonidiums, and miltassias do fairly well in warm temperatures. Many can be grown successfully in South Florida or in other areas where high summer temperatures overwhelm odontoglossums and the cool-growing hybrids.

Beauty has not been compromised in the creation of warmth-tolerant hybrids. *Aliceara* Hawaiian Delight *(Miltassia* Cartagena × *Oncidium crispum)* is a fine aliceara, producing 6-inch-wide cream and brown flowers with large ruffled lips. Brassidiums such as *Brassidium* Florida Gem *(Brassia* Rex × *Oncidium tigrinum)* have the starry shapes of brassias with the yellow and brown markings of oncidiums.

The following hybrids often have cool-growing species in their backgrounds and thus grow better in cool conditions: *Odontioda (Odontoglossum × Cochlioda), Odontobrassia (Odontoglossum × Brassia), Odontonia (Odontoglossum × Miltonia),* and *Vuylstekeara (Miltonia × Cochlioda × Odontoglossum).*

As for some other genera and groups in the Orchidaceae, there is a specialty group dedicated to odontoglossums, the Odontoglossum Alliance. Group meetings and newsletters regularly update members on these breathtaking orchids.

Culture

Their showy flowers have made odontoglossums popular with hobbyists, despite the plants' sometimes exacting temperature requirements. Most species originate high in the Andes, where they are continually

bathed in cool, moist fog. They thrive in nighttime low temperatures of 45° F and daytime highs of 60° F, conditions similar to those required by cymbidiums. Outside of the Pacific Northwest, where hobbyists grow odontoglossums to perfection, most areas of the United States are too warm for these plants. Good results may be obtained under the right conditions in the San Francisco Bay area or with the warmer-growing *Odontoglossum*-type hybrids. Odontoglossums benefit from bright light, whether grown in a greenhouse or on a windowsill with an eastern or a shaded southern exposure. If day temperatures rise above recommended levels, increase the humidity and air circulation to compensate.

Odontoglossums should be kept from drying out completely between waterings. Pot size, medium, light, temperatures—all contribute to determining how often plants need to be watered. Like miltonias, odontoglossums may develop accordion pleating on the leaves if kept too dry. Adding more water will leave the wrinkle unaffected, but correcting watering practices will prevent future problems. Many growers use a mixture containing

Odontoglossum crispum

one part coarse sand, one part shredded peat, one part coarse perlite, and four parts fine bark to create a moist, well-drained medium.

Repot only when necessary to replace the growing medium. Odontoglossums grow poorly if their roots are frequently disturbed. When repotting, remove the old, leafless pseudobulbs with heat-sterilized clippers. Check the cut surface of the pseudobulb for rot. Rotted areas are light to dark brown; healthy tissue is white. Remove all rotten growth and sear the cut surfaces of the healthy growths with the heated blade of the clippers before repotting. After repotting, keep the medium barely moist and provide ample humidity until new roots show. Then resume regular watering.

Species

■ *Odontoglossum crispum:* This breathtaking beauty has captured the fancy of orchid enthusiasts since it was described by John Lindley in 1852. More than 1,000 varieties of *Odm. crispum* have been named. As many as twenty 3- to 4-inch-wide flowers—white, sometimes flushed with purple—decorate each inflorescence, which may be branched at the base. The edges of the flower parts—sepals and petals— may be smooth or serrated, giving

them a shaggy appearance. Two leaves top each of the 3-inch-tall pseudobulbs of this epiphyte. Native to Colombia.

■ *Odontoglossum pulchellum* (syn. *Osmoglossum pulchellum*):* Given time, this plant will form a large, handsome clump about 15 inches tall. The white flowers are rounded and fragrant. At the center of each flower is a yellow callus with reddish brown spots. Three to 10 flowers are borne on a slim, erect inflorescence in the spring. Native to Mexico, Guatemala, El Salvador, and Costa Rica.

Intergeneric hybrids

■ *Beallara* Marfitch (*Miltassia Charles M. Fitch × Odontiode Fremar*): (Abbreviation Bllra.) The name of this genus recognizes the Beall Orchid Company on Vashon Island, Washington, a longtime family business famous for its miltoniopsis and paphiopedilums. The grex name, Marfitch, honors the orchid photographer Charles Marden Fitch. This intergeneric hybrid has *Brassia, Cochlioda, Miltonia,* and *Odontoglossum* in its parentage, resulting in an orchid that is adaptable to a wide range of conditions and that can flower twice each year. It produces many large, beautiful deep plum-purple, attention-getting flowers. Provide low to medium light and intermediate to warm temperatures. Allow it to dry slightly between waterings.

Odontoglossum pulchellum

■ *Odontioda* Allan Long (Point Lonsdale × Joe's Drum): (Abbreviation: Oda.) Electric colors in outstanding patterns draw attention to the best odontioda hybrids, including the *Oda.* Allan Long clone shown here, 'Berrymore', AM/AOS. Lush, full rustic orange flowers watermarked fuchsia pink make an exciting contrast with the lip, which is usually white, flushed hot pink, marked with orange, and touched off by a golden crest. The complex lineage of odontiodas traces back to high-altitude, cool-growing species. They will grow best when temperatures remain between 75° to 80° F during the day and 55° to 60° F at night. Eastern exposure suits these beauties, as they need bright light to bloom well. Keep them evenly moist and allow them to dry only slightly between waterings.

Beallara Marfitch

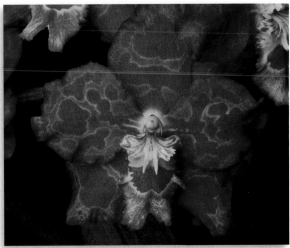

Odontioda Allan Long

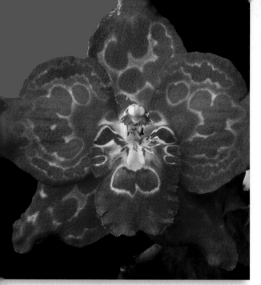

Odontioda Drummer Joe

Odontoglossum
continued

■ **Odontioda Drummer Joe (Joe's Drum × Lingway):** *Oda.* Drummer Joe—including this clone, 'Galactic Queen'—is a robust grower that bears long-lasting, bright flowers with intricate patterns in spring. It is a parent to a number of successful odontioda hybrids. A sunshine yellow callus accents its wild raspberry petals that have pink, orange and deep raspberry markings. Robert Dugger created this hybrid in 1989. Dugger was instrumental in generating interest in odontoglossum hybrids and created more than 8,000 crosses. The Robert B. Dugger

Odontoglossum Award, of the American Orchid Society, recognizes his contributions.

■ **Vuylstekeara Aloha Passion (Vuyl. Memoria Mary Kavanaugh × Oda. Alcatraz):** (Abbreviation: Vuyl.) *Vuylstekeara* is an intergeneric hybrid, the species parents of which are in the genera *Cochlioda, Miltonia* and *Odontoglossum*. All of the species are from higher elevations, indicating that this genus requires intermediate to cool conditions. At more than 3 inches across, the flowers of *Vuyl.* Aloha Passion, a hybrid made by Tom Perlite of Golden Gate Orchids in the San Francisco Bay area, are large. They last up to three months. A mature plant can bear as many as 20 flowers each spring and, in cooler climates, in the autumn as well. Its flowers draw attention with their dramatic combination of dark plum-purple, decorated with lavender-pink and blotched burgundy, with a bright yellow crest. The time to repot this beauty is after flowering.

■ **Vuylstekeara Cambria (Vuyl. Rudra × Odm. Clonius):** An immensely popular intergeneric hybrid, *Vuyl.* Cambria was first registered in 1931 and is still widely available. The clone 'Plush' has received the highest possible award of flower quality—FCC, or First Class Certificate—from both the American

Vuylstekeara Aloha Passion

Orchid Society and the Royal Horticultural Society. There are numerous mericlones available from orchid nurseries and catalogs, in colors ranging from white to gold, all with exotic patterning in shades of scarlet, raspberry, brick red, and brown, accented with a touch of sunny yellow in the throat. These clones share several characteristics with the hybrid, including a full, rounded shape and stunning color combinations.

■ **Wilsonara Christmas Candy (Oncidium Tai × Oda. Fireflower):** (Abbreviation: *Wils.*) Registered by Everglades Orchids of Belle Glade, Florida, this grex is part of that nursery's focus on warmth-tolerant cymbidiums and *Oncidium* intergeneric hybrids. For more than 40 years, Everglades has

Vuylstekeara Cambria

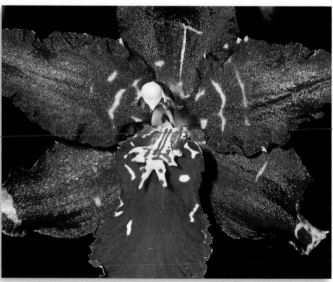

Wilsonara Christmas Candy

been breaking new ground in hybrids from traditionally cool-growing genera that can withstand Florida's summer heat. *Wils.* Christmas Candy is aptly named for its crimson-red flowers with washes of fuchsia, accented in gold and cinnamon. The flowers are large and full in form, reaching nearly 3 inches across. This grex is more temperature tolerant than many wilsonaras, adapting to summer days up to 90° F when full air circulation and humidity are provided.

■ *Wilsonara* Native Girl (*Wils.* Bubba Mock × *Oncidium* Illustre):

The Everglades Orchids creation *Wils.* Native Girl puts on quite a show in flower with satiny cadmium yellow flowers heavily overlaid in burgundy, beautifully displayed on inflorescences that can reach 4 feet tall. Wilsonaras do well potted in fine bark mix with ample drainage and some moisture-retentive material such as sphagnum moss or rockwool. This hybrid needs intermediate light, such as an eastern exposure.

Relatives

■ *Aspasia principissa* (syn. *Odontoglossum principissum*):

(Abbreviation: Asp.) Eight species of *Aspasia* (ah-SPAY-zee-a) grow naturally as epiphytes from Guatemala to Brazil. Compact and a pretty green, the plants are easy to flower. *Asp. principissa* bears striking 3-inch-wide flowers, each tan striped with purple, on 10- to 12-inch-tall inflorescences. Aspasias grow well under the same conditions as cattleyas: bright light, warm temperatures, and a porous medium that is allowed to dry slightly. Keeping the plants slightly potbound may coax a better flower display. Native to Costa Rica, Panama, and Colombia.

■ *Rossioglossum grande* (syn. *Odontoglossum grande*):

(Abbreviation: Ros.) About half a dozen species of *Odontoglossum* that grow in cool to intermediate conditions were moved to their own genus, *Rossioglossum*. Among the members is *Rossioglossum grande*, an epiphyte that bears waxy flowers anywhere from 5 to 9 inches across. This plant gets its common name—

Aspasia principissa

tiger orchid—from its coloring: golden yellow with reddish-brown bands and flecks. The callus looks like a small fat doll or clown, inspiring a second common name, clown orchid. The plant grows about 15 inches tall and flowers anytime from autumn to spring. In the summer, keep this species on the intermediate to warm side and give copious water and fertilizer. During winter, provide cooler, drier conditions; plants will withstand temperatures to 40° F. *Ros. grande* requires filtered light, rather than direct sun. Be vigilant against snails and slugs. Native to Mexico and Guatemala.

Wilsonara Native Girl

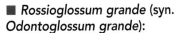

Rossioglossum grande

ONCIDIUM

on-SID-ee-um

Abbreviation: Onc.

Growth: Sympodial

Light: Medium to high

Temperature: Intermediate

Flowering: Varies

Care: Beginner

Dancing ladies is an appropriate name for many members of the genus *Oncidium,* a large grouping of about 150 species native to the New World tropics. The robust, shimmering sprays of the larger oncidiums are dramatic and elegant, while the dainty spikes of the smaller species are delightful. Yellow and brown are the predominant flower colors, though white, purple, pink, and green hues also are available.

Oncidium is a large genus, embracing plants with tremendous diversity in their growth habits as well as flower types. Many of the terms chosen to describe the leaves or plant type capture their shapes: rat-tail types have slender pencil-shaped leaves, while the mule-ear oncidiums grow upright, thick, leathery leaves.

Since it was established in 1800, *Oncidium* has been a catch-all genus for hundreds of species that bear a superficial resemblance to one another. In the past decade, however, DNA studies on *Oncidium* and its allies carried out by Mark Chase at the Jodrell Laboratory at the Royal Botanic Gardens, Kew, London, have generated new data. When combined with other details about the plants, such as their flower structure, these findings reveal more accurate relationships. Norris Williams and Mark Whitten at the Florida Museum of Natural History in Gainesville have been carrying out similar experiments. The result has been renaming of species in several genera in the *Oncidium* Alliance— *Oncidium, Miltonia, Miltoniopsis, Odontoglossum, Rossioglossum, Zelenkoa, Cyrtochilum,* and *Tolumnia,* among others.

Oncidiums come in many sizes, shapes, and colors. With proper care these easily grown orchids can be kept small or allowed to grow into dramatic specimens, depending on the desires of the grower and the size limits of the environment in which the plants will be raised. Garden designers in tropical climates plant oncidiums directly onto trees such as oaks, tabebuias, and palms to create fluffy clouds of seasonal color. The fragrances of some species add another dimension to the landscape, stimulating the senses during a walk through a garden, often before the dancing ladies come into view.

Culture

Oncidiums are generally easier to grow than their relatives in the genera *Odontoglossum* and *Miltoniopsis.* They adapt well to intermediate temperatures and tolerate an occasional missed watering without damage. Like other epiphytic orchids, they require a well-drained medium and should be allowed to dry slightly between waterings. The leaves indicate how much dryness the plants will tolerate. Thin-leaved species such as *Onc. sphacelatum* need to be watered more frequently than species with thick leaves, such as *Onc. carthagenense.* Oncidiums tend to be robust, good choices for the beginner because they quickly develop into full specimens and put forth lovely flower displays when provided with ample fertilizer, regular watering, and bright light.

In addition to thriving in containers, many oncidiums adapt well to life on a plaque, such as a piece of wood, driftwood (washed to remove any salts), or tree fern. Hanging baskets are another option, especially for developing large specimens that will be impressive in flower. Use wood-slat, wire, or plastic mesh baskets for oncidiums. *Onc. crispum* and *Onc. macranthum* grow best in temperatures at the cool end of the intermediate range, while other

species do better when provided with intermediate to warm conditions. Oncidiums benefit from being outside during the summer. In warm climates they can be grown outdoors year-round. As you return plants indoors before the first frost, inspect them carefully, taking the time to lift each plant from its pot and see whether there are insects in the root zone or in the leaves.

Species

■ *Oncidium ampliatum:* The pseudobulbs of this species are large and rounded. The leaves are about 15 inches long up to 5 inches wide. In spring, arching 4-foot-long sprays bear bright yellow flowers about 1 inch across. *Onc. ampliatum* var. *majus* is a winter-flowering yellow species. It needs intermediate to warm temperatures and grows easily indoors. Native to Guatemala, Venezuela, and Bolivia.

Oncidium ampliatum

Oncidium carthagenense

vivid yellow, waxy, and deliciously fragrant—are arrayed in dense clusters on 6-inch-tall spikes from autumn through winter. Native to Nicaragua, Costa Rica, Panama, and the highlands of Colombia.

■ *Oncidium crispum:* The large, ruffled petals of *Onc. crispum* and its huge dorsal sepal are nearly as big as the lip. The sepals, petals, and lip are coppery red to greenish brown. The lip has a yellow patch at the base and a crest decorated with warty red protuberances. This plant's oval leaves grow two to three to a pseudobulb and reach about 9 inches long. It flowers autumn through winter. Native to Brazil.

■ *Oncidium carthagenense:* A beautiful example of a mule-ear oncidium, this species has thick upright leaves 6 to 24 inches long, spotted with tiny reddish-brown dots. In summer the spikes, to 5 feet, bear ½-inch-wide ruffled purple and white flowers. Native to Florida, the West Indies, and from Mexico to Venezuela and Brazil.

■ *Oncidium cheirophorum:* This is a charming plant with shiny, tightly clustered pseudobulbs. The thin leaves are short; the plants reach 4 inches tall. The flowers—

Oncidium cheirophorum

Oncidium crispum

Oncidium *continued*

■ **Oncidium luridum:** This plant is a large mule-ear type. *Onc. luridum* has stout 2-foot-tall leaves. The branching flower stalk, which reaches about 4 feet tall, bears showy white flowers that are marked with rose in spring. The lip is tinged with orange and the crest is yellow with a pattern of orange lines. Native to South Florida and the West Indies, and from Mexico to Peru.

■ **Oncidium ornithorhynchum:** Tiny pinkish-purple, rose, or mauve flowers with an eye-catching yellow crest spill in masses above the leaves of this compact-growing oncidium. Dozens of buds on the wiry inflorescence serve up a cloud of color and fragrance when it flowers in autumn and winter. Cooler conditions suit this epiphyte that puts on an incredible show, even in a 4-inch pot. Native to Mexico and portions of Central America.

Oncidium luridum

bottom and shorter at the top, giving the flower stalk an appealing symmetry. This vigorous orchid does well mounted or in a basket. In tropical gardens, it makes an excellent subject for mounting directly onto a tree with rough bark, such as a yellow tabebuia. Native to Mexico, Honduras, Guatemala, and El Salvador.

Oncidium splendidum

Oncidium ornithorhynchum

■ **Oncidium sphacelatum:** This robust species has 6-inch pseudobulbs with leaves growing more than 2 feet long. An upright, branched inflorescence bears golden yellow and brown flowers November to June, but especially in the spring. The side branches are longer at the

Oncidium sphacelatum

■ **Oncidium splendidum:** One of the largest mule-ear oncidiums, *Onc. splendidum* has leaves that are about 3 feet tall, although they can be much shorter on plants in cultivation. The showy flowers, in spring to early summer, are 3 inches across, with lemon yellow and brown sepals and petals. The large, clear yellow lip is smooth and rounded. Native to Guatemala and Honduras.

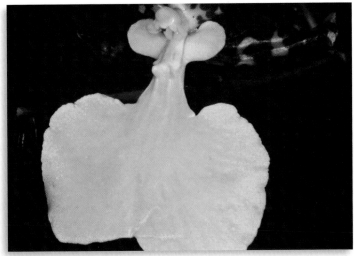

Oncidium tigrinum

Oncidium Gower Ramsey

■ *Oncidium tigrinum:* When this plant blooms in autumn, the greenish-yellow and brown sepals of its fragrant 2-inch-wide flowers that appear on 2-foot spikes provide a dark background for the striking yellow lip. The narrowed portion in the center of the colorful lip lends it an asymmetrical hourglass shape. Native to Mexico.

■ *Oncidium varicosum:* Although the name dancing ladies is applied to many oncidiums, it best describes this pseudobulbous species. From autumn through winter, yellow and brown flowers dance like ballerinas in troupes of 200 on lacy, branched stems up to 5 feet long. Native to Brazil.

Hybrids

■ *Oncidium* **Gower Ramsey (Goldiana × Guinea Gold):** This grex makes an excellent orchid for beginners. It is easy to grow on a bright windowsill, forgiving of imperfect culture, and a prolific bloomer. Even on a young plant, its ½-inch-wide, chrome yellow flowers appear in profusion on tall, branching spikes to resemble cheery dancing ladies in full, brightly colored skirts. A widely sold hybrid, it will grace its growing area with glowing inflorescences twice each year. In spike, one of these orchids will reach over 2 feet tall, so it may be less than ideal for light gardens.

Similar to *Onc.* Gower Ramsey is *Onc.* Sweet Sugar (Aloha Iwanaga × *varicosum)*, one of the most desirable dancing-lady orchids. *Onc.* Sweet Sugar flowers prolifically on compact, upright, heavily branched inflorescences with larger, more fully shaped sunshine yellow flowers than many comparable hybrids.

■ *Oncidium* **Sharry Baby (Jamie Sutton × Honolulu):** An exceptional orchid, *Onc.* Sharry Baby is popular for its heady white-chocolate fragrance and ease of culture. It has vigorous growth and blooming tendencies. Its heavy perfume fills the air with rich scent. While an individual flower may fail to impress, a mature and well-grown plant can produce 3-foot-tall, branching inflorescences covered in clouds of hundreds of flowers perfuming an entire greenhouse. This hybrid tends to develop dry leaf tips and small black spots on its leaves. Although unsightly and irreversible once present, they are harmless to other orchids in the collection.

Oncidium varicosum

Oncidium Sharry Baby

Oncidium *continued*

■ **Oncidium Twinkle (cheirophorum × ornithorhynchum):** Registered nearly 50 years ago by W. W. Goodale Moir, a Hawaiian pioneer in oncidium hybridizing, this petite beauty is an excellent choice for a light garden or windowsill cultivation. It usually flowers in the spring and again in autumn, with showers of dainty blossoms in shades of red, pink, lavender, cream, or white, with an intense and deliciously spicy fragrance. This primary hybrid stays compact and requires only low to moderate illumination. An eastern exposure is ideal. It is easy to grow, needing intermediate temperatures and evenly moist conditions. It is important to keep the plant from drying completely between waterings, especially when in bloom, as this can cause the inflorescences to abort or buds to drop.

Oncidium Twinkle

Burrageara Nelly Isler

Intergeneric hybrids

■ **Burrageara Nelly Isler (Burr. Stefan Isler × Miltoniopsis Kensington):** (Abbreviation: Burr.) An intergeneric member of the *Oncidium* Alliance, *Burr.* Nelly Isler combines *Oncidium, Miltoniopsis,* and *Vuylstekeara*. Such varied parentage provides for an easy grower that will thrive under a wide range of conditions. Its ideal temperatures fall in the intermediate range. A 10° F drop at night helps this complex hybrid set buds. Abundant flowers are beautifully displayed on upright inflorescences (which may appear two to a pseudobulb), eye-catching in color and lightly fragrant. Cultivate this orchid in medium light, such as an eastern exposure. It should be kept from drying out completely between waterings.

■ **Colmanara Wildcat (Colm. Rustic Bridge × Odcdm. Crowborough):** (Abbreviation: Colm.) *Colmanara* is a complex hybrid genus created by crossing *Miltonia, Odontoglossum,* and *Oncidium.* This combination generates a vigorous fast-growing, temperature-tolerant, and easy to care for orchid. It has impressive displays of vibrantly colored flowers of heavy substance on long branching inflorescences. Plants generally flower twice each year. Colors range from cream through brilliant gold, with red, brown, and burgundy spotting to nearly complete coverage. The plants are tall with relatively young plants reaching 3 feet. Repot *Colm.* Wildcat after flowering is complete, usually in the spring or early summer, in a well-drained mix that has some moisture-retentive materials, such as sphagnum moss or rockwool, added.

Colmanara Wildcat

■ *Odontocidium* Mitsuishi (*Onc.* Splinter × *Odm.* Moselle): (Abbreviation: Odcdm.) This lovely hybrid is capable of flowering twice each year and bears up to 25 waxy chrome yellow flowers with a creamy white lip, covered in attractive chocolate markings. With parentage in the genera *Odontoglossum* and *Oncidium,* it adapts to a wide range of temperatures and should be comfortable in a range from 60° to 85° F. It can tolerate a variation of 5 degrees in either direction for short periods. Southern or eastern exposures provide the best light levels for this orchid. Dark spots at the tips of the leaves indicate that the plant is receiving too much light.

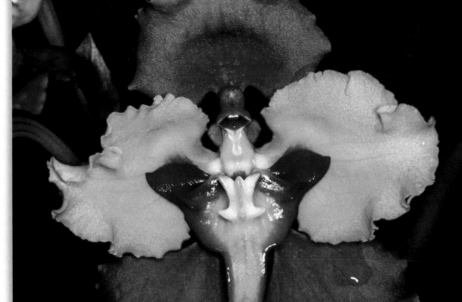

Cyrtochilum macranthum

Odontocidium Mitsuishi

■ *Odontocidium* Susan Kaufman (*Odcdm.* Wera Stolze × *Onc.* flexuosum): These petite and attractive plants are fast growers, flower when young, and produce abundant flowers. The vivid yellow-chartreuse flowers are heavily overlaid in shades of crimson to chestnut, while the brilliant chrome yellow lip is generously speckled with burgundy. Although the flowers are small compared with *Odcdm.* Susan Kaufman's larger cousins, it is common to find up to fifty

1- to 1½-inch flowers on each branching inflorescence.
In addition, this grex has inherited its *Onc. flexuosum* parent's characteristic of producing two inflorescences from a single pseudobulb. A temperature tolerant plant, this hybrid will accept a range of 55° F winter nights to 90° F summer days. Provide humidity of 50 to 80 percent and an eastern exposure.

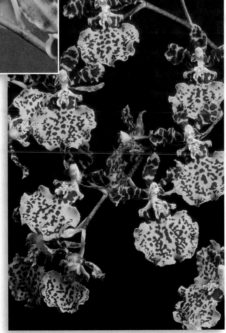

Odontocidium Susan Kaufman

Relatives

■ *Cyrtochilum macranthum* (syn. *Oncidium macranthum*): (Abbreviation: Cyr.) Previously classified as an *Oncidium,* this species is now part of the genus *Cyrtochilum* (sir-toh-KY-lum), which has about 120 species native to Costa Rica, Colombia, Ecuador, and Peru.

The 4-inch-wide flowers of *Cyr. macranthum,* which appear in early summer, are probably the largest in the genus. They are held on a branched, vining inflorescence that reaches 8 to 12 feet long. If trained on a wire hoop as it develops, this vining inflorescence will form a wreath of flowers. The flower sepals are brown and the petals are golden yellow. The bloom's complex lip has violet side lobes and a yellow midlobe.

These handsome and very rewarding orchids require ample space to grow. A cool-growing orchid from upper-elevation cloud forests, this species will thrive in the following conditions: intermediate light, night temperatures of 50° to 55° F, daytime highs in the low 70s year-round, high humidity, and plentiful moisture. This orchid should be allowed to dry only slightly between waterings. Native to Ecuador and Peru.

Psychopsis papilio

Oncidium *continued*

■ *Psychopsis papilio* (syn. *Oncidium papilio*): (Abbreviation: Pyp.) Five species of *Psychopsis* (sye-KOP-sis) are native to portions of Central and South America. The flower of *Pyp. papilio* looks like a large hovering insect, giving it the common name butterfly orchid. The dorsal sepal and petals are long and narrow, curving up and forward like antennae. The lateral sepals and lip are yellow with brown markings. A pure yellow form is also available. The 10- to 15-inch-tall inflorescences produce new flowers at the tip. Throughout the year, as the oldest flower fades, a new one opens to take its place. In its native habitat, the butterfly orchid receives fairly even temperatures year-round, with daytime highs around 80° F, and night temperatures in the low 60s, making it a good indoor plant if you provide enough light and humidity. During the growing season, typically spring through autumn for this species, it requires copious water. Allow the plant to dry between waterings. Fertilize and keep humidity at 50 to 75 percent. Mounted plants need higher humidity and more frequent watering, at least once a day in hot weather. Reduce frequency of watering and fertilizing

during winter. *Psychopsis* species need a medium with rapid drainage. They may be mounted or grown in baskets or shallow pots, such as azalea pots.

■ *Tolumnia* **species and hybrids:** (Abbreviation: Tolu.) Once part of the genus *Oncidium,* the vargiegata-type oncidiums have been moved to their own genus, *Tolumnia* (toh-LUM-nee-ah), which contains about 35 species.

Among the species is *Tolumnia bahamensis,* which is found in the Bahamas and a small area of southeast Florida, where it grows on rosemary scrub close to the lichen-covered ground. Discussion continues as to whether or not the Florida colony was begun from wind-blown seed originating in the Bahamas, or from plants brought by Bahamian immigrants to adort the graves of a nearby cematary.

Although species are in cultivation, garden centers and stores stock mostly hybrids, which have short sprays of bright-colored jewel-toned flowers. Frequently, these charming little orchids are sold in tiny clay pots with only a few pieces of horticultural-grade charcoal tucked among the roots. The fan-shaped plants also may be mounted. Most catalogs and garden centers call these plants equitant oncidiums even though botanists have moved them to the genus *Tolumnia.*

Tolumnia Pelican Island

Tolumnia bahamense

Tolumnias have a reputation as confidence builders and outstanding houseplants. In fact, most interspecific oncidium hybrids are equitants. One of the first equitant hybrids was *Tolumnia* Golden Glow (*triquetra* × *urophylla*). *Tolumnia* Golden Sunset, another fairly old hybrid, results from the combination of several species, among them *Tolu. pulchella, Tolu. triquetra,* and *Tolu. urophylla.* The equitant species *Tolu. pulchella* is one of the easier orchids to grow. It is native to Jamaica.

Tolumnias, like many oncidiums, generally do well outdoors in summer, benefiting from rain or, in its absence, showering with the hose. Bring them inside before temperatures drop below 50° F. These miniatures also grow well under lights and on windowsills with a bright exposure.

■ *Tolumnia* **Pelican Island (Sundowner × Sammy Ray) (syn.** *Oncidium* **Pelican Island):** Tolumnia hybrids are highly variable. Their colors and patterns differ from clone to clone and even from one blooming to the next on the same plant. The amount of light that developing flowers receive affects color intensity and patterning on fully open blossoms. Anita Aldrich of Sundance Orchids in Texas, one of the premier hybridizers of tolumnias or equitant oncidiums, created this grex. At its peak flowering season in the spring, this easy bloomer produces many flowers in shades of sparkling scarlet, hot pink, brick red, gold, and cream with spots, speckles, flushes, and blushes of color.

■ *Tolumnia* Popoki (Puff × Phyllis Hetfield) (syn. *Oncidium* Popoki):

This miniature is also an equitant oncidium. Its narrow pointed fanlike leaves are long, fleshy, and nearly succulent. The boldly patterned flowers sport festive color combinations and full lips that resemble a dancer's flowing skirt. A single inflorescence will produce a cluster of little blooms, sometimes on branching stems. A well-grown plant may bear numerous spikes. Because their species ancestors are twig epiphytes, these plants need excellent air circulation and should dry between waterings. Keep water out of the leaf crevices to avoid rot.

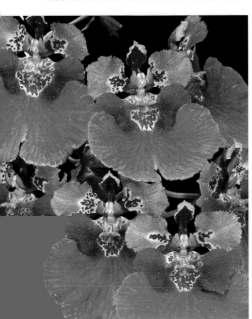

Tolumnia Popoki

■ *Tolumnia triquetra* (syn. *Oncidium triquetrum):* Gardeners who wish

to try species tolumnias have several options, among them *Tolu. triquetra.* Thick three-sided leaves overlap at the base and are arranged in a fan about 3 inches tall. The petals and lip of the 1-inch-wide flowers are white, dotted with maroon. The contrasting sepals are greenish brown, lighter around the edges. Each 7-inch-tall inflorescence

bears 5 to 15 flowers. This species usually flowers in summer, but some specimens are almost everblooming. Refrain from cutting the spikes after flowering; they often branch and bloom again. Native to Jamaica.

■ *Zelenkoa onusta* (syn. *Oncidium onustum):*

(Abbreviation: Zel.) Originally described as an *Oncidium* in 1836, this species was moved to its own genus—*Zelenkoa*— in 2001. The genus name honors artist Harry Zelenko, who has painted hundreds of oncidiums and their relatives, many of which have been reproduced in his book

Zelenkoa onusta

Orchids: The Pictorial Encyclopedia of Oncidium. Zelenkoa (zel-en-KOW-ah) contains a single species, which grows naturally in dry lowland regions as an epiphyte on tree cactus or as a lithophyte. This small-growing but vigorous plant—with 1-inch oval pseudobulbs tightly spaced along the rhizomes—bears light, airy sprays of 1-inch-wide pure yellow flowers with broad, flaring notched

lips. Frequently, the inflorescences are branched, multiplying the impact of the dazzling show. To master its cultural needs, provide bright light, allow the plant to dry slightly between waterings, grow zelenkoa in a pot or slat basket using a well-draining medium (possibly with chunks of charcoal) or on a mount, such as cork or tree fern. Native to Ecuador and Peru.

Tolumnia triquetra

PAPHIOPEDILUM

paff-ee-oh-PED-ih-lum

Abbreviation: Paph.

Growth: Sympodial

Light: Low to medium, depending on species

Temperature: Intermediate to cool, depending on species

Flowering: Generally autumn to spring, though plants are available in bloom year-round

Care: Beginner to advanced

Paphiopedilums differ from most other orchids in their fan leaf arrangement and in flowers. One feature that sets the flowers apart is the lip, which is a cup-like pouch. The common name slipper orchid often is applied to paphiopedilums. (Lady's-slipper orchid is reserved for the related genus *Cypripedium*.) About 70 species of *Paphiopedilum* are native to the Old World tropics, with new species still being discovered, especially in China and Vietnam. Among the contemporary researchers is Phillip Cribb, deputy keeper of the Orchid Herbarium at the Royal Botanic Gardens, Kew near London.

Another showy part of a paphiopedilum flower is the dorsal (uppermost) sepal, usually shaped like an upside-down heart and colorfully marked with distinct lines or spots. The two lower sepals are fused and may be almost completely hidden by the pouch. The long, narrow petals may stick straight out at the sides of the flower or may hang down like a long mustache. Tufts of black hairs sprout from the upper edges of the petals in some species.

In the modern hybrids the flower parts are thick and waxy, often taking on the texture of rubbery plastic. Green, brown, white, and pink hues predominate in the species with some vivid shades of red and purple. These colors may be subtly blended or patterned in bold stripes and spots. Paphiopedilum flowers are usually borne singly on thick stalks. A few species bear as many as six flowers on a single stalk.

Paphiopedilums are terrestrial orchids, living in the shade of the forest floor. Because this environment is always moist, these plants have no water-storing stems, or pseudobulbs. Their leathery leaves join at the base of the plant, forming fans of three to seven leaves.

Culture

The leaves of paphiopedilums may be pure green or mottled with silvery green, light green, or dark green. Green-leaved paphiopedilums and mottled-leaved paphiopedilums may have different temperature requirements. Species and hybrids with green leaves generally need cool night temperatures, especially in the autumn when the flower buds are developing.

The strap-leaved multifloral hybrids derived from species such as *Paph. rothschildianum* and *Paph. philippinense*, however, require intermediate temperatures year-round. Plants with mottled leaves bloom freely with intermediate night temperatures. Day temperatures between 70° and 80° F are ideal for both types.

Both types of paphiopedilums also do well in light ranging from 800 to 1,200 foot-candles. The light should be at the low end of the range in the summer when temperatures are high to prevent plants from drying out too quickly.

Leaf yellowing can be a sign of too much light. The foliage of the green-leaved forms should be a medium green; the darker patches in mottled-leaved forms should be dark green. Multifloral species and hybrids, again, are exceptions to the rule, requiring light on the higher end of the range all year to encourage flowering.

Paphiopedilums are excellent orchids for fluorescent light gardens. Their undemanding light and temperature requirements and free-blooming habits also make the mottled-leaved paphiopedilums some of the best orchids for the beginning window gardener. The plants flower

Paphiopedilum Anhinga

frequently with no special treatment, and the flowers last in perfect form on the plant or in a vase for at least a month. Some may linger up to three months. Their attractive foliage makes them decorative even when blooms are gone.

Avoid letting paphiopedilums to dry out between watering. Seedlings need even more constant attention to moisture. Paphiopedilums require humidity to range between 60 and 70 percent. In the home, place plants on trays of moistened pebbles if conditions are too dry. In a greenhouse, use a humidifier.

Paphiopedilums are more likely than other orchids to grow and flower on a low-fertilizer diet. However, because potting media provide few nutrients, fertilize plants on a regular basis. The fertilizer to use depends on the mix in which the plant is growing. A good rule to follow is to apply a balanced fertilizer, such as 10-10-10 or 12-12-12, weakly, weekly. Dilute the fertilizer to one-fourth the rate recommended on the product label and apply once a week.

Although paphiopedilums are classified as terrestrials, their roots usually ramble through the moist, well-aerated humus on the surface rather than penetrating the soil. Simulate this environment with a variety of potting media. Fine fir bark amended with a little perlite is traditional.

Water plants frequently enough to keep them moist but avoid letting them be soggy. Use plastic pots to retain moisture.

When watering paphiopedilums, avoid splashing water into the growing points and leaf axils. If water collects and remains in these places, bacterial rot can kill the growing points and young leaves. Overzealous misting can also encourage bacterial infections.

Paphiopedilums are sensitive to salt accumulations. Leach the medium occasionally with plain water and fertilize lightly. Water thoroughly, allowing water to run freely through the medium, to prevent salt accumulation.

Too much salt or too much mineral accumulation in water is a major impediment to successful culture. Proper watering is especially important where water quality may be poor, as in arid regions of the Southwest.

Paphiopedilums do best when allowed to grow into large specimen plants. They may be divided if they grow too large, if they die out in the center, or if you want more plants. It is better to break (rather than cut) the plants apart, creating divisions with at least three growths.

Repot paphiopedilums every one to two years, before the mix deteriorates. You can repot them at almost any time of year. Use a water-retentive potting mix that drains well.

It's important to pot for the size of the root ball rather than the size of the plant. Select a pot size that is appropriate for the root mass, ignoring the size of the leaf mass. This allows the frequent watering and slight drying the plants require while avoiding soggy medium around the roots. Because the plants need frequent repotting, there is little reason to allow excess room for new growth.

All of the paphiopediliums on the market are seedlings or old clones that have been multiplied through conventional division. A method for propagating paphiopedilums through meristemming has yet to be developed.

Species

■ *Paphiopedilum armeniacum:* Mottled-leaved species. A relatively recent introduction from China, this species has narrow leaves that are jewel-like in their beauty. Tall, thin stems bear large brilliant chrome-yellow blooms singly. The rhizomes of this species can be several inches long, resulting in a plant that crawls beyond the rim of the pot. Shallow pans or baskets are often used to allow for this tendency. *Paph. armeniacum* is a beautiful and highly desirable species that should be more widely propagated from seed to prevent plants from being overcollected in their native habitats.

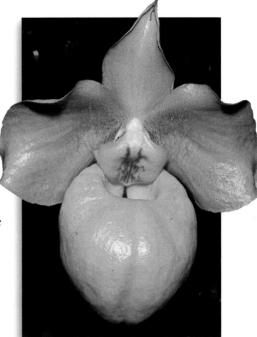

Paphiopedilum armeniacum

■ *Paphiopedilum bellatulum:* Mottled-leaved species. The dark green leaves of this unusual spring-flowering species are sparingly mottled on their upper surfaces and have purple spots below. The short inflorescences bear flowers right on top of the leaves. The entire flower is white or pale yellow, liberally spotted with purplish brown. Unlike those of most other paphiopedilums, the petals of this species are rounded and are larger than the dorsal sepal. An exceptionally fine orchid for growing in a light garden, it remains short, even when in flower. It is sensitive to overwatering, poor-quality water, and bacterial rots. Messrs. Low & Co. of Clapton, England, first introduced *Paph. bellatulum* into cultivation in 1888. Native to Burma and Thailand.

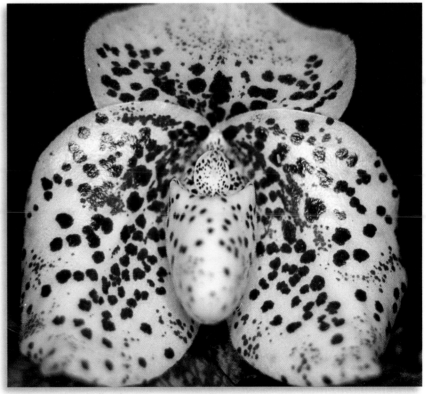

Paphiopedilum bellatulum

Paphiopedilum callosum

■ **Paphiopedilum chamberlainianum:** Green-leaved species. Although this species has green leaves, some light tessellation, particularly on the undersides of the leaves, may be present. The shell-like dorsal offsets a pink spotted pouch and corkscrewlike twisted petals. A sequential blooming habit—with more than 20 flowers appearing over a period of months—makes this an excellent orchid for home growing. Although some botanists classify it as *Paph. victoria-regina*, it is most often found under the name *Paph. chamberlainianum*. It needs a little more warmth and shade than most paphiopedilums. Native to Sumatra.

Paphiopedilum concolor

Paphiopidilum *continued*

■ **Paphiopedilum callosum:** Mottled-leaved species. The leaves of this species are a light bluish-green with darker mottling. The long-lived flowers, about 4 inches across, have a large rounded dorsal sepal that is white and green with purple streaks. The petals point downward at a 45-degree angle. They are greenish at the base and suffused with purple at the tips. The lip is brownish purple. This species, which flowers in spring to summer, was discovered by Parisian Alexandre Regnier in Thailand and introduced into cultivation in 1885. *Paph. callosum* is one of the most satisfactory and easiest to grow slipper orchids. Native to Thailand, Laos, and Cambodia.

Paphiopedilum chamberlainianum

■ **Paphiopedilum concolor:** Mottled-leaved species. Related to *Paph. bellatulum,* this orchid has flowers that are not dissimilar, although they are yellow in color with tiny red pepper-size spotting throughout. The flowers are typically smaller than those of *Paph. bellatulum,* with the stems slightly longer and more upright, sometimes bearing two or three flowers. Equally as compact as its cousin *Paph. bellatulum,* this is a more forgiving plant, good for the home grower. Native to Burma and China.

■ **Paphiopedilum delenatii:** Mottled-leaved species. *Paph. delenatii* is one of the most beautiful and popular slipper orchids. The flowers are a subtle soft pink and round on a strong medium-length inflorescence that may have two flowers at a time.

The foliage is particularly fine and jewel-like. Improved seed-raised plants have been plentiful for many years. This plant was recently rediscovered in the wild. Avoid wild-collected plants and purchase only the seed-grown variety. *Paph. delenatii* needs to be grown in warmer temperatures than most other slipper orchids. Native to Vietnam.

Paphiopedilum delenatii

Paphiopedilum fairrieanum: Green-leaved species. This small plant has ornate flowers about 2 inches across. The dorsal sepal is white with violet lines and netting. It is notably large in proportion to the rest of the flower and has wavy edges. The upward-curling petals have the same pattern and coloration as the lip with the addition of a greenish tinge. The green and violet lip has purple veins. It flowers from summer to early autumn. A man named Fairrie in Liverpool, England, introduced *Paph. fairrieanum* into cultivation in 1857. Native to India.

Paphiopedilum fairrieanum

Paphiopedilum glaucophyllum: Although this is a green-leaved species, the under-sides may show some light tessellation. Another sequential bloomer, similar to *Paph.chamberlainianum,* this orchid has flowers that are often larger with more muted coloration. The plants also are somewhat larger than *Paph. chamberlainianum* and lack the distinctive hairy leaf edges. Native to Java.

Paphiopedilum insigne: Also a green-leaved species. Although this species sometimes bears two flowers on a stem, most of the time it produces a single 4- to 5-inch-wide flower. The brownish tinge and shiny surface of its apple-green flowers give them a varnished appearance. The dorsal sepal is yellow to light green with slightly darker green lines and brown to purple spots. The undulating petals and helmet-shaped lip have a color scheme similar to that of the dorsal sepal, but with more brown or purple. Plants may flower at any time from autumn to spring. *Paph. insigne* first flowered in the West in 1820 in the Liverpool Botanic Garden in England. An albino form, var. *sanderae,* is entirely yellowish green. The dorsal sepal has a white margin without the brown pigmentation of the species. *Paph. insigne* is the key species behind the modern bulldog-type hybrid paphiopedilums, which have been developed over 100 years and through a dozen or more generations of intensive hybridization. Native to India and Nepal.

Paphiopedilum malipoense: Mottled-leaved species. Another of the recently discovered Chinese group, this species has flowers that are among the largest in the genus.

Paphiopedilum insigne

The flowers are green, often with some slight brownish-red reticulation on the petals. The pouch is inflated, like those of its close relatives *Paph. armeniacum* and *Paph. micranthum. Paph. malipoense* plants are beautiful, with distinctive dark tessellation on the broad, dark green leaves. The flower stem can be more than 24 inches tall and slow to develop. Native to China and Vietnam.

Paphiopedilum glaucophyllum

Paphiopedilum malipoense

Paphiopedilum micranthum

Paphiopidilum *continued*

■ *Paphiopedilum micranthum:*
Mottled-leaved species. Plants are generally petite, with narrower leaves than many of its relatives. *Paph. micranthum* has the same tendency as *Paph. armeniacum* to grow over the edge of the container. The flowers are perhaps best known for their large, round pink pouch, which often is compared to a pink toilet bowl. *Paph. micranthum* grows well under the same general conditions as other plants in its group. Native to China.

■ *Paphiopedilum philippinense:*
Green-leaved species. The dorsal sepals of these pleasingly triangular flowers are white with reddish-brown lines. The long, twisted reddish-purple petals are the most striking aspects of the flower, dangling to 6 inches below the center of the flower. The lip is yellow with faint brown markings, a stunning contrast to the rest of the flower. A well-grown plant can have up to six (though four or five is more common) of its striking flowers on each upright inflorescence from summer to autumn. It was discovered by English plantsman J. G. Veitch on Guimaras Island in the Philippines in 1865. This species typically occurs in the wild near the sea on limestone and even on the roots of other plants, such as *Vanda batemanii*. Native to the Philippines.

■ *Paphiopedilum rothschildianum:*
Green-leaved species. Often known as the king of the slipper orchids, *Paph. rothschildianum,* named after the famed banking house, has excited passions and higher prices. Tall, sturdy stems of four to six immense birdlike flowers may be 12 inches or more across. Yellow dorsal and ventral sepals are heavily striped with mahogany, while the outstretched petals can be nearly black. The outthrust pouch is darker

Paphiopedilum philippinense

yellow with brown veins. When it is used as a parent in hybrids, this paphiopedilum has a strong record of consistency. Seedling plants, some years from flowering size, are generally available and are preferable to the more expensive divisions or to wild-collected plants, which should not be purchased in any event. Specimens of this species can grow quite large and require more light than other paphiopedilums. Native to Borneo.

■ *Paphiopedilum sanderianum:*
Green-leaved species. This is an orchid of legendary proportions, lost to cultivation for nearly 100 years and only recently rediscovered. The most notable

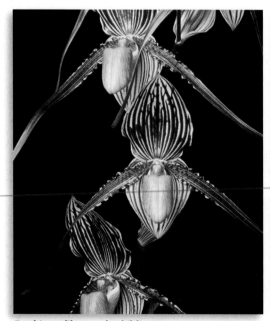

Paphiopedilum rothschildianum

Paphiopedilum sanderianum

feature is its petals, which can measure 36 to 40 inches long or more. Seed-raised plants are still hard to find and seem to be slower growing than related species such as *Paph. philippinense* and *Paph. rothschildianum*. However, the spectacular spike of six or more long-petaled flowers, spaced along the gently arching stem, amply rewards the search and the wait. It is often used in hybridizing but is not as good as *Paph. rothschildianum*. Native to Borneo.

■ ***Paphiopedilum sukhakulii:***
Mottled-leaved species. The leaves of this species are dark green mottled with light green. The dorsal sepal is pale green with well-defined lines of much darker green. The petals are

Paphiopedilum sukhakulii

stiff, nearly flat, and point slightly downward. They are pale green, spotted all over with dark purple. The lip of this exotic and unusual species is pale green, mottled, and veined with purple. The flowers are produced in summer. It was introduced in Germany in 1964. Native to Thailand.

■ ***Paphiopedilum venustum:***
Mottled-leaved species. The leaves of this species are particularly attractive. The upper surfaces are dark green with pale mottling; the undersides are dark purplish green. The dorsal sepal is white with green lines. The petals are similarly colored at their bases. The ends look as if they have been dipped in red lacquer, and

Paphiopedilum venustum

their wavy edges bristle with black hairs. The lip is orange to bronze veined with green. This orchid blossoms from late winter to early summer. *Paph. venustum* was one of the first *Paphiopedilum* species introduced into the West in England in 1819. Native to Nepal, Bangladesh, and India. Subsequently, *Paph. venustum* was one of the first orchid species to be hybridized when a man named Cross, gardener to Lady Ashburton of Melchett Court, Hampshire, England, crossed it in 1871 with *Paph. insigne* to create *Paph.* Crossii.

Paphiopedilum Fanaticum

Hybrids

■ ***Paphiopedilum* Edna Ratcliffe (Saint Swithin × *glanduliferum*):** Green-leaved plant. This multifloral hybrid has all the advantages of its parent, *Paph.* St. Swithin—one of the top slipper hybrids of all time—with the added advantage of the generally smaller stature of the *Paph. glanduliferum* parent. The result is a lovely cream-colored flower with mahogany markings. *Paph.* Edna Ratcliffe makes a good choice for anyone with limited growing space, such as on a windowsill or under lights.

Paphiopedilum Edna Ratcliffe

■ ***Paphiopedilum* Fanaticum (*malipoense* × *micranthum*):** Mottled-leaved plant. This is a naturally occurring hybrid that has been remade in cultivation and registered. Its flowers, at 3 inches, are large and light green or dusky pink atop 12-inch stems. Typically intermediate between the two parents, *Paph.* Fanaticum is often easier and faster growing, with added hybrid vigor.

Paphiopidilum *continued*

- **Paphiopedilum Magic Lantern (*micranthum × delenatii*):** Mottled-leaved plant. One of the prettiest of all slipper hybrids, *Paph.* Magic Lantern has uniformly beautiful flowers with equally attractive foliage. The good-sized round flowers are pink with darker pink tessellation throughout. This orchid surpasses *Paph.* Vanda M. Pearman (*delenatii × bellatulum*) as one of the best pink slipper hybrids. This fine slipper orchid is easy to grow for the beginner and beautiful enough to warrant a place in even the most experienced grower's collection.

Paphiopedilum Magic Lantern

- **Paphiopedilum Maudiae (*lawrenceanum × callosum*):** Mottled-leaved plant. This is the best paphiopedilum—some would say the best orchid—for the beginner. Its beautiful foliage, superb flowers, and ability to thrive in low light and average home temperatures make this hybrid a best bet. *Paph.* Maudiae was first produced in 1900 by a cross of the album (white and green) forms of *Paph. lawrenceanum* and *Paph. callosum.*

These still-popular, widely available forms of *Paph.* Maudiae have white dorsal sepals with clearly defined bright green veins. The white-tipped 5-inch petals are light green, with veins of darker green. The pouch is yellow-green with faint green veining.

Paphiopedilum Maudiae

The flowers, borne on 14-inch long stems above the light and dark green mottled foliage, last for two to three months.

Many *Paph.* Maudiae hybrids have green and white flowers but two other color forms—coloratum and vinicolor—are also available. The coloratum forms, produced by crossing normally pigmented *Paph. lawrenceanum* and *Paph. callosum* plants, have red flowers with darker red veins. Tufts of jet black hairs sprout from the upper edges of the petals. Two excellent clones are 'Los Osos', AM/AOS, and 'St. Francis', AM/AOS.

The richly hued vinicolor forms are the most recent *Paph.* Maudiae hybrids. Their flowers are deep burgundy or nearly black with purple-red pigments. The heavy coloration comes from two clones of *Paph. callosum,* 'Jac', AM/AOS, and 'Sparkling Burgundy', FCC/AOS.

In order for a plant to be classed as a vinicolor rather than merely as a deeply hued coloratum, the flower must be a clear purple-red showing no trace of brown, with the tip of the pouch nearly black.

The darkest types are easily identified even when they are not in flower by their darkly pigmented leaf bases.

Fortunately, excellent vinicolor cultivars are no longer expensive. *Paph.* Maudiae 'Diamond Jubilee' is an excellent vinicolor, earning a First Class Certificate.

Paph. Maudiae has been crossed with species paphiopedilums to produce stunning results. For example, *Paph.* Faire-Maude (Maudiae × *fairrieanum*) is best described as a *Paph.* Maudiae that has an Oriental appearance. *Paph.* Makuli (*sukhakulii* × Maudiae) has the straight, simple lines of *Paph. sukhakulii* and the easygoing cultural requirements of *Paph.* Maudiae.

- **Paphiopedilum Norito Hasegawa (*malipoense × armeniacum*):** Mottled-leaved plant. Intermediate between the two well-known species parents, *Paph.* Norito Hasegawa has lovely large brilliant chartreuse-green flowers. A fine shape coupled with tall stems adds to the allure of this hybrid that was registered in 1992 and named after famous slipper orchid aficionado Norito Hasegawa. He was among the first to bring new species such as *Paph. malipoense* and *Paph. armeniacum* into cultivation.

- **Paphiopedilum Saint Swithin (*philippinense × rothschildianum*):** Green-leaved plant. This orchid was registered in 1901. More than 100 years later clones continue to receive

Paphiopedilum Norito Hasegawa

awards from remakes that use superior parental stock. For anyone desiring just one multifloral-type paphiopedilum, there is no better hybrid than *Paph*. St. Swithin. Possessing the best traits of both parents, this hybrid is faster growing than either and much easier to flower. The 25-tall, strong inflorescences bear four to six, or occasionally more, large flowers combining the massive character of *Paph. rothschildianum* with the grace of *Paph. philippinense*. The dramatic 8-inch flowers can be nearly as large as those of *Paph. rothschildianum,* with petals that vary from straight out to completely downswept.

Paphiopedilum Saint Swithin

■ *Paphiopedilum* Sierra Sunrise (**Via Luna Este** × *charlesworthii*)**:** Green-leaved plant. Registered in 1999, this plant's luscious full-shaped flowers are a delightful blend of pink, raspberry, green, and mahogany. This is an example of crossing a multi-generational hybrid with an improved form of a species, resulting in what is called a bulldog-type paphiopedilum. The best of this type will have the vigor and size of the complex hybrid parent, in this case *Paph*. Via Luna Este, with the indescribable charm of the species, here *Paph. charlesworthii*. This hybrid is more compact in habit than other bulldog paphiopedilums.

Paphiopedilum Sierra Sunrise

PHALAENOPSIS

fal-en-OPP-sis

Abbreviation: Phal.

Growth: Monopodial

Light: Low to bright

Temperature: Intermediate to warm

Flowering: Autumn to spring, some year round

Care: Beginner

Phalaenopsis orchids—commonly called moth orchids for their enchantingly pretty flowers with oversize petals—are some of the easiest for the beginner to grow. Like the mottled-leaved paphiopedilums, phalaenopsis thrive in intermediate to warm temperatures and bright low light. Their low, compact growth makes them ideal plants on windowsills or under fluorescent lights. Their undemanding culture as well as their attractive foliage and beautiful long-lasting flowers make phalaenopsis very popular.

Phalaenopsis are monopodial, producing new leaves at the top of the plant year after year, rather than producing new growth from the base. In theory, this should make them grow increasingly taller without spreading out. Because the lower leaves tend to die and fall off as the plant grows taller, most growers remove the tops of their plants and repot the upper portion long before the plant reaches 1 foot tall.

Nurseries, big-box stores, florists, and commercial growers fill their benches with colorful phalaenopsis hybrids in myriad colors and patterns. Those with large, rounded white flowers now offered everywhere can be traced back to *Phal. amabilis* and *Phal. aphrodite.* Through years of hybridizing, the sepals and petals have been enlarged so that they overlap to give the flower a more rounded form. They've also been thickened to make them sturdier and longer lasting. The overall size of the flowers has also been enlarged from the 3-inch spread found in

the species to saucer-sized flowers measuring more than 5 inches across the sepals.

Many of the pink-flowered plants commonly available get their large rounded forms from *Phal. amabilis* and their flower coloration from *Phal. sanderiana* and *Phal. schilleriana.*

Other improvements were made using *Phal. lueddemanniana,* which imparts red-purple color, and *Phal. gigantea,* which gives roundness and fullness to the offspring. Both have excellent substance and have contributed to the dark pink—almost purple—novelty hybrids seen today.

As another example, the yellow flowered *Phal. lueddemanniana* was crossed with white complex hybrids to produce creamy yellow flowers with pink spots such as *Phal.* Golden Sands (Fenton Davis Avant × *lueddemanniana*).

Hybridizers have also added the markings and yellow coloration seen in the flowers of *Phal. amboinensis* to white-flowered hybrids to make the yellow and pink flowers of *Phal.* Solar Flare (Golden Sands × Golden Pride). Similar results have occurred with *Phal. venosa* through the hybrids *Phal.* Brother Lawrence (Taipei Gold × Deventeriana) and *Phal.* Venimp (*venosa* × Malibu Imp).

A good deal of the interest in phalaenopsis breeding concerns the red-flowered hybrids. *Phal. violacea,*

Phal. amboinensis, and *Phal. venosa* figure in the genetic backgrounds of these striking flowers. Other species with pink or yellow flowers are used as well.

Intergeneric hybrids that include phalaenopsis are also becoming common. One of the most important is *Doritaenopsis* (page 136), the result of *Phalaenopsis* being crossed with *Doritis pulcherrima.* It has rose-pink to deep purple flowers borne on an upright, sometimes well-branched inflorescence up to 2 feet tall.

Doritaenopsis hybrids have smaller, often more deeply colored flowers than those of the phalaenopsis parent. The upright inflorescence of doritis also appears in the progeny, improving the presentation of the flowers. The hybrids grow under the same easy conditions as phalaenopsis.

Visit any orchid grower who has an up-to-date selection of phalaenopsis and you will see an amazing array of color. *Phal.* Mary Brooks (Lyndsay × Mary Crocker) is white with a rose-pink blush in the center of the 4½-inch flower. *Doritaenopsis* Pretty Heart (*Dtps.* Pretty Nice × *Phal.* Heart of Gold) is an even-colored 3½-inch-wide red flower on an upright inflorescence.Apricot-colored *Asconopsis* Irene Dobkin (*Phal.* Doris × *Ascocentrum garayi*) may look like a phalaenopsis. The label tells the difference.

Phalaenopsis Zumita Blush

To celebrate these plants in all of their colors and glory, enthusiasts established the International Phalaenopsis Alliance, which is a worldwide organization of more than 800 members who have a particular interest in the genus.

Founded in 1990 by four orchid growers, the organization is affiliated with the American Orchid Society and is the largest orchid specialty group that convenes when the AOS holds its members meetings twice a year in spring and autumn. Regional meetings are held throughout the year, with an annual symposium of speakers and information on phalaenopsis held each summer in various cities throughout the United States. *Phalaenopsis*—the journal of the International Phalaenopsis Alliance —is published quarterly for its members and includes articles on breeding trends, as well as color pictures of the latest hybrids and listings of awards from the American Orchid Society.

Culture

Generally speaking, phalaenopsis are better house or greenhouse plants in temperate climates, although they can be grown outdoors in tropical regions and in the warmer parts of subtropical climates: Florida, along the Gulf Coast, Southern California, and Hawaii.

Phalaenopsis, the closely related doritis, and the hybrids of the two, doritaenopsis, do well in the same conditions in which African violets thrive. They adapt to bright window light (with little or no direct sun) or fluorescent light (at least two 40-watt tubes) and consistently warm temperatures. Consistency with watering—no extremes of wet or dry—and fertilizing keeps the handsome foliage in perfect condition and fends off the scale insects that take advantage of stressed phalaenopsis.

Like paphiopedilums, phalaenopsis plants lack pseudobulbs. They are more sensitive to low humidity or a dry growing medium than are the

pseudobulbous orchids such as cattleyas. Keep the medium moist but not soggy, and maintain a high humidity—a minimum of 60 percent.

Phalaenopsis plants can be infected with a bacterial rot if water stands in the center of the plant or in the leaf axils for long periods of time. This rot is particularly disastrous for a phalaenopsis plant because it can kill the only growing point. To prevent rot, water and mist the plants in the morning so that the excess water will evaporate quickly. Check plants at nightfall on the days they have been watered. If water is still in the growing point, gently soak it up with a twisted piece of tissue or paper towel.

The leafy part of a phalaenopsis plant is low and compact. The inflorescences of popular species and hybrids are erect and arching, often reaching between 2 and 3 feet tall. Cool temperatures in the autumn are necessary to initiate spiking. Stake spikes when they begin to grow, inserting a bamboo or wire stake next to the inflorescence. As the spike grows, gently tie it to the stake with soft twine or other fastener. Keep the plant in the same place once budding begins or you will change the flower orientation.

Although phalaenopsis cannot be divided, many types, such as *Phal. lueddemanniana* and its hybrids, produce keikis (see page 79) at the ends of their inflorescences. Remove these and pot them up individually once they have several well-developed roots. If keikis do not form on their own, induce them by removing the bracts from the nodes at the end of the flower stem and treating the buds with a hormone paste for keikis. (See Keikigrow Plus in Orchid Resources, page 216.) Usually the paste makes the bud grow into a keiki, although it may form flowers or a callus instead. Sometimes old plants produce keikis

Phalaenopsis **Bill Goldberg**

at their bases. Remove these and pot them the same as flower-stem keikis. Old, leggy plants can be topped to form two or more new plants. This procedure is the same as for other monopodial orchid plants. (See pages 79–80 for instructions.)

Most phalaenopsis can be repotted after they have finished flowering, often in spring or summer. Some summer-blooming species and hybrids that flower and grow during the warm summer months can be repotted while in flower, though care should be used to avoid damaging the plant's tender root tips.

Several media are available, although some hobbyists mix their own medium. When potting, decant the plant, remove all medium, and, using a sterilized cutting tool, remove dead roots.

Many growers pour plastic foam peanuts into the new container to facilitate good drainage. A single layer of the plastic foam will suffice if you use a well-drained medium. However, if the medium is a heavier one, fill the container about one-third full of peanuts. After the plastic foam peanuts are in place, add more medium and then the plant. Once the plant is centered in the container, fill in around it with the medium, leaving the rootball ½ to 1 inch below the rim of the container. Firm the medium carefully, and water thoroughly.

Phalaenopsis *continued*

Species

■ **Phalaenopsis amabilis:** This species and several of its varieties are used to breed large white hybrid moth orchids. In the last quarter of the 20th century, the hybrids became so popular that it may now be difficult to find specimens of the species. The flowers of *Phal. amabilis* are up to 3 inches across and have pure white sepals and petals. The intricate lip is yellow and white striped, spotted with red. *Phal. amabilis* usually flowers from October to January. Native to Indonesia, northern Australia, New Guinea, and the Philippines.

■ **Phalaenopsis amboinensis:** The petals and sepals of this species are marked with bold reddish-brown patterns against a yellow background. The almost leathery flowers are substantial, about 2 inches across, and appear in succession on spikes that may

Phalaenopsis amabilis

Phalaenopsis amboinensis

reach 18 inches in length. *Phal. amboinensis* flowers in the spring. Native to the island of Ambon, west of New Guinea.

■ **Phalaenopsis cornu-cervi:** This orchid's inflorescences flower almost year-round, but mostly in early summer. The characteristic zigzag blooming pattern of the inflorescence is a hallmark of this species. As the inflorescences grow

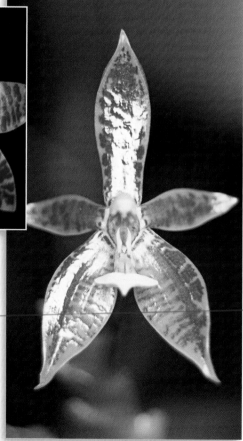

Phalaenopsis cornu-cervi

longer, the small yellow and brown-blotched flowers of *Phal. cornu-cervi* continue to appear. The inflorescences should not be cut because they will continue to flower year after year as new ones are produced from the base of the plant. *Phal. cornu-cervi* readily lends itself to being mounted. Its thick fleshy roots appear healthiest when allowed to hang freely. A daily drenching during warm weather will keep the roots plump and actively growing. Pot culture requires a well-drained potting medium, but the roots will still grow readily outside the pot. Native to Sumatra.

■ **Phalaenopsis equestris:** This species has three distinct color forms, each with ½-inch-wide flowers. One form is white with a lavender blush on its sepals and petals, while a second is medium pink with a white picotee along the sepal and petal margins (var. *rosea*). There are two pure white forms—one with yellow color on the lip and callus (var. *aurea*) and one without the yellow color (var. *alba*). Cultural care is the same for all varieties.

Phal. equestris is one of the easiest species to grow successfully. Keikis grow at the ends of the inflorescences after flowering is completed for the summer. Keikis should have three roots, each at least 3 inches long, before the plantlet is removed and potted. Native to the Philippines and Taiwan.

Phalaenopsis gigantea

Phalaenopsis equestris

■ *Phalaenopsis fasciata:* Often overlooked, this plant is actually one of the easiest to flower, putting forth delightfully fragrant 2-inch-wide yellow flowers with brown markings on long inflorescences. As with *Phal. equestris,* this species produces keikis on the older inflorescences. When left intact, they too will flower, producing a spectacular display. A standard well-drained potting medium works well for this species. Native to the Philippines.

■ *Phalaenopsis gigantea:* The name for this species originates from the plant's extremely large leaves, which have reportedly grown to a length of 6 feet on plants in the jungle. Fortunately, cultivated plants can flower when the leaves are only

12 inches long. Like their counterparts growing in the wild, however, they continue to reach the larger size. The pendent inflorescences creep across the pot and over the side to hang away from the plant. Maturing plants often do not completely develop their initial inflorescence to flower the first year. This inflorescence should not be removed because it will bloom the second year and each year thereafter. Older spikes on a mature plant bear up to twenty 2½-inch flowers from late summer through autumn and early winter. Flowers are fleshy and usually white or almost white, although some yellow forms exist. Be careful when repotting, because the plants are sensitive to movement, especially if their roots are damaged. Repot during the active growing season. This plant should fit snugly in its new pot, so avoid using too large a pot. Native to East Malaysia.

Phalaenopsis fasciata

Phalaenopsis
continued

■ **Phalaenopsis lueddemanniana:** The 2½-inch-wide flowers of *Phal. lueddemanniana* are fragrant creamy white with red-lavender spots and bars. Generally, three to five flowers are borne on each inflorescence. Some clones display more red coloration in the spots and bars and have been used by hybridizers trying to develop true red phalaenopsis flowers. The species is easy to grow in a standard potting medium. It readily produces keikis on its long inflorescences. These bloom, usually each spring, year after year. Native to the Philippines.

■ **Phalaenopsis mannii:** Similar in growth habit to *Phal. cornu-cervi,* this species produces long, branching, densely flowered

Phalaenopsis mannii

inflorescences of 1½-inch yellow flowers with brown markings. The flowers—up to 70 per inflorescence—usually appear in March and April. The plant's exceptionally shiny, medium-green leaves are attractive. The species adapts easily either to mounting or to potting in an open mix with adequate drainage. Native to India, Nepal, China, and Vietnam.

Phalaenopsis lueddemanniana

■ **Phalaenopsis philippinensis:** This species features some of the finest traits of all phalaenopsis. Many hobbyists consider it one of the best of the best. The plant has long dark-green leaves with silvery mottling, giving an attractive look to the plant when not in flower. Its spring-blooming 3-inch-wide flowers are produced in great quantities—typically 30 to 50, and up to

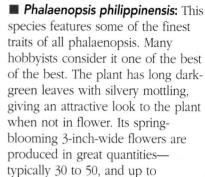

Phalaenopsis philippinensis

100 on a large, mature plant—on branched inflorescences. The flowers are clear white. The form often has a slight reflex, and the lip features varying intensities of bright yellow. The flattened roots are silvery and grow aggressively into neighboring pots. Grow in an open mix, allowing for good air penetration while maintaining constant moisture. When repotting, handle the roots carefully to avoid damage. Native to the Philippines.

■ **Phalaenopsis pulchra:** This small-growing plant—with an 8-inch leafspan—produces 2-inch-wide flowers that are shiny deep purple with the lateral lobes of the lip bright yellow. Two types of inflorescences are present: one is

Phalaenopsis pulchra

Phalaenopsis schilleriana

2 feet long and produces keikis at its tip; the other is a shorter flowering inflorescence. This summer-flowering phalaenopsis is easy to grow in a standard potting mix. It is adaptable to most phalaenopsis growing conditions. Native to the Philippines.

■ *Phalaenopsis schilleriana:* The leaves of this species are particularly attractive—dark green mottled with silvery gray, usually with a tinge of magenta underneath. In ideal conditions with sufficient humidity, they may reach over 12 inches long and 5 inches wide. Dozens of 2½-inch flowers may be carried on the long, drooping inflorescences. The color of the sepals and petals varies. Most are white with a rosy blush. *Phal. schilleriana* is an easy-to-grow old favorite. It usually flowers in the spring. Native to the Philippines.

■ *Phalaenopsis stuartiana:* This species is similar to *Phal. schilleriana,* but its leaves are smaller and narrower. The flowers are white and tinged on the lip and lower portions of the bottom sepal with golden yellow and marked with reddish-brown patches. In some plants the upper sepal and petals have spotty patches at their bases. This plant is recommended for beginners because it is easy to grow and its winter-blooming flowers last a particularly long time. Native to the Philippines.

■ *Phalaenopsis venosa:* As a relatively new introduction made in 1979, this species has already set the standard for producing nonfading yellow flowers. Though small—the flowers are 2½ inches across—it has been bred with a variety of standards and novelties to produce flower colors from clear yellows to orange and red. The species features glossy light green leaves and inflorescences that bloom with three to five flowers year after year, usually in autumn. Its fragrance resembles that of a crushed centipede—sweetly pungent and not particularly pleasant. Standard culture for the other species applies to this one. Because there appears to be no resting season for the plant, water and fertilize it year-round. Native to Indonesia.

Phalaenopsis stuartiana

Phalaenopsis venosa

Phalaenopsis *continued*

■ ***Phalaenopsis violacea:*** *Phal. violacea* is more difficult to grow than most other phalaenopsis species. It has lovely, delightfully fragrant flowers borne on stout 5-inch stems, enough to make the species popular for growing in fluorescent light gardens. The star-shaped purple or pink flowers open successively over a long period. At any given time during the blooming season, two or three fragrant flowers will be on display. A variation of this species formerly called *Phal. violacea* var. *bellina,* or the Borneo form, is now considered a separate species and is listed as *Phal. bellina.* It, too, has fragrant flowers. The top sepal and petals are mostly greenish white, with the lower half suffused with pink to purplish rose. It flowers from spring through summer. Native to Borneo and Malaysia.

Phalaenopsis violacea var. coerulea

Hybrids

■ ***Phalaenopsis* Baldan's Kaleidoscope (Hausermann's Candy × Daryl Lockhart):** This hybrid presents nonfading yellow flowers with vivid red striping. Mature plants feature branching inflorescences up to 3 feet long with many well-presented and long-lasting flowers that are almost 4 inches across.

■ ***Phalaenopsis* Be Glad (Swiss Miss × Cassandra):** This grex was made in 1978 by the late Herb Hager, in whose name the Herbert Hager Phalaenopsis Award was established. His friends and members of the International Phalaenopsis Alliance endowed this award, given annually by the trustees of the American Orchid Society to the best phalaenopsis judged by AOS judges the previous

Phalaenopsis Baldan's Kaleidoscope

Phalaenopsis Be Glad

■ *Phalaenopsis* Brother Orange Runabout (Timothy Christopher × Brother Sara Gold): Combining the multifloral traits of the white-flowering *Phal.* Timothy Christopher with the distinctive yellow-orange color of *Phal.* Brother Sara Gold produced a unique multifloral with light orange 3-inch-wide flowers. The small growth habit of this hybrid makes it a wonderful pot plant, perfect on windowsills or under lights.

year. The 2½-inch flowers—which set the standard for small-flowered multifloral phalaenopsis—are white with a reddish blush and a red lip. Plants can produce more than 100 flowers on multiple inflorescences.

■ *Phalaenopsis* Brecko Elfinfrost (Summit Frosty Jewel × Riverblend Elfinfrost): This multifloral hybrid features 2½-inch light pink flowers abundantly produced on branching inflorescences. Both *Phal. equestris* and *Phal. stuartiana* played significant roles in this hybrid.

Phalaenopsis Brother Orange Runabout

Phalaenopsis Brecko Elfinfrost

Phalaenopsis Golden Peoker

Phalaenopsis Ho's Amaglad

Phalaenopsis *continued*

■ *Phalaenopsis* Golden Peoker (Misty Green × Liu Tuen-Shen): This hybrid, made in 1983, is one of the classic phalaenopsis crosses developed in Taiwan. Its original form was a white flower with fuchsia spotting. During meristemming, the flower color mutated to produce a completely different look in the 3-inch flowers—irregular raspberry splotching on a white background. This mutated form is the cornerstone for breeding harlequin-type phalaenopsis .

■ *Phalaenopsis* Ho's Amaglad (Be Glad × *amabilis*): Introducing the species *Phal. amabilis* into this multifloral hybrid enhanced the size and roundness of the flowers and shortened the inflorescence while retaining many of the desirable characteristics of the seed-bearing parent, *Phal.* Be Glad. The 3-inch-wide flowers are mostly white and very round with firm substance. The plant retains its small size, growing comfortably in a 5- to 6-inch pot.

■ *Phalaenopsis* Kathleen Ai (Waimanalo Sunrise × Wendel George): This hybrid is characterized by 3½-inch white flowers (sometimes pink) overlaid with vivid red stripes and a red lip, produced on strong branching inflorescences on mature plants. Though small-flowered by today's

Phalaenopsis Kathleen Ai

Phalaenopsis Taisuco Pixerrot

standards, the hybrid has been a valuable contributor to the breeding of striped phalaenopsis.

■ *Phalaenopsis* Taisuco Pixerrot (Zauberrot × Carmela's Pixie): This multifloral orchid, with 2½-inch-wide medium to dark pink flowers, combines an older pink hybrid of excellent quality—*Phal.* Zauberrot,

Phalaenopsis Windsong's Sonnet

made in 1975—with a modern multifloral known for its branching habit and excellent flower presentation.

■ *Phalaenopsis* World Class (Mae Hitch × Kathy Sagaert): Both parents of this hybrid feature *Phal.* Kathleen Ai as a "grandparent." Vivid red stripes are the result. The uniqueness of the *Phal.* World Class 'Bigfoot,' JC/AOS, clone shown here is the shape of the lip that has mutated to form a wide petal-like lip. Observers compare the look of this phalaenopsis, which bears 3½-inch flowers, to the look of another orchid genus, *Miltoniopsis*—the pansy orchid—which also features a large, colorful lip.

■ *Phalaenopsis* Windsong's Sonnet (Zuma Poem × *equestris*): This phalaenopsis shows an example of a peloric flower, that is, the lip structure is expressed wholly or partially on the flowers' petals. Petals may appear distorted but the effect is pleasing if there is a certain regularity to the patterns and colors on the petals. The seed-bearing parent, *Phal.* Zuma Poem, is a cross of a striped phalaenopsis with a large clear white one. While the hybrid has reduced striping, the flowers gained increased size, substance, and texture. When bred with the species *Phal. equestris,* the result has a pink striped flower with round, flat form as well as excellent substance and texture.

Relative

■ *Paraphalaenopsis labukensis:* (Abbreviation: Pps.) Though once listed as phalaenopsis, the four species in this genus are distinctly different from the phalaenopsis described above. The leaves of *Paraphalaenopsis* (par-ah-fayl-ee-NOP-sis) are terete—rounded, pencil-like—with flowers typically clustered on short inflorescences at the base of the leaves. *Pps. labukensis* has 2-foot-long leaves and grows mostly pendulously. Velvety 3-inch-wide flowers are

Phalaenopsis World Class

Paraphalaenopsis labukensis

golden brown with a reddish lip facing upward, in clusters of up to 10 flowers. Treat this orchid like a phalaenopsis, providing warmth, high humidity, ample moisture during active growing, and drier conditions during rest. Native to Borneo.

PHAIUS

FAY-us

Abbreviation: P.

Growth: Sympodial

Light: Medium to high

Temperature: Intermediate to warm

Flowering: Spring

Care: Beginner

*P*haius includes 45 species widely distributed in the Old World tropics and is related to *Calanthe* and *Spathoglottis*. Until recently, *P. tankervilleae* was the star attraction in this genus of showy terrestrial orchids. But hybridizing efforts by George Hausermann, a fourth-generation orchid grower at E.F.G. Orchids in DeLand, Florida, have yielded dramatic new crosses. They are generating interest in these fast-growing plants that perform equally well indoors or in the garden where warm weather permits. Hausermann has developed new colors, starting with red and then setting his sights on oranges and yellows. Incorporating calanthes into his hybridizing program led to the dramatic eye-catching hybrid *Phaiocalanthe* (*Phaius* × *Calanthe*). Some of these have been meristemmed, making them widely available and taking the risk out of buying unflowered seedlings. A small plant in a 2- or 3-inch pot may put up only one spike, but in two years it can produce as many as 12 inflorescences at a time. Phaius hybrids have taller spikes with larger flowers and a higher flower count, about 15 to 30 on a stem, whereas the phaiocalanthes have more spikes but fewer flowers, perhaps 18 to 25.

Culture

Copious water is the key to success with phaius. They are terrestrial orchids that do best in partial to full sun in warm temperatures. Outdoors, position the plants no deeper than they were in the container and, if placed in the garden, set plants about 2 feet apart. Be sure the soil drains well and the area is irrigated regularly.

Indoors, pot in sphagnum moss in a clay or plastic pot. Keep the medium moist at all times. Fertilize with each watering at the rate of 2 teaspoons per gallon of water. Once a month use plain water to flush out any accumulated salts.

Phaius and phaiocalanthes are evergreen plants. However, once an individual phaiocalanthe growth has flowered, that growth will die back. When that growth withers, remove it to allow the new growths to prosper.

Species

■ **Phaius tankervilleae:** Commonly called the nun's orchid, this large

Phaius tankervilleae

terrestrial orchid with palmlike leaves sends up 3- to 4-foot-tall inflorescences each spring. When they emerge above the leaves, the spikes look like plump asparagus spears. As they elongate and the flowers open, the drama begins: Over a period of weeks, about two dozen fragrant 2-inch-wide red to brown flowers unfold, revealing pretty pink lips. This fast-growing orchid benefits from liberal applications of fertilizer and does best when provided with some shade and ample moisture. It makes a dramatic focal point planted in masses or set into an ornamental container. Native from Australia to the Himalayas.

Intergeneric hybrids

■ ***Gastrophaius* (syn. *Phaius*) Dan Rosenberg (*P. tankervilleae* × *Gastrorchis tuberculosa*):** (Abbreviation: Gaph.) A truly outstanding orchid when in flower, *Gaph.* Dan Rosenberg commands attention with its bronzy yellow-orange blooms and full rose to burgundy lips on tall, upright inflorescences. This cross has received numerous awards from the American Orchid Society. The plant makes a great landscape ornamental. When grown in a container, it requires a large growing area because a healthy specimen can reach more than 4 feet at maturity.

Gastrophaius Dan Rosenberg

Gastrophaius Micro Burst

it grows bountiful long-lasting 2-inch-wide magenta flowers. Keep it within a temperature range of 55° to 85° F, and provide 50 percent humidity. It should receive bright indirect light as well as regular water and fertilizer during active growth from spring through autumn. Once the leaves begin to yellow and die, cease fertilizing and water plants sparingly to keep the pseudobulbs from dehydrating. Large plants may be divided during spring repotting.

Calanthe Rozel

■ *Gastrophaius (syn. Phaius)* **Micro Burst** *(Gastrorchis pulchra* × *P. tankervilleae):* An excellent orchid for potted or landscape growing, this hybrid stays on the small side, reaching only about 2 feet. The variable hues of its flower may favor either parent, ranging from fresh yellows and sunset tones to rich caramels through shades of burgundy, with mauve to red lips. This hybrid was registered in 2001. Propagate it by dividing clumps of pseudobulbs from established plants when repotting.

■ *Phaiocalanthe* **Kryptonite** *(Calanthe Rozel* × *P. tankervilleae):* (Abbreviation: Phcal.) The flower colors for this rewarding orchid vary from whites through yellows to rosy mauve and into deep burgundy. Some flowers exhibit combinations of those colors. A popular new hybrid, *Phcal.* Kryptonite is easy to grow and temperature tolerant, capable of withstanding brief periods of near-freezing lows. This makes it an ideal landscape plant for tropical and subtropical climates. It will naturalize in an outdoor area that receives abundant light without direct afternoon sun, consistent moisture, and good drainage. It also grows well in containers using a commercial potting mix. Cut back slightly on water and fertilizer as new foliage matures.

Relatives

■ *Calanthe* **Rozel (Grouville** × **Saint Aubin):** (Abbreviation: Cal.) About 150 species of *Calanthe* (kal-AN-thee) are widely distributed in Madagascar, Asia, and the Pacific Islands. Plants in the genus are either evergreen or deciduous. *Calanthe* Rozel is a deciduous hybrid, dropping its leaves in early autumn in preparation for a dry winter rest. When properly cared for,

Phaiocalanthe Kryptonite

Calanthe vestita

■ *Calanthe vestita:* This deciduous spring-flowering species puts forth graceful inflorescences bearing about a dozen flowers in shades of white with pink or white with red. The flowers emerge before the leaves appear. Provide bright light, frequent waterings, and regular applications of dilute fertilizer during growth. In the autumn, when the leaves are shed, water sparingly until new sprouts appear in the spring. Native to Thailand and Burma.

PHRAGMIPEDIUM

frag-mi-PEE-dee-um

Abbreviation: Phrag.

Growth: Sympodial

Light: Medium to high

Temperature: Intermediate

Flowering: Spring to autumn

Care: Beginner to intermediate

Phragmipediums are Latin American relatives of the Asian paphiopedilums (the lip forms a pouch). Although the dorsal petal of a phragmipedium is not as broad and brightly marked as a paphiopedilum, the lateral petals may be fantastically long, in some cases dangling more than 2 feet. In the wild, these petals may serve as ladders for pollinating insects.

About 20 species have been discovered, varying from terrestrial plants that grow in the moist, well-drained loam of stream banks to true epiphytes that live in trees or on mossy rocks where they receive high humidity. Each inflorescence bears several flowers. The leathery leaves arch gracefully upward and outward from the base. There are no pseudobulbs.

Phrag. kovachii (pictured on page 13), described as new to science in 2002, has captivated the orchid world. Native to Peru, this flamboyant orchid commands attention with its 7- to 8-inch pink to purple flowers. However, until government officials grant permission to import specimens, plants of this species are unattainable in the United States. *Phrag. kovachii* has excited hybridizers in the United States with its potential, but they must wait until it can be grown legally.

Meanwhile, enthusiasts can focus instead on hybrids derived from another Peruvian beauty, *Phrag. besseae,* which was introduced by the Marie Selby Botanical Gardens in Sarasota, Florida. The plant's brilliant red flowers immediately caught the attention of orchid afficionados. When first sold at auction in the United States, bidders paid thousands of dollars. As a result, the pollen—hybridizers' gold—was available only to a few.

The introduction of *Phrag. besseae* to the horticultural trade spurred hybridizing in this genus of New World slipper orchids. Since then, *Phrag. besseae* has been used as a seed or pollen parent in more than 50 crosses.

Mixing *Phrag. besseae* with other species and hybrids, breeders have developed exciting new types that offer a palette of breathtaking colors. Seed-grown plants of the species make this dazzling orchid available at reasonable prices. Also, the plants raised in cultivation are more robust.

Hybrids that are derived from *Phrag. besseae* are remarkably easy to bring into flower, and their names—*Phrag.* Inca Embers (Andean Fire × *longifolium*) and *Phrag.* Sunset Glow (Eric Young × Memoria Dick Clements)—reflect their beauty.

Culture

Pot terrestrial species, such as *Phrag. longifolium,* in a mix of sand and peat or in sphagnum moss. Epiphytes, such as *Phrag. caudatum,* grow well in fir bark or tree-fern fiber. The terrestrials need constant moisture and excellent drainage. The epiphytes are not harmed if the medium dries out slightly between waterings. In general, a well-drained mix suits phragmipediums, which also benefit from frequent applications of a dilute fertilizer during active growth.

Although most orchids will die from overwatering, terrestrial phragmipediums flourish when given a constant supply of moisture. Some growers even set pots in saucers with water and replenish the water often to ensure there is always moisture at the plants' roots.

When the inflorescences begin to emerge, carefully insert a wire or slender bamboo stake into the medium. As the spike grows upward, gently attach it to the support. Taking time to stake the inflorescences correctly ensures the best presentation when the buds open. An inflorescence will typically bear several long-lasting flowers and may be in bloom for months.

Species

■ ***Phragmipedium besseae:***
Phrag. besseae was discovered by plant explorer Libby Besse in Peru in 1981. Originally it was thought to be scarce. Subsequent exploration has shown this species

Phragmipedium besseae

is widespread northward into Ecuador. This fan-type orchid bears dark green strap-shaped leaves about 10 inches long. Each inflorescence bears several brilliant-red flowers that are slightly more than 2 inches across. In addition to the typical form, two varieties of *Phrag. besseae* are also in cultivation—var. *flavum* and var. *dalessandroi.* Native to Ecuador and Peru.

■ ***Phragmipedium caudatum:***
Commonly called the mandarin orchid, this plant has an epiphytic habit that is forgiving of occasional drought. For this reason, it is recommended for windowsill culture. The flower stalk grows to about 2 feet tall and holds one to six flowers. The dorsal sepal is about 6 inches long and is pale yellow with light green veins. The petals are crimson, dangling up to 3 feet like narrow, twisted ribbons. The slipper-shaped lip is yellowish white. The most popular forms have crimson

Phragmipedium caudatum

markings around the rim of the lip. *Phrag. caudatum* blooms at any time from spring to autumn. Native from Mexico to Peru.

■ **Phragmipedium longifolium:** This terrestrial has long, narrow leaves to 32 inches. The inflorescence may bear more than 10 flowers, produced in succession over a long period. The individual flowers are waxy, yellow, and green with rose markings. They measure about 8 inches across. The flowering season is usually autumn. Native to Panama, Costa Rica, and Colombia.

Phragmipedium longifolium

Hybrids

■ **Phragmipedium Grande (caudatum × longifolium):** A hybrid with staying power, the original *Phrag.* Grande was registered by Veitch & Sons in 1881. It has taken several awards and remained popular with growers. Its dramatic rich caramel and garnet colored flowers have long, gracefully down-swept twisted petals that can reach up to 32 inches in length. When those flower petals begin to elongate, position them to dangle over the edge of the surface on which the plant is grown, as they will stop growing when they contact a surface.

Phragmipedium Jason Fischer

■ **Phragmipedium Jason Fischer (Memoria Dick Clements × besseae):** *Phrag.* Jason Fischer is one of the most heavily awarded phragmipedium hybrids—no surprise considering its brilliant reds on full, rounded, velvety-looking flowers. Flowers appear at any time of year on the plant, but show most often during spring and autumn. Plants are successive bloomers, and a single inflorescence may continue to bloom for the better part of a year. Provide cooler temperatures (55°–75° F) for the plants to produce their highest-quality flowers.

Phragmipedium Grande

■ **Phragmipedium Memoria Dick Clements (sargentianum × besseae):** With lovely deep crimson coloration from its *Phrag. besseae* parent and large flower size from the *Phrag. sargentianum* parent, this primary hybrid is a winning combination. Its sizable, well-shaped flat flowers have been recognized with many flower-quality awards. It is a sequential bloomer that often has many flowers open concurrently. Plants may be unsuitable for windowsill culture because inflorescences can reach 3 feet tall on a well-grown plant. *Phrag.* Memoria Dick Clements is an easier hybrid to grow. Although intermediate temperatures suit it best, it will tolerate more warmth than many phragmipediums.

Phragmipedium Memoria Dick Clements

SOBRALIA

so-BRAL-ee-ah

Abbreviation: Sob.

Growth: Sympodial

Light: Medium to high

Temperature: Varies according to species, cool to intermediate

Flowering: Generally summer

Care: Intermediate

Approximately 100 species of this fascinating tropical New World genus have been identified. Once considered collectors' items, sobralias are gaining mainstream status as plants become more readily available. The study of sobralias both in cultivation and in their native habitat is solving name problems and making new introductions possible.

One of the chief problems with identifying species is the ephemeral nature of the flowers, which seldom last more than a day (though flowers of some species may last several days under the right circumstances.) The delicate flowers make up for their short-lived nature by their size and showiness. They bloom sequentially over a period of several weeks from the tops of the canes or from the axils of the terminal leaves.

Sobralias are terrestrial and may form sizable colonies where conditions permit because of their reedy, clumping habit and canelike stems clothed with narrow to broad fan-folded leaves.

Plant size varies enormously, from 8 inches up to some of the tallest orchids known, including *Sob. altissima* from Peru, reported to grow 40 feet tall. The species most commonly cultivated are more compact but are still unsatisfactory windowsill plants. Two small-growing sobralias are *Sob. callosa,* which may be as little as 8 inches tall, and *Sob. mariannae,* which has a pretty white flower.

Most sobralias do best in greenhouses or, in tropical climates, in the garden, where they can be grown in containers or even planted if there is adequate protection.

Sobralias are rarely seen in collections for several reasons: the short flower life, the large plant size (up to 3 feet tall), and the difficulty of obtaining plants.

Imported plants are difficult to establish because most of the fleshy roots, which also function as storage organs, are lost in bare-rooting and in transit, resulting in weakened plants that often die. More and more growers are taking the time to grow plants from seeds even though established seedlings are easier to handle. From seed to flowering can take seven or more years, resulting in uniformly high prices for flowering-size plants. Despite the challenge of finding plants, sobralias are being more widely grown by fans who are enthusiastic about the graceful flowers.

Culture

In their native habitats, sobralias are generally found in open or disturbed areas. They require fairly high light. The temperature range depends on the species, though many come from places with a climate similar to what cattleyas need—55° to 60° F at night and 80° to 85° F during the day.

Sobralias lack pseudobulbs. Because the reedy stems have little water storage capability, the roots have evolved to provide the plant with water. The plants will do best if kept evenly moist and not allowed to dry out. Their terrestrial habit dictates a potting medium similar to that suggested for paphiopedilums, cymbidiums, and zygopetalums. Pot after flowering when new growths are about half mature. Divide carefully to avoid injuring the large, fleshy roots.

In Southern California and similar coastally moderated climates, sobralias make excellent garden subjects, doing well alongside cymbidiums. The bamboolike foliage

forms a dramatic backdrop to the large, showy, sequentially produced flowers. Where conditions are favorable, sobralias make attractive subjects for planting in specially amended garden beds.

Species

■ *Sobralia crocea:* One to three tubular orange flowers appear on 20-inch-tall plants. Although the flowers are small for the genus, the unusual color and presentation make for a desirable horticultural subject. Even when out of flower, this species is attractive with its leafy stems that resemble a small bamboo. Originally from elevations of about 5,200 feet, *Sob. crocea* needs cool to intermediate temperatures. Native to South America.

Sobralia crocea

■ *Sobralia decora:* This species often grows into large clumps composed of 40-inch-tall canes. Conelike terminal inflorescences produce a succession of 4-inch-wide rose-pink flowers resembling those of cattleyas. Common in nature, this species grows best under intermediate conditions. It makes a wonderful potted flowering plant, where the foliage complements the sequentially produced flowers. It is one of the

Sobralia decora

Sobralia macrophylla: One of the shorter members of the genus, *Sob. macrophylla* reaches about 20 inches, making it easy to grow in a 6- to 8-inch pot. The leaves are proportionately large, hence the specific epithet, *macrophylla*. The tips of the canes bear fleshy, delightfully scented large flowers with colors ranging from cream to light yellow, usually with a darker yellow center in the throat. Native to Central America.

■ Sobralia virginalis:

This is one of the most beautiful flowers in the genus. Its soft and appealing color often approaches pure white, although the flowers may be lightly flushed rose. It resembles a hybrid cattleya flower, with its delicate color offset by a rich yellow throat. Grow this moderate-size plant in a container or, in warm frost-free climates, in the garden. *Sob. virginalis* is one of the problematic white-flowered sobralias for which experts are trying to clarify names and identification. Native to South America.

few species to branch and form keikis. Native to Central America.

■ Sobralia macrantha:

One of the largest flowered of the genus, this beauty puts forth 9-inch-wide flowers resembling those of a cattleya. The flowers come in a variety of shades from pale pink and nearly white through dark rose, often with a crepelike texture. The lip is particularly large and showy. *Sob. macrantha* is a moderate-size plant, with canes reaching about 4 feet tall.

This widely cultivated sobralia does well with cymbidiums. During the flowering season, which is often July, the huge flowers attract attention from quite a distance. Native from Mexico to Nicaragua.

Sobralia virginalis

Sobralia macrantha

Sobralia macrophylla

SOPHRONITIS

sof-roh-NIGH-tiss

Abbreviation: S.

Growth: Sympodial

Light: Medium

Temperature: Intermediate

Flowering: Autumn to winter

Care: Intermediate to advanced

Sophronitis species are best known for the scarlet-red they contribute to the flowers of hybrid cattleyas and laeliocattleyas. Their diminutive size and well-formed blossoms make the plants worthwhile collectibles. All sophronitis—six or seven species—are native to Brazil, where they cling to moist, mossy rocks and dead tree branches. Some species, such as *S. cernua,* grow at low elevations and thus tolerate temperatures at the warm end of the intermediate range. *S. coccinea,* the most popular species, is from higher altitudes and suited to the low end of the inter-mediate range.

Sophronitis are related to laelias and cattleyas. Hybridizers interested in creating red hybrid cattleyas began crossing sophronitis with species cattleyas and with hybrids of laeliocattleyas. The genus *Sophrolaelia* (*Sophronitis × Laelia*) combines the compact habit and vivid colors of sophronitis with the attractive flower shapes and free-blooming habit of laelias. These plants thrive under fluorescent lights. Another popular combination is the genus *Sophrolaeliocattleya* (*Sophronitis × Laelia × Cattleya*). The flowers of these small plants range from clear yellow to cherry red.

Culture

Sophronitis are touchy about water. They must have high humidity and a moist medium. In nature, some

of the plants often grow in living sphagnum moss above a carpet of terrestrial bromeliads. Pot them in pure sphagnum moss or in fine fir bark with a top-dressing of sphagnum. Keep the medium moist but not soggy.

The light requirements of sophronitis are similar to those of cattleyas. They adapt to a wide range but flower best in bright light. You can propagate sophronitis plants by division, but many growers prefer growing them as specimen plants. When buying species, opt for artificially propagated plants raised from seeds, which often are more vigorous than wild-collected plants, which should be avoided.

Species

■ **Sophronitis brevipedunculata:** This species comes from drier habitats than the other species in the genus. Its leaves, pseudobulbs, and

Sophronitis brevipedunculata

growth habit resemble those of *S. cernua,* while its flowers are more closely related to those of *S. coccinea. S. brevipedunculata.* Flowers can be up to 3 inches across. Native to Brazil.

■ **Sophronitis cernua:** The flat, tightly clustered pseudobulbs of this species bear rigid oval leaves about 1 inch long. *S. cernua* has bright red flowers borne in clusters of two to five blossoms, each about 1 inch across. A yellow-orange patch

Sophronitis cernua

decorates the base of the lip and column. It flowers in the winter. Native to Brazil.

Sophronitis coccinea

■ **Sophronitis coccinea:** Although the pseudobulbs and leaves of *S. coccinea* are a little longer and narrower than those of *S. cernua,* the plants are still only between 2 and 4 inches tall. The flowers are borne singly and vary in size and color. Most plants have flowers that are about 1 to 2 inches across, with the flowers in some forms reaching 3 inches. Colors range from a rare yellow through shades of orange to scarlet and rosy purple. The lip is usually orange with scarlet streaks. The flowers appear in autumn and winter from the newest mature growths. Native to Brazil.

Sophrolaeliocattleya Fire Lighter

Intergeneric hybrids

■ *Sophrolaeliocattleya* Fire Lighter
(Slc. Bright Angel × *Sophrolaelia*
Orpetii): (Abbreviation: Slc.)
A miniature, *Slc.* Fire Lighter was
registered in 1998. The hybrid is
aptly named: Reds, oranges, and
deep magenta tones are electric,
packing a visual punch on petite
plants. Given proper
culture (similar to
cattleyas), they display
colors twice a year in
round, full-shaped
flowers that are large
in relation to the plant
size. Although flowers
resemble their
S. coccinea ancestor,
this hybrid is more
heat-tolerant and much
easier to grow.

■ *Sophrolaeliocattleya*
Hazel Boyd (California
Apricot × Jewel Box):
For decades, the Rod
McLellan Co. was a San Francisco
orchid landmark, developing new
hybrids and introducing thousands
of orchid fans to exciting species
and hybrids. Among the nursery's
contributions was *Slc.* Hazel Boyd,
which is often found at orchid shows
and sales, and through commercial
nurseries. Many plants have garnered
AOS quality awards. Colors and
patterns include gorgeous sunset
shades of reds, roses, oranges, and
golds. Some clones boast flared
petals or contrasting lips and
petals. All are compact growers
that benefit from bright light and
intermediate temperatures. Water
and fertilize regularly when these
orchids are actively growing and
less often during winter.

■ *Sophrolaeliocattleya* Jewel
Box (Cattleya aurantiaca
× *Slc.* Anzac): Stewart Orchids,
a nursery known for its
cattleya hybrids, registered
this dependable-flowering
hybrid in 1962 when the nursery
was located in Santa Barbara,
California. This compact hybrid,
which has large flowers in
relation to the plant size, remains
widely available. It is popular
because of its compact size, ease
of culture, and rich, eye-catching
flower color. In addition, it has
sired a number of lovely
miniature and compact progeny,
many of which have earned
AOS awards.

Relative

■ *Sophronitella violacea:*
(Abbreviation: Soph.) The genus
Sophronitella (sof-roh-NI-tell-ah)
contains one species and is named
because of its similarity to the genus
Sophronitis. The 4- to 5-inch-tall
plants have narrow green leaves
and inflorescences with one or two
¾-inch-wide violet flowers with
white in the center. *Sophronitella*
flowers are best grown on a slab
of cork, wood, or tree fern in bright
light. Allow it to dry slightly between
waterings. If grown in a container,
choose a porous, well-drained
medium. Native to Brazil.

Sophronitella violacea

Sophrolaeliocattleya Jewel Box

Sophrolaeliocattleya Hazel Boyd

SPATHOGLOTTIS

spath-oh-GLOT-tis

Abbreviation: Spa.

Growth: Sympodial

Light: Medium

Temperature: Intermediate to warm

Flowering: Spring and summer

Care: Beginner to intermediate

From a field of 40 species of *Spathoglottis*—commonly called ground orchids—several stand out as excellent landscape plants for subtropical and tropical gardens. Excellent as ground covers when planted in masses, these terrestrial orchids brighten the scene with colorful cluster-borne flowers. Their palmlike foliage hugs the ground, creating a lush green carpet that remains attractive even when the plants are not in flower.

Complementing the species are hybrids with flowers in delicious hues that multiply the joy of tending these sometimes fragrant, resilient orchids. While some nurseries label plants with their full hybrid names, others may offer the plants by flower color only, such as peach or lavender.

Culture

Spathoglottis grow best when placed where they will receive light shade, although they will grow in brighter conditions. Water and fertilize heavily during spring and summer. In early autumn, reduce the amount of water and fertilizer, increasing it again as spring approaches and the plants begin another cycle of growth. Overwatering may create fungus problems.

In the garden, avoid planting deeper than they were in the container. Spathoglottis come in containers of various sizes. Half-gallon and gallon containers provide a good start for garden use, although plants in smaller containers are commonly found. Depending on the species or hybrid, space plants about 18 inches apart to allow them room to grow, yet keep plants close enough together to cover the ground and prevent weeds from creeping in.

Indoors, pot in a mixture of peat moss, perlite, and bark. Choose deep pots with roomy interiors that can accommodate the robust root system. Provide warmth with day temperatures above 75° F. Water and fertilize regularly.

Species

■ **Spathoglottis plicata:** The lavender flowers of this rapidly growing orchid are often self-pollinating. An alba form bears 1¾-inch white flowers with a yellow lip. Clusters of buds open over several weeks, providing an extended show in the landscape, whether planted in the ground or in containers. Native to Southeast Asia, the Philippines, and India.

Spathoglottis unguiculata

■ **Spathoglottis unguiculata:** The fragrance of *Spa. unguiculata* flowers is reminiscent of grape juice. This terrestrial's upright spikes carry 10 or more 1-inch-wide purple flowers. Native from New Caledonia to Fiji.

Hybrid

■ **Spathoglottis Lueng Aroon (Primson × aurea):** Sunny golden blooms, many accented with shades of carmine and orange, await the

Spathoglottis Lueng Aroon

attentive grower of this hybrid. A terrestrial, or ground orchid, *Spa.* Lueng Aroon produces multiple flowers that open in succession on each upright inflorescence. Its cormlike pseudobulbs sit at the surface of the growing medium. The plant can be grown in a pot in well-drained soil or as a landscape ornamental in tropical and subtropical areas.

Spathoglottis plicata

STANHOPEA

stan-HOPE-ee-ah

Abbreviation: Stan.

Growth: Sympodial

Light: Medium

Temperature: Intermediate

Flowering: Spring to autumn

Care: Beginner to advanced

Exotic stanhopea flowers pull out all the stops—fragrance, channels, speckles, and spots—to attract their pollinators, euglossine bees. Although the flowers may be short lived, lasting only two days to a week, a plant will often bear several dangling inflorescences that prolong the show.

About 50 species of *Stanhopea* grow as epiphytes in the New World tropics from Mexico to Brazil. Botanists group *Stanhopea* under the name *Stanhopeinae* with other curiosities, among them *Acineta* (a-sin-EE-ta), *Coryanthes* (ko-ree-AN-theez), and *Paphinia* (pa-FIN-ee-ah). Any orchid collection can benefit from having a stanhopea species or hybrid. They are becoming more readily available as seed-grown plants from conservation-minded nurseries such as Tropical Orchid Farm in Maui, Hawaii. There, Jeffrey Parker artificially propagates stanhopea and its relatives to reduce the demand for their being collected in the wild.

Although stanhopeas tend to be large plants, there are smaller-growing look-alikes, such as *Kegeliella* (keg-el-ee-EL-ah) *atropilosa*. For a scent of vanilla, try *Stan. oculata*.

Culture

Plant stanhopeas in hanging baskets to allow normal development of the flowers, which dangle on pendent inflorescences. A popular choice is to line a wire basket with moistened sphagnum moss and fill it with a porous medium. Stanhopeas may require repotting every few years. The specimens will grow larger the longer they remain undisturbed.

Stanhopeas in baskets can be suspended in a greenhouse or in a window. In a greenhouse's brighter light, it's necessary to provide some shade during the summer to prevent leaf burn. Air movement and abundant water and fertilizer during the growing season will encourage growth and flowers. Keep humidity less than 80 percent to prevent leaf spotting.

Species

■ **Stanhopea reichenbachiana:** Many stanhopeas bear bold-colored flowers, but those of *Stan.*

Stanhopea reichenbachiana

Gongora armeniaca

Stanhopea tigrina

reichenbachiana are pure porcelain white, usually two on each inflorescence. This species is one of several white-flowering stanhopeas, among them *Stan. candida*. Native to Colombia.

■ **Stanhopea tigrina:** Bold and beautiful, this large, husky plant presents its flowers in pairs, each one white splashed with maroon blotches. Described by John Lindley in 1838, the plant is temperature tolerant and flowers in the summer. Native to Mexico.

Relative

■ **Gongora armeniaca:** (Abbreviation: Gga.) About 50 species of *Gongora* are found as epiphytes in the New World tropics. *Gongora* (gon-GOR-ah) has been hybridized with *Stanhopea* to create the intergeneric genus *Stangora*. *Gga. armeniaca* bears a few to more than a dozen 2-inch yellow or yellow-orange flowers on the pendent inflorescences of plants that are small for the genus. Like stanhopeas, gongoras benefit from bright light, plentiful moisture, and fertilizer while growing. Grow them in a hanging container to show off the flowers that hang beneath the plant. Native to Panama, Nicaragua, and Costa Rica.

VANDA

VAN-dah

Abbreviation: V.

Growth: Monopodial

Light: High

Temperature: Intermediate to warm

Flowering: Any season; most species spring to summer

Care: Beginner to intermediate

Vandas are some of the most popular cultivated orchids. The broad spectrum of their flower colors includes purple, brown, yellow, white, red, and blue—colors that have been mixed in fantastic combinations and patterns by hybridizers. Hybrid vanda flowers are large and long-lived, often appearing more than once a year. They are produced on spikes that grow from the points where the leaves join the stem.

Vanda plants have an interesting shape: The thick, generally upright stems bear opposite ranks of stiff leaves nourished by a tangle of aerial roots. As with other monopodial orchids, new growth takes place at the top of the plant. Some species grow very tall—up to 6 feet—but can be kept at a manageable size by topping. Many of the hybrids have more compact growth habits.

There are two basic types of vandas, distinguished by the shape of the leaves. Most of the species have straplike leaves, folded into a V near the point where the leaf joins the stem. The other group has cylindrical leaves, called terete leaves. Some taxonomists place these into their own genus, *Papilionanthe* (pap-ill-ee-oh-NAN-thee).

Hybridizers have created a third group with semiterete leaves by crossing strap-leaved species with terete-leaved species. Vandas with terete or semiterete leaves need intense sun and flower well only outdoors in full sun in warm climates. Strap-leaved types, however, perform well in greenhouses or lath houses, and in bright windows if their other cultural needs are met.

Because flowers are the focus of hybridization, hybrid vanda flowers are generally larger and more colorful than those of the species. In many cases, the hybrid plants are also more vigorous. Undoubtedly, the most famous hybrid is V. Rothschildiana (*coerulea* × *sanderiana*). The *V. coerulea* parent imparts the hint of blue and the netted pattern of color, while *V. sanderiana* contributes a particularly attractive flower shape and an intriguing lip structure. V. Rothschildiana does best with intermediate temperatures.

Vandas have also been crossed with a number of other closely related genera. Some of these intergeneric hybrids are easier to grow than the pure vanda hybrids because they require less space and less light.

Smaller hybrids made between vandas and ascocentrum species, known as ascocendas, are especially well-suited to light gardens and other small spaces.

The quarter-sized flowers of some ascocendas are smaller than those of the vandas but make up in color and form what they may lack in size. Another small hybrid genus suited to growing in windowsills and under light gardens is *Vascostylis* (*Rhynchostylis* × *Vanda* × *Ascocentrum*).

Vandas grow to perfection in subtropical and tropical climates, often outdoors in the garden.

A superb collection of hybrids has been developed at the Singapore Botanic Gardens, where mass plantings bloom in profusion, adorning a hilltop with their lovely colorful flowers.

Culture

Wooden slat baskets are the preferred container for vandas, but pots can work. Coarse bark and tree-fern fiber are the most widely used growing media, if any medium is used. Or use a few large chunks of horticultural-grade charcoal. If humidity is high and the plants are watered correctly, vandas will grow in slat baskets with no additional medium. Because these fast-growing plants should not have their roots crowded or confined, young plants do well in small plastic baskets that can later be placed inside larger baskets without disturbing the roots. Repotting stresses the plants. Use long-lasting containers and media, and repot only if absolutely necessary. The thick roots are brittle when dry. Soaking them for a few minutes in 85° F water will make them more pliable and easier to work with.

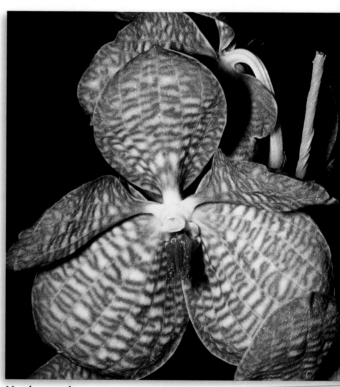

Vanda coerulea

The plants need abundant water and plentiful fertilizer during the growing season. In warm climates, such as South Florida, you may need to water vandas every day during the summer. When watering the growing medium, water the aerial roots as well.

Vandas offered in baskets present a challenge for indoor growers in temperate climates. The plants require high humidity—a minimum of 60 percent—and regular watering, conditions sometimes difficult to provide indoors during the colder months. To increase the amount of moisture available to vanda roots in baskets, some growers tuck the basket inside a larger one and add a small amount of coarse bark, charcoal, or some tree-fern chunks to the space between the baskets.

It is best to avoid placing potting material of any kind directly in contact with the stem of the plant to prevent problems with rot. The plants should be watered thoroughly, so the basket and roots are dripping wet, then allowed to dry before watering again. Under warm or dry conditions, daily watering may be necessary.

A weekly application of a dilute balanced fertilizer enhances growth and improves flowering.

Most vandas, whether species or hybrids, are warm-growing and need temperatures above 65° F at all times. They will tolerate brief periods of cooler temperatures, but extended exposure to temperatures below about 55° F slows their growth and may inhibit flowering.

Species

■ *Vanda coerulea:* This famous blue flower is widely grown and extensively hybridized. The symmetrical, rounded petals and sepals are pale blue, netted with veins of deeper blue. The flower sprays are dramatic, with 5 to 15 blossoms on each inflorescence. The individual flowers may be up to 4 inches across. The plants reach 4 feet tall but are easily kept below 2 feet. The strap-shaped leaves are about 10 inches long and 1 inch wide. Many fine clones are available, with flower colors ranging from pale blue to midnight blue. A rare pink-flowered variety also exists. *V. coerulea* requires cool night temperatures and flowers in autumn and winter.

As a result of serious overcollecting and habitat destruction, *V. coerulea* is considered endangered in the wild. Although international trade is prohibited, a number of excellent clones exist in collections in the United States.

Careful line breeding has produced populations of plants with flowers superior to those of wild-collected specimens. These plants have, in turn, been used extensively in hybridizing. *V. coerulea* is the source of the blue-violet pigments and netlike patterns in the flowers of many modern hybrids.

In addition to *V. Rothschildiana,* some well-known descendants include *V. Gordon Dillon (Madame Rattana × Bangkok Blue), V. Sansai Blue (Crimson Glory × coerulea),* and *V. Tokyo Blue (Chindavat × coerulea).* Native to Burma, Thailand, and India.

■ *Vanda dearei:* This vanda produces stems of three to six fragrant, waxy 2-inch-wide flowers in the summer. Flower color is variable, ranging from creamy ivory to shades of tan. The best ones are clear yellow. Well-established plants can grow to more than 8 feet tall. Cultivated plants are usually much shorter. Unlike many other species vandas, *V. dearei* can bloom several times a year. It is one of the important ancestors of modern yellow vandas such as *V.* Fuchs Oro (Pong

Vanda dearei

Tong × Bangkhunsri). Native to Borneo.

■ **Vanda sanderiana (syn. *Euanthe sanderiana*):** Although some botanists place this species in genus *Euanthe* because of its unusual lip, most horticultural books and catalogs still list it with the vandas.

Vanda sanderiana

Whatever it is called, this is one of the most magnificent of all orchids, producing lightly fragrant, well-shaped flowers 3 to 4 inches across. The petals and sepals are broad and rounded, and open flat. The typical color is an exquisite combination of white, yellow, crimson, and brown in a distinctive pattern. The species has many variously colored forms, with base flower color ranging from pure white to bright pink, marked in shades of green to rich mahogany brown or purplish red. Each inflorescence bears 4 to 10 flowers. The strap-shaped leaves are about 15 inches long. Warm conditions are necessary for this autumn-flowering vanda. Native to the Philippines.

Vanda tricolor

It was discovered as a natural hybrid in the Singapore garden of Agnes Joaquim and was registered in 1893. Although some botanists classify this hybrid and its parents in the genus *Papilionanthe*, they are still widely referred to as vandas. The lovely pink and white flowers are used for fresh-flower leis in Hawaii. The stiffly upright plants grow

Vanda Miss Joaquim

Vanda *continued*

■ **Vanda tricolor:** These plants, which bear sweetly-scented flowers, are popular garden subjects throughout the species' native range. The plants have inflorescences of 7 to 12 flowers, usually in the winter months, and can grow 2 or 3 feet tall. The 2-inch flowers are white to pale yellow, tipped and spotted with reddish brown. They have a contrasting deep fuchsia lip. Native to Borneo and Java.

Hybrids

■ **Vanda Kasem's Delight (Sun Tan × Thospol):** This stunning hybrid is an ancestor of many of the best modern vandas. It produces large, beautifully formed flowers in a range of colors from rich maroon to deep indigo-violet. The plants can begin blooming at a modest size of about 18 inches. *V.* Kasem's Delight imparts excellent shape and intense color to its progeny.

■ **Vanda Miss Joaquim (*hookeriana* × *teres*) (syn. *Papilionanthe* Miss Joaquim):** This terete-leaved hybrid has been a popular tropical garden plant for more than 100 years and is the national flower of Singapore.

Vanda Kasem's Delight

as flowering hedges in many parts of the tropics.

■ **Vanda Robert's Delight (Kasem's Delight × Madame Rattana):** One of the finest modern large-flowered vandas, this cross produces immense, intensely colored flowers on relatively small plants. The 10 or more long-lived flowers on upright inflorescences are 4 to 6 inches across. They range from electric pink through deep cranberry red and brilliant blue-violet. The

Vanda Robert's Delight

plants begin blooming at about 18 inches in height. Most produce flowers at least twice a year. *Vanda* Robert's Delight exemplifies the hybridizer's goals for large, brilliantly colored, long-lasting flowers on relatively compact plants.

Intergeneric hybrids

■ *Ascocenda* **Crownfox Yellow Sapphire (Crownfox Sunshine × Fuchs Gold):** (Abbreviation: Ascda.) This ascocenda showcases the flat, overlapping shape of its vanda ancestors coupled with the brilliant clear yellow color and tall, cylindrical inflorescence habit from its ascocentrum heritage. *Ascda.* Crownfox Yellow Sapphire is among the larger-flowered hybrids, with many 2½-inch flowers on tall spikes above the 18-inch plants. Ascocendas require the same care as that given to vandas.

■ *Ascocenda* **Yip Sum Wah (V. Pukele × Asctm. curvifolium):** Ancestor of most of the best modern ascocendas, this hybrid blooms in shades of brick red to brilliant orange. The flowers have excellent round shape and intense color.

Christieara Crownfox Sundowner

■ *Christieara* **Crownfox Sundowner (Aer. lawrenciae × Ascda. Udomchai):** (Abbreviation: Chtra.) Crossing ascocendas with *Aerides* brings out the best of all the ancestral genera. The ascocenda background tames the large, rampant plant size and sideways-leaning inflorescence of *Aer. lawrenciae.* The resulting sweetly fragrant hybrid flowers have a heavier substance than most ascocendas. The aerides parent also contributes a splash of deeper color at the tips of the sepals and petals.

Ascocenda Yip Sum Wah

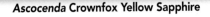

Ascocenda Crownfox Yellow Sapphire

■ *Ascocenda* **Su-Fun Beauty (V. Bangkapi × Ascda. Pralor):** One of the most free-flowering hybrid orchids available, *Ascda.* Su-Fun Beauty produces upright inflorescences of long-lasting, brilliant orange flowers four or more times a year. The plants are compact and easy to grow, and adaptable to bright windows.

Ascocenda Su-Fun Beauty

Christieara Renee Gerber

■ **Mokara Razzmatazz (Mkra. Khaw Phaik Suan × Ascda. Guo Chia Long):** (Abbreviation: Mkra.) The vanda relative in this intergeneric mix is the Southeast Asian *Arachnis* (uh-RACK-niss), a genus of tall, warm-growing orchids with spiderlike flowers. Crossing them with ascocendas can reduce the plant size considerably, although many mokaras are still large plants. *Mokara* Razzmatazz is an example of one of the smaller-growing hybrids. Mokaras are among the most important orchids in the Asian cut-flower trade. The plants are popular for gardens in the tropics because of their frequent flowering. They require warm conditions at all times and will adapt to full sun.

Vanda *continued*

■ **Christieara Renee Gerber (Ascda. Bonanza × Aer. lawrenciae):** Combining *Aer. lawrenciae* with a heavily spotted ascocenda produces attractively spotted flowers on upright inflorescences. The aerides influence adds the splash of color on the petal and sepal tips, heavier substance, and a light fragrance. In this hybrid, the flowers also have a dramatic deep fuchsia lip.

■ **Kagawara Samrerng (Ren. Nancy Chandler × Ascda. Madame Panni):** (Abbreviation: Kgw.) Adding renantheras to the hybrid mix produces some of the most brilliant red hues in the Vanda Alliance. Renanthera hybrids are less cool-tolerant than many vanda relatives and require about the same light as semiterete vandas. The species are native to the hot tropical lowlands in parts of Southeast Asia. Keep these plants in the warmest part of the growing area and provide maximum light.

Mokara Razzmatazz

Kagawara Samrerng

Vascostylis Kaleidoscope

■ **Aerides multiflora:** This is one of the more compact-growing species in the genus. Adult plants rarely grow taller than about 10 inches, although they may form dense clumps of multiple plants over time. The leaves are no more than about 1 foot tall. In early summer plants produce one or more densely flowered, foxtail-like inflorescences of extremely fragrant, 1-inch-wide magenta and white flowers. Native to mainland Southeast Asia, including parts of Burma, Thailand, Laos, and Vietnam.

Aerides multiflora

■ **Vascostylis Kaleidoscope (*Ascda. David Peterson* × *Rhynchostylis coelestis*):** (Abbreviation: Vasco.) Vascostylis hybrids are a wonderful direction in intergeneric breeding. Most have the best ancestral characteristics: full flower shape, brilliant color, multiple upright inflorescences, and a compact habit. This vascostylis can produce two or three inflorescences of 25 flowers or more on a plant only 6 inches tall. The more compact varieties adapt well to bright windowsills.

Relatives

■ **Aerides lawrenciae:** (Abbreviation: Aer.) This species is one of some 15 to 20 members of the genus *Aerides* (ay-air-EE-dees) found throughout Southeast Asia. *Aer. lawrenciae* grows to a large size—4 or 5 feet—with leathery, straplike leaves as much as 1 foot long. Despite their size, the plants are much sought-after as they produce the largest flowers in the genus. The waxy, extremely fragrant flowers are borne on long, arching inflorescences in the summer. Each flower is about 1½ inches across and glossy white with bright pink to deep magenta markings on the sepals and petals. Grow aerides like vandas but with slightly reduced watering during the winter months. Native to the Philippines.

Aerides lawrenciae

Aerides odorata

Vanda *continued*

■ **Aerides odorata:** This robust plant can grow 5 feet tall in nature. As the name suggests, the flowers are extremely fragrant. Long, arching inflorescences bear 1-inch-wide waxy white flowers, variably marked with pink to magenta. Native from northeastern India across the Indochinese peninsula to the Philippines and south into Indonesia and Malaysia.

■ **Ascocentrum ampullaceum:** (Abbreviation: Asctm.) Native to mainland Southeast Asia and parts of Malaysia and Indonesia, the 10 or so species in the genus *Ascocentrum* (ass-koh-SEN-trum) are closely related to and strongly resemble miniature vandas. They grow under the same general conditions. A brief period of slightly reduced watering during the winter will stimulate flowering. *Asctm. ampullaceum* is compact. Adult plants are typically less than 8 inches tall, with stiff 5- to 6-inch leaves. Multiple upright inflorescences of small bright

magenta to pink flowers appear in the late spring to early summer. A rare white-flowered form is known; these plants bloom about a month later than the colored forms. In bright conditions, the foliage is often freckled with reddish or purple-brown spots. Native to northeast India, Nepal, and northern Southeast Asia.

Ascocentrum ampullaceum

Ascocentrum garayi

■ **Ascocentrum curvifolium:** This species has taller stems—to about 1 foot—and long, gracefully arching 10-inch leaves freckled with brownish spots. In late spring to early summer, the tall inflorescences bear bright cinnabar red to intense orange flowers. The lip is usually the same color as the petals and sepals, but with bright yellow side lobes. *Asctm. curvifolium* is the ascocentrum most commonly used in hybridizing and appears in the pedigree of nearly all modern ascocendas. A clear yellow form exists but is rare. Native to northern Southeast Asia.

Ascocentrum curvifolium

■ **Ascocentrum garayi (syn. Ascocentrum miniatum):** This plant rarely grows more than about 6 inches tall. The thick 4-inch-long leaves may be speckled with red-brown under highlight conditions. In late spring to early summer, the plants produce multiple upright inflorescences of small bright orange to orange-yellow flowers. Over time, the plants may grow into dense clumps as young offset plants at the base mature to flowering size. This species is commonly identified as *Asctm. miniatum* in lists and catalogs. Native to mainland Southeast Asia.

Renanthera storiei

■ **Renanthera storiei:** (Abbreviation: Ren.) One of about 15 species of *Renanthera* (ren-ANN-ther-ah) native to Southeast Asia from India to New Guinea and the Philippines, *Ren. storiei* is a tall-growing, vinelike species. This climber has narrow 4-inch leaves. Support the plant because it may grow to more than 10 feet tall. Horizontal branching inflorescences produce a profusion of brilliant red 2-inch flowers during the summer. The plant requires warm conditions and may grow too large for confined indoor spaces. Its brilliant red flowers contribute intense color to hybrids. Native to the Philippine islands of Luzon, Mindanao, and Palawan.

■ **Rhynchostylis coelestis:** (Abbreviation: Rhy.) The four species in this genus are native to mainland

Sarcochilus hartmannii

Southeast Asia, Malaysia, and the Philippines. Closely related to vandas, *Rhynchostylis* (rink-oh-STYE-liss) produce densely flowered inflorescences of fragrant flowers on short-stemmed, thick-leaved plants. *Rhy. coelestis* is a compact grower, flowering in the summer with upright inflorescences with waxy white flowers tipped in blue-violet. Much used in hybridizing vascostylis crosses, *Rhy. coelestis* contributes compact plant size and densely flowered upright inflorescences to its progeny. Native to Thailand, Cambodia, and Vietnam.

■ **Sarcochilus hartmannii:** (Abbreviation: Sarco.) Native to Australia and New Caledonia, the 15 or so species in the genus

Sarcochilus (sar-coh-KYL-us) are small epiphytes or lithophytes. Most grow in slightly sheltered conditions at low to moderate altitudes. *Sarco. hartmannii* is a charming lithophyte from moderate elevations and grows best under intermediate temperature conditions with strong air movement and excellent drainage. The 6-inch stems grow into large clumps. The plants produce erect to arching inflorescences with up to twenty-five 1-inch-wide flowers in the spring. The typical color is white with a red-spotted throat. Many sarchochilus hybrids are known, including *Sarco.* Rachael (Heidi × *hartmannii*) and *Sarco.* Fitzhart (*hartmannii* × *fitzgeraldii*). Hybridizers are experimenting with crosses involving other genera such as *Phalaenopsis*. Native to eastern Australia.

Rhynchostylis coelestis

VANILLA

va-NIL-la

Abbreviation: Vl.

Growth: Monopodial

Light: Medium

Temperature: Intermediate to warm

Flowering: Spring

Care: Beginner

Although most orchids dazzle the eye, vanilla excites the taste buds and nose. From ice cream, baked goods, and beverages to cosmetics and air fresheners, vanilla is used to flavor and scent countless products. The flavoring is extracted from the vanilla bean or pod (capsule, to be botanically correct) that is harvested by hand and then cured, during which time the vanilla flavor develops.

In the New World, the first reference to orchids appeared in the 1552 Aztec herbal *Badianus Manuscript*. Known as *tlilxochitl* to the Aztecs, vanilla was used s a flavoring, such as in the beverage *chocolatl* (which combined vanilla with cacao seeds), perfume, and a lotion to prevent fatigue.

Vanilla is now widely cultivated commercially in the tropics in such exotic destinations as Madagascar and Indonesia. Exporting vanilla has grown into a multimillion-dollar business, with more than 2 million pounds of vanilla beans imported annually into the United States.

One hundred species of vanilla are native to the Old World and New World tropics. While some vanilla vines are clothed with leaves, others are leafless. They carry out photosynthesis in their green pencil-thick stems. In addition to the standard green-leaved types, there are some forms with variegated foliage—marbled with light and dark green or with green and white.

Culture

Vanilla is easy to grow in a home or greenhouse, where it is more likely to flower because it is easier to meet light demands.

Many orchids grow best when grouped together so their specific needs can be met, but vanilla mixes in perfectly with other houseplants. Position a container near a well-lit kitchen window and allow the vine to grow upward, perhaps mingling with a hoya or a nematanthus.

When growing vanilla plants by a window, you may need to provide them with some protection from cold winter nights by inserting a piece of cardboard or bubble wrap between the pane and vine.

Pot vanilla in a well-drained mix, water frequently, and fertilize often with a dilute solution. A clay pot provides stability for what may become a top-heavy plant. Plastic also works well.

As the vine grows, train it in place, around a stake, totem, or curtain rod. Although you may coax your vanilla to bloom, to set the fruits chefs treasure, the flowers are pollinated by hand.

To share your vanilla vine with friends, propagate new plants by stem cuttings, which root easily when inserted into a pot or flat of always moist sphagnum moss. Once roots form, you can pot up plants individually.

Vanilla planifolia is the main source of commercial vanilla today.

Species

■ *Vanilla planifolia:* Six-inch thick green leaves are set alternately along the lanky zigzag stems of this robust vine. In the spring, several 5-inch-wide yellow or yellowish-green

Vanilla planifolia

flowers appear near the base of each leaf. Despite the flowers' ephemeral nature—they last only one day— a vine often produces enough to be dotted with color for several weeks. In subtropical and tropical gardens, vanilla vines will grow outdoors on trees, especially on rough-barked oaks and tabebuias, where the vines' roots will grow into the fissures while the stem grows upward toward the light source. Pinch unbranched vines if you want several stems.

Enjoy the pretty glossy foliage and, if your plant flowers, enjoy your good fortune. Native to the West Indies and Central America.

ZYGOPETALUM

zye-go-PET-a-lum

Abbreviation: Z.

Growth: Sympodial

Light: Medium

Temperature: Cool to intermediate

Flowering: Late autumn and winter

Care: Intermediate

Approximately 15 species of this New World genus occur in the mid-elevations of northern South America, where they are among the first to populate disturbed areas such as road cuts. Only a few species are generally seen in cultivation. These are almost always nursery-raised from select populations. *Z. mackayi* and *Z. intermedium,* particularly, are popular garden companions for cymbidiums on the West Coast. Their boldly blue-veined lip dramatically offsets their exotic green and mahogany flowers. There is a distinctive look to zygopetalums that carries through to most hybrids. A striking feature is their lovely perfume, which will scent the entire growing area. Some hybrids flower twice a year.

The plants are of moderate size with golf ball-size pseudobulbs on generally short rhizomes and 24-inch-long broad light green leaves. The most common types have four to eight flowers 2 to 3 inches across on inflorescences requiring support for better viewing. The inflorescences come from emerging growths, usually in the late autumn and early winter, though it is not unusual to see another flush of spikes in late winter in some hybrids.

Culture

The most commonly available species and hybrids in this group are easy to grow. Avoid species on the market that are difficult to flower. Look at the size of the flowering plant. If it is quite large—with many pseudobulbs, and few flower spikes or no sign of having previously flowered—you should keep looking before you buy.

Hybridizers are concentrating on ease of flowering to eliminate this problem.

Zygopetalums grow well in anything from a mix used for paphiopedilums or cymbidiums to a more commercial peat moss-based medium. These plants should be kept evenly moist. Allow them to dry partially before watering again. Watering can range from every other day in warmer months and smaller pots to once a week in cooler months or larger pots. Potting is best done in spring when you see new growths. New roots will come from the emerging growths when they are about half mature. As with most sympodial orchids, the best flowering is achieved when plants are allowed to grow into sizable specimens with multiple pseudobulbs. When dividing, you should have a minimum of three to five pseudobulbs per division.

In nature, zygopetalums are opportunistic and can tolerate a variety of light regimes, though the bright light provided for cattleyas and oncidiums will bring out the most robust growth and best flowering. Strong light will encourage maximum flower production as well as prevent diseases. The leaves should be erect and light green, rather than droopy and darker green. Plants respond well to regular fertilization with a formula appropriate to the medium being used. For example, plants grown in a bark-based mix will need a ratio with higher nitrogen than those grown in a peat-based medium.

Species

■ **Zygopetalum crinitum:** This is a typical zygopetalum, with erect inflorescences carrying mahogany-barred green flowers with a blue-veined lip. The flowers are approximately 2 inches across on 24-inch-tall spikes. *Z. crinitum* will tolerate somewhat warmer conditions. Native to Brazil.

■ **Zygopetalum intermedium:** This species is similar to, and often confused with, *Z. mackayi*. In the autumn, robust plants push up 30-inch-tall inflorescences, each

Zygopetalum crinitum

Zygopetalum intermedium

one carrying six or more flowers. The green flowers are barred with mahogany brown and have a blue-veined lip. *Z. intermedium* makes a good companion plant for cymbidiums. The plants do well in the garden and are free flowering. Native to Brazil.

Hybrids

■ **Zygopetalum Artur Elle (Blackii × B. G. White):** These relatively compact plants are most often seen as sibling crosses—one plant of *Z. Artur Elle* crossed with another plant of *Z. Artur Elle*. Plants grow less than 24 inches tall. Each new growth produces multiple spikes. This hybrid might be best described as an improved version of *Z. mackayi,* with the darker markings and brighter colors that are characteristic of the smaller-growing *Z. maxillare.*

Zygopetalum Artur Elle

■ **Zygopetalum B.G. White (Blackii × mackayi):** One of the earlier hybrids made in this genus, *Z. B. G. White* remains a desirable selection. The good-sized flowers are typical for zygopetalums: green with dark brown markings and a blue-veined lip.

Zygopetalum B.G. White

■ **Zygopetalum Imagination (Artur Elle × Kiwi Geyser):** Good vigor is a trademark of this

Zygopetalum Imagination

hybrid that reflects the efforts to improve standard zygopetalums, resulting in larger flowers with darker markings. The intriguing lip can be more velvety purple than blue.

Intergeneric hybrid

■ **Zygoneria Adelaide Meadows (Z. Titanic × Zga. Dynamo):** (Abbreviation: Zga.) The brilliant apple-green background of this

Zygoneria Adelaide Meadows

orchid contrasts with darker markings on the sepals and petals and the purple-veined white lip. This hybrid's more compact habit differentiates it from a pure zygopetalum. Intergeneric hybrids in this group may be more difficult to grow, with some experiencing foliar problems and shy flowering.

Relative

■ **Promenaea stapelioides:** (Abbreviation: Prom.) One of the many genera related to *Zygopetalum*, *Promenaea* (pro-men-EE-ah) is a genus of dwarf plants, often less than 6 inches tall, with proportionately large flowers to 2 inches wide. Some

hybridization has been done both within this genus and with other genera, including *Zygopetalum*. *Prom. stapelioides* has 2-inch-wide yellow flowers with concentric red-brown markings, resembling the famous carrion flower stapelia, hence the epithet *stapelioides*. But *Prom. stapelioides* plants lack the foul odor of the carrion flower.

Prom. stapelioides is a ompact plant that will make a pleasing display of single flowers on short stems ringing a 4-inch pot. It does well on the cool end of intermediate temperature conditions, under lights, or on a windowsill. Native to Brazil.

Promenaea stapelioides

Orchid Terms

AD (Award of Distinction): An award that recognizes worthy new trends in hybridizing.

Aggregates: Products used in potting media that are artificially made from clay or shale that has been fired to form nuggets of a porous material similar to lava rock, such as Aliflor.

Albus, -a, -um: Usually a white form of a flower, although sometimes it is pale green or yellow.

Alliance: A group of genera sharing characteristics that can interbreed, such as the *Vanda* Alliance, which includes *Vanda, Ascocentrum,* and *Rhynchostylis,* among others.

AM (Award of Merit): A flower-quality award granted to flowers scoring 80 to 89 points on a 100-point scale.

Angraecoid: An orchid belonging to a group of 50 genera with 750 species that typically come from Africa, Madagascar, and surrounding islands; many have nocturnally fragrant white flowers with a spur.

Anther: Male reproductive structure bearing pollen.

AQ (Award of Quality): A judging award that recognizes improved quality in hybrids.

Apical growing point: The meristem from which stems and leaves originate.

Backbulb: An old pseudobulb, sometimes leafless, as in cymbidiums.

Bare-root: An orchid with no medium around its roots; often refers to orchids being sold out-of-pot and ready for the customer to pot or attach to a plaque.

Barring: Stripes on a petal that extend the width of the petal, from one side to the other, as in some phalaenopsis.

Bifoliate: Bearing two leaves, as in the bifoliate cattleyas that have two leaves on a pseudobulb, such as *Cattleya guttata.*

Bud: An unopened flower or an embryonic point on a stem that could eventually grow.

Callus: A thick or hard protuberance, especially on the lip.

Calyx: The sepals collectively.

Capsule: A dry dehiscent fruit commonly called a seed pod.

CBR (Certificate of Botanical Recognition): Granted to rare and unusual species of educational interest.

CCE (Certificate of Cultural Excellence): A cultural award recognizing the grower's skill granted to a plant scoring 90 to 100 points.

CCM (Certificate of Cultural Merit): A cultural award recognizing the grower's skill granted to a plant scoring 80 to 89 points.

CHM (Certificate of Horticultural Merit): Awarded to a well-grown and well-flowered species or natural hybrid with characteristics that contribute to the horticultural aspects of orchidology.

CITES (Convention on International Trade in Endangered Species): An international trade agreement, established in 1973, to protect and govern the movement across international boundaries of plants and animals that are endangered or may become so. Today, there are 150 signatories to this treaty. Orchids are on Appendix I and Appendix II of CITES, which makes it illegal to import or export them without the proper documents.

Clone: An orchid that is genetically identical to the plant from which it was derived, indicated as such by placing a clonal name in single quotation marks following the grex name, such as *Miltassia* Royal Robe 'Jerry's Pick', AM/AOS.

Column: A floral structure in which the stamen and pistil are fused together.

Community pot (compot): A pot or small tray containing several to more than a dozen young seedlings, often recently transplanted out of a flask, offering hobbyists a means to buy plants at low cost.

Cool-growing: Orchids that grow best with day temperatures of 60° to 70° F and night temperatures of 50° to 55° F.

Corolla: The petals collectively.

Cross: Pollinating a flower with pollen from a different plant to produce hybrid offspring.

Crown: The center of a plant formed by the leaf bases, as in the crown, or center, of a phalaenopsis.

Cultivar: A named horticultural variety, such as *Brassavola nodosa* 'Orchidglade'.

Deciduous: Plants that lose their leaves or leaves that are lost.

Diploid: Having two sets of chromosomes.

Division: A piece of a sympodial orchid plant that is genetically identical to the plant from which it was separated. A process for separating a plant into several smaller plants.

Dormancy: The rest period during which plants are not actively growing. Some plants lose their leaves when dormant.

Dorsal sepal: An element in the outer whorl of flower parts (calyx); the dorsal sepal is opposite the lip and may look like a petal.

Epiphyte: A plant that uses another plant (host) for support, but does not derive any nutrition from it; also called air plant.

Equitant oncidiums: Now called tolumnias, this group of dancing-lady orchids, their diminutive leaves arranged into a fan-shaped growth, was previously known as variegata oncidiums.

Family: The top level of classification for a group of related plants, such as the Orchidaceae, or orchid family.

FCC (First Class Certificate): A flower-quality award granted to flowers scoring 90 to 100 points on a 100-point scale.

Flask: A glass or plastic container in which orchid seeds and meristems are grown on a sterile medium.

Floral tube: A small plastic tube filled with water and sealed with a plastic cap into which a cut flower orchid stem is placed, such as a cut cymbidium.

Floriferous: Producing an abundance of flowers.

Flower spike: A stem bearing flowers, also called a spray or inflorescence.

Foot-candle: A unit for measuring light defined as the amount of light falling on a 1-square-foot surface located 1 foot away from one candle.

Free-flowering: An orchid that is easy to bring to flower.

Genus (plural: genera): A taxonomic group below the level of subtribe consisting of species and hybrids with shared characteristics and the ability to be easily crossed with one another.

Grex: A plant group representing the offspring from a cross.

HCC (Highly Commended Certificate): A flower-quality award granted to flowers scoring 75 to 89 points on a 100-point scale.

High light: Illumination of 3,000 to 4,500 foot-candles, which is suitable for some dendrobiums, oncidiums, and vandas.

Hybrid: Progeny resulting from crossing a hybrid or species with another hybrid or species.

Inflorescence: A stem bearing flowers; also called a spray or spike.

Intergeneric: A hybrid made between two or more genera that are often closely related, such as *Laeliocattleya* (*Laelia × Cattleya*) and *Darwinara* (*Ascocentrum × Neofinetia × Rhynchostylis × Vanda*).

Intermediate-growing: Orchids that grow best with day temperatures of 70° to 80° F and night temperatures of 55° to 65° F.

Internode: The space between two nodes on a stem, rhizome, or inflorescence.

JC (Judges Commendation): Given to orchids for distinctive characteristics that judges feel should be recognized but that cannot be scored in customary ways.

Keiki: From the Hawaiian meaning little child, referring to a plantlet, such as those that develop on some phalaenopsis inflorescences.

Labellum: The lip of an orchid flower, which is often showy, as in a cattleya.

Lateral sepal: Most orchid flowers have two lateral sepals and one dorsal sepal in the outer whorl of flower parts. The sepals often resemble the petals.

Lip: A common name for the labellum of an orchid flower, which is often showy, as in a cattleya.

Lithophyte: An orchid growing on rocks or in rocky terrain in nature.

Low light: Illumination of 500 to 1,500 foot-candles, which is suitable for masdevallias and miltonias.

Medium (plural: media): The potting mix in which orchids are grown, such as fir bark, rockwool, or sphagnum moss.

Medium light: Illumination of 1,500 to 3,000 foot-candles, which is suitable for most orchids, including brassavolas, cymbidiums, epidendrums, odontoglossums, and paphiopedilums.

Mentum: The combination of the extended foot of the column and sepals that forms a projection at the base of an orchid flower.

Mericlone: An orchid plant resulting from meristemming; the plant is genetically identical to its parent.

Meristem: A group of undifferentiated dividing cells, such as those at the tip of a stem.

Micropropagation: Growing meristems in a sterile environment to generate plants by the thousands from a single superior specimen.

Monopodial: An orchid that grows predominantly upward, such as vandas and renantheras.

Mount: A plaque or other support o which orchids can be attached, such as a piece of cork, wood, or tree fern.

Multifloral: An inflorescence with many flowers, as in multifloral phalaenopsis.

Natural hybrid: A hybrid in nature between two species, with a multiplication sign preceding the specific epithet, which is written in lower-case italics, such as *Cattleya ×guatemalensis*.

Nomenclature: The naming of organisms. Orchids are governed by two codes of nomenclature, one for natural genera and species and another for cultivated plants.

Osmunda fiber: Once popular as a potting medium for orchids, but rarely used today, osmunda fiber comes from the roots of ferns in the genus *Osmunda*.

Panicle: A branched inflorescence.

Pendulous: Hanging downward.

Perianth: Collectively the sepals and petals, including the lip.

Perlite: An inert potting-medium ingredient with no nutritive value sometimes used in soilless mixes.

Petal: A flower part, often showy, which collectively makes up the corolla.

pH: The acidity of water based on a scale of 1 to 14, with 7 being neutral.

Plantlets: Also called keikis, these small plants, which develop on some inflorescences and on the stems of some orchids, can be removed as a means of vegetative propagation.

Pod: A dehiscent capsule containing seeds.

Pollen: Contains male reproductive cells.

Pollination: Placing pollen onto a stigma.

Pollinia (singular: pollinium): Pollen grains gathered into clumps. The number of pollinia in an orchid flower ranges from 2 to 12.

Pseudobulb: A modified stem that is often swollen and capable of storing water, as in cattleyas and schomburgkias.

Raceme: An unbranched inflorescence with flowers borne along the axis.

Rachis: Axis of an inflorescence.

Resupinate: In the majority of orchids, a developing flower bud rotates 180 degrees so when the bud opens the lip is pointing downward. However, in some orchids, such as *Dendrobium cuthbertsonii*, the flowers are not resupinate, so when the buds open the lip is uppermost.

Rhizome: A modified stem that usually grows horizontally across the potting medium, as in a cattleya, but can grow upward, too.

Rhizome clip: A short horizontal length of metal wire that clips onto the edge of a pot to help anchor a plant in the medium.

RHS (Royal Horticultural Society): The International Registration Authority for orchid hybrids, and as such the sole organization that registers names of orchid hybrids.

Rockwool: An artificially made ingredient for potting media with a neutral pH used either alone or in combination with other ingredients for potting media. Wear a mask to prevent inhaling the particles, which can be harmful.

Rostellum: A divider in the column that separates the stamens from the pistil and prevents self-pollination. A gland that exudes a viscid substance to assist insects with removing the pollinia.

Seed-grown: An orchid propagated from seed.

Seedling: A very young unflowered orchid grown from seed.

Seed pod: A fertilized orchid fruit.

Semiterrestrial: Orchids in their native habitats may grow in leaf litter on the ground but not directly in the soil. For example, some cymbidiums and paphiopedilums are semiterrestrial.

Sepal: A member of the outer whorl of flower parts, collectively called the calyx.

Sib cross: A cross between two siblings of the same progeny.

Siblings: Progeny derived from a cross with the same parents.

Species: .A natural group of plants that breeds true with offspring that look like the parents. The basic unit in plant and animal classification.

Specimen: A well-grown, often mature plant, illustrating the potential of the species or hybrid and reflecting good cultural practices.

Sphagnum moss: A natural water-absorbing plant material available in several forms; used in potting mixes and for wrapping around the roots of orchids attached to mounts.

Spike: An upright inflorescence with the flowers attached directly to the stem or on very short stalks.

Spur: A tubular extension of the base of the lip, often filled with nectar, as in *Angraecum sesquipedale.*

Stamen: Male reproductive organ.

Stem: An axis bearing leaves or flowers and occasionally roots.

Stigma: The female receptive area for reproduction.

Sympodial: An orchid that grows outward along the surface of the growing medium; its stem, called a rhizome, is often horizontal, although sympodial orchids attached on mounts grow vertically and in almost any direction.

Terete: Pencil-shaped, as in terete-leaved vandas, such as *Vanda* Miss Joaquim, which some experts now place in the genus *Papilionanthe.*

Terrestrial: Plants rooted in soil, such as *Spathoglottis plicata.*

Throat: Cavity inside a tubular lip.

Tissue culture: A propagation method to multiply orchids by placing meristems in a sterile environment provided with light and a nutrient source, such as a flask filled with agar.

Tree-fern fiber: A material harvested from tree ferns and used in potting mixes that comes in various grades; tree fern is also available in slabs and as small pots in which to grow orchids.

Tribe: In plant classification, an intermediate level between that of family and subtribe.

Unifoliate: Bearing one leaf, as in the unifoliate cattleyas that have one leaf on a pseudobulb, such as *Cattleya labiata.*

Vandaceous: Orchids similar to the genus *Vanda* in their appearance and cultural needs, including the genera *Ascocenda, Rhynchostylis,* and *Sarcochilus,* among others. These plants also create intergeneric hybrids readily.

Variety: In taxonomy, a level below species that is abbreviated as var. In botany, variety refers to variations found within a species in nature, such as *Phragmipedium besseae* var. *dalessandroi.* For cultivated plants, variants of a species or hybrid are recognized by the use of cultivar names.

Vegetative propagation: Multiplying orchids through cuttings, offsets, and divisions to create offspring genetically identical to the parent.

Velamen: A layer of tissue around orchid roots that absorbs water.

Warm-growing: Orchids that grow best with day temperatures of 80° to 90° F and night temperatures of 65° to 70° F.

Orchid Resources

Societies

American Orchid Society
16700 AOS Lane
Delray Beach, FL 33446-4351
561-404-2000
TheAOS@aos.org
www.aos.org
A nonprofit membership organization established in 1921 to extend the knowledge, production, use, preservation, perpetuation, and appreciation of orchids.

Benefits include the monthly 80-page magazine *Orchids,* the *Orchid Source Directory*, a 10 percent discount in the Orchid Emporium gift shop, free admission to the Society's Visitors Center and Botanical Garden, and discounts at select gardens and arboreta in the United States. First-time members also receive a free copy of *Your First Orchid.*

Awards Quarterly

The American Orchid Society publishes *Awards Quarterly* with both color and black-and-white photographs and descriptions of orchids awarded by AOS judges. Subscription information available from American Orchid Society (see above).

Specialty groups

(Additional specialty groups can be found at www.aos.org.)

International Phalaenopsis Alliance
mcrna2go@aol.com
www.phal.org

The Odontoglossum Alliance
info@odontoglossumalliance.org
www.odontoglossumalliance.org

The Pleurothallid Alliance
freespirit@pleurothallids.com
www.pleurothallids.com/The_Pleuroth
allid_Alliance.htm

Orchid events

A three-month calendar of orchid events is printed in each issue of *Orchids*, or visit www.aos.org for an extended calendar of events.

Hybrid information

The Royal Horticultural Society is the official registrar of orchid hybrids. To identify any grexes from particular seed and pollen parents search this site: www.rhs.org.uk/research/registerpages/orchid_parentage.asp. To find the parentage of particular grexes search this site: www.rhs.org.uk/research/registerpages/orchidsearch.asp.

Orchid ailments

AOS Guide: Orchid Pests and Diseases A 124-page reference to the identification and control of insects, diseases, and viruses. Available from the American Orchid Society (www.aos.org).

National Pesticide Information Center
Oregon State University
800-858-7378
npic@ace.orst.edu
www.npic.orst.edu

Ailment identification services for most states can also be found online at http://apsnet.org/directories/univ_diagnosticians.asp.

A list of specialists who deal in plant pathology and plant nematology is maintained jointly by the American Phytopathological Society and the USDA at www.apsnet.org/directories/extension/alctdir.htm.

Plants

In addition to the sources below for plants and supplies, check www.aos.org for additional listings in the United States and abroad.

A & P Orchids
110 Peters Road
Swansea, MA 02777
508-675-1717
aporchid@aandporchids.com
www.aandporchids.com

Cal-Orchid, Inc.
1251 Orchid Drive
Santa Barbara, CA 93111
805-967-1312
calorchid@cox.net
www.calorchid.com

Carmela Orchids
P.O. Box 277
Hakalau, HI 96710
808-963-6189
carmelaorchids@hawaii.rr.com

Carter and Holmes Orchids
629 Mendenhall Road
P.O. Box 668
Newberry, SC 29108
803-276-0579
orchids@carterandholmes.com
www.carterandholmes.com

E.F.G. Orchids
4265 Marsh Road
DeLand, FL 32724
386-738-8699
powergrown@aol.com
www.efgorchids.com

Everglades Orchids, Inc.
1101 Tabit Road
Belle Glade, FL 33430
561-996-9600
milton@evergladesorchids.com
www.evergladesorchids.com

Exotic Orchids of Maui
3141 Ua Noe Place
Haiku, HI 96708
808-575-2255
www.mauiorchids.com

Fordyce Orchids
1330 Isabel Avenue
Livermore, CA 94550
925-447-1659
fordyceorchids@comcast.com
www.fordyceorchids.com

Haiku Maui Orchids
2612 Pololei Place
Haiku, HI 96708
808-573-1130
www.haikuorchids.com

H&R Nurseries, Inc.
41-240 Hihimanu Street
Waimanalo, Oahu, HI 96795
808-259-9626
www.hrnurseries.com

Hoosier Orchid Co.
8440 West 82nd Street
Indianapolis, IN 46278
317-291-6269
orchids@hoosierorchid.com
www.hoosierorchid.com

Krull-Smith
2815 West Ponkan Road
Apopka, FL 32712
407-886-4134
www.krullsmith.com

J&L Orchids
20 Sherwood Road
Easton, CT 06612
203-261-3772
jlorchid@snet.net
www.jlorchids.com

Norman's Orchids
11039 Monte Vista Avenue
Montclair, CA 91763
909-627-9515
sales@orchids.com
www.orchids.com

Oak Hill Gardens
37W 550 Binnie Road
Dundee, IL 60118
847-428-8500
oakhillgardens@sprintmail.com
www.oakhillgardens.com

Orchids of Waianae
86-345 Halona Road
Waianae, HI 96792
808-696-6923
orchidsofwaianae@hotmail.com

Orchids Limited
4630 N. Fernbrook Lane N.
Plymouth, MN 55446
763-559-6425
orchids@orchidweb.org
www.orchidweb.com

Parkside Orchid Nursery, Inc.
2503 Mountainview Drive
Ottsville, PA 18942
610-847-8039
parkside@ptd.net
www.parksideorchids.com

Piping Rock Orchids
2270 Cook Road
Galway, NY 12074
518-882-9002
pipingrock@aol.com
www.pipingrockorchids.com

R.F. Orchids, Inc.
28100 S.W. 182nd Avenue
Homestead, FL 33030
305-245-4570
rforchids@aol.com
www.rforchids.com

Santa Barbara Orchid Estate
1250 Orchid Drive
Santa Barbara, CA 93111
800-553-3387
www.sborchid.com

Tropical Orchid Farm
P.O. Box 170
Haiku, Maui, HI 96708
808-572-8569
www.tropicalorchidfarm.com

Supplies

Applied Science Center
P.O. Box 5168
Central Point, OR 97502
jewing1@earthlink.net

Calwest Tropical Supply
11614 Sterling Avenue
Riverside, CA 9250
800-301-9009
www.orchid-supplies.com

Charley's Greenhouse Supply
17979 SR 536
Mt. Vernon, WA 98273
800-322-4707
www.charleysgreenhouse.com

Full Spectrum Innovations
27 Clover Lane
Burlington, VT 05401
802-863-3100

Garden Indoors
4538 Indianola Avenue
Columbus, OH 43214
800-833-6868
Columbus@gardenindoors.com
www.gardenindoors.com

Hydrofarm, Inc.
755 Southpoint Boulevard
Petaluma, CA 94954
707-765-9990
info@hydrofarm.com
www.hydrofarm.com

Indoor Gardening Supplies
P.O. Box 527
Dexter, MI 48130
734-426-9080
igsmi@indoorgardensupplies.com
www.indoorgardensupplies.com

Interior Water Gardens, Inc.
615 Long Beach Boulevard
Surf City, NJ 08008
609-494-1900
orchidannie@interiorwatergardens.com
www.interiorwatergardens.com

Kelley's Korner
P.O. Box 6
Kittery, ME 03904
207-439-0922
info@kkorchid.com
www.kkorchid.com

Keikigrow Plus
Box 354, McMaster University
Hamilton, Canada L8S 1C0
jbrasch@mcmaster.ca
www.orchidmall.com/hormones

OFE International, Inc.
12100 SW 129th Street
Miami, FL 33186
305-253-7080
sales@ofe-intl.com
www.ofe-intl.com

Orchidarium
16708 Third Street
Riverton, MN 56455
218-546-7700
www.orchidarium.com

U.S. Orchid Supplies
1621 S. Rose Avenue
Oxnard, CA 93033
805-247-0086
sales@usorchidsupplies.com
www.usorchidsupplies.com

Sunlight Supply
5408 N.E. 88th Street, #A-101
Vancouver, WA 98665
888-478-6544
www.sunlightsupply.com

Verilux, Inc.
9 Viaduct Road
Stamford, CT 06907
203-921-2430
info@healthylight.com
www.healthylight.com

Index

Note: Page references in **bold regular type** indicate gallery entries and always include a photograph. Page references in ***bold italic type*** indicate other photographs, illustrations, or text in captions.

Root-rot fungus, 88, **88**
Roots
  of epiphytes, 18, **18**
  of lithophytes, 19
  mounting, 68, **69**
  repotting and, 61, 62
  of terrestrials, 19
Rossioglossum grande, 22, **163**
Rostellum, 22
Rotenone, 94, 95
Royal Botanic Gardens, 8
Royal Horticultural Society, 12, 27, 215
Rubbing alcohol, 94

S
Sander, Frederick K., 8
Sander's List of Orchid Hybrids, 8, 27
Sarcochilus, **207**
  hartmannii, **207**
  Fitzhart, 207
  Rachael, 207
Sarcopodium affine, 110
Scale insects, 84, 85, **85,** 94, 95
Schlecter, Rudolf, 103
Schomburgkia tibicinis, **121**
Sedirea japonica, 37, **37**
Seedlings, in flasks, 26, 81, **81**
Seeds, starting and sowing, 10, 26
Slipper orchids, 8, 12, 13, 22
Slugs, 87, **87**
Snails, 87
Sobralia, 35, **194–195**
  altissima, 194
  callosa, 194
  crocea, **194**
  decora, **195**
  macrantha, **195**
  macrophylla, **195**
  mariannae, 194
  virginalis, **195**
Soil-heating cable, 51
Soilless mixes, 67
Solite, 66
Sophrolaelia, 196
Sophrolaeliocattleya, 196
  bigeneric hybrid, 27
  Fire Lighter, **197**
  Hazel Boyd, **197**
  Jewel Box, **197**
Sophronitella violacea, **197**
Sophronitis, 35, **196–197**
  acuensis, 68
  brevipedunculata, **196**
  cernua, **196**
  coccinea, 21, **196**
  in light garden, 47
  light range for, 44
  night temperature range for, 50
Spathoglottis, 34, **198**
  Lueng Aroon, **198**
  plicata, **19,** **198**
  unguiculata, **198**
Species names, 24, 25

Sphagnum moss
  growing medium, 67, **67, 69,** 77, 90
  mounting orchids, 68, **69**
Spider mites, **85,** 85–86, 94, 95
Spider orchids. *See Brassia*
Spotlights, 48
Staking, 63–64, **64**
Stamen, 22
Stanhopea, **199**
  reichenbachiana, **199**
  tigrina, **199**
Stelis, **153**
Stenorrhynchos speciosum, 37, **37**
Subtribe name, 24, 25
Summering outdoors, 59, 82
Sunburn, **43,** 91, **91**
Sympodial orchids
  dividing, 76–77, **77**
  growth patterns, 16, **17**
  potting, **62,** 62–63

T
Temperature
  bottom heat, **51**
  bud drop and, 92
  measuring, **50**
  nighttime, 50, 51
  outdoor plants, 82, 83
  windowsill garden, 59
Terrestrial orchids, 19, **19,** 72, 74
Theophrastus, 7
Thermometer, maximum-minimum, **50**
Thrips, 86, **86,** 94, 95
Tiger orchid, 22
Tissue culturing, 80
Tokyo Dome Show, 31
Tolumnia, **170**
  Pelican Island, **170**
  Popoki, **171**
  triquetra, **171**
Tree-fern fiber, 65, **65,** 74
Tribe names, 24, 25
Trichocidium Elvena, 68
Trudelia, 14, 19

U
Underwatering, **90**
United States, history of orchid-
  growing in, 10–11

V
Vanda, 10, 11, 14, 35, **200–207**
  coerulea, **201**
  dearei, **201**
  Gordon Dillon, 201
  growing medium, 19
  Kasem's Delight, **202**
  light range for, 44
  Miss Joaquim, 10, **202**
  night temperature range for, 50
  Robert's Delight, **202–203**
  Rothschildiana, 200, 201
  sanderiana, **201**
  tricolor, **202**

Vandofinetia Virgil, **159**
Vanilla, **208–209**
  planifolia, **208–209**
Variety names, 24
Vascostylis, 200
  Kaleidoscope, **205**
Veitch (James) & Sons, 8
Velamen, 18, **18**
Ventilation, 54, 59, 92
Viruses, 89
Viscum album, 18
Vuylstekeara
  Aloha Passion, **162**
  bigeneric hybrid, 27
  Cambria, **162**

W
Warscewiczella discolor, **36**
Watering
  bag-packaged plants, 39, **39**
  disease control, 89
  epiphytic orchids, 18
  fertilizing and, 75
  how to water, 71–72
  mineral concentration, 91
  outdoor plants, 83
  overwatering, 70, **70,** 90
  after planting, 69
  tips, 71
  underwatering, **70,** 90, **90,** 92
  when to water, 70, 70–71
  windowsill garden, 59
Web ordering, 40–41, **41**
Weed control, 93, **93**
Wells, H.G., 9
Whiteflies, 86, **86,** 94, 95
Wild orchids, 12–13, 34
Wild Orchids (film), 10, **10**
Wilsonara
  Christmas Candy, **162**
  Native Girl, **162–63**
Wind orchid, 7
Windowsill garden, **58**
  air circulation, 54, 59
  light for, 58
  seasonal care, 59
  setting up, 58–59
Wire mounting, 68–69
Wood flats, 51
World Orchid Conference, 31

Y
Yamadara, 16
Young (Thomas) Nurseries, 10

Z
Zelenkoa onusta, **171**
Zygoneria Adelaide Meadows, **211**
Zygopetalum, 16, **210–211**
  Artur Elle, **210–211**
  B.G. White, **211**
  crinitum, **210**
  Imagination, **211**
  intermedium, **210**

Ortho Complete Guide to Orchids
Editor: Michael McKinley
Contributing Editor: Veronica Lorson Fowler
Contributing Writers: Elvin McDonald, James B. Watson
Photo Researcher: Harijs Priekulis
Copy Chief: Terri Fredrickson
Publishing Operations Manager: Karen Schirm
Edit and Design Production Coordinator: Mary Lee Gavin
Editorial and Design Assistants: Kathleen Stevens,
 Kairee Windsor
Marketing Product Managers: Aparna Pande, Isaac Petersen,
 Gina Rickert, Stephen Rogers, Brent Wiersma,
 Tyler Woods
Book Production Managers: Pam Kvitne,
 Marjorie J. Schenkelberg, Rick von Holdt, Mark Weaver
Contributing Copy Editor: Lorraine Ferrell
Contributing Proofreaders: Susan Brown, Fran Gardner,
 Mindy Kralicek
Contributing Map Illustrator: Jana Fothergill

**Additional Editorial Contributions from
 Lark Productions**
Project Manager: Robin Dellabough
Principal Garden Writer: James B. Watson
Designers: Oxygen Design
Photo Editor: Ilene Bellovin
Indexer: Marilyn Flaig

Meredith® Books
Executive Director, Editorial: Gregory H. Kayko
Executive Director, Design: Matt Strelecki
Executive Editor/Group Manager: Benjamin W. Allen
Senior Associate Design Director: Tom Wegner

Publisher and Editor in Chief: James D. Blume
Editorial Director: Linda Raglan Cunningham
Executive Director, Marketing: Jeffrey B. Myers
Executive Director, New Business Development:
 Todd M. Davis
Executive Director, Sales: Ken Zagor
Director, Operations: George A. Susral
Director, Production: Douglas M. Johnston
Business Director: Jim Leonard

Vice President and General Manager: Douglas J. Guendel

Meredith Publishing Group
President: Jack Griffin
Senior Vice President: Bob Mate

Meredith Corporation
Chairman and Chief Executive Officer: William T. Kerr
President and Chief Operating Officer: Stephen M. Lacy

In Memoriam: E.T. Meredith III (1933–2003)

Note to the Readers: Due to differing conditions, tools,
and individual skills, Meredith Corporation assumes no
responsibility for any damages, injuries suffered, or losses
incurred as a result of following the information published
in this book. Before beginning any project, review the
instructions carefully, and if any doubts or questions remain,
consult local experts or authorities. Because codes and
regulations vary greatly, you always should check with
authorities to ensure that your project complies with all
applicable local codes and regulations. Always read and
observe all of the safety precautions provided by
manufacturers of any tools, equipment, or supplies,
and follow all accepted safety procedures.

Thanks to: Greg Allikas, Janet Anderson, Staci Bailey,
Thomas E. Blackett, Dr. Raymond Cloyd, Dr. Calaway
Dodson, Dr. Robert Dressler, Robert Fuchs, Gina Hale, Tom
Harper, Susan Jones, Downs Matthews, Jane Mengel, Ned
Nash, Dr. Henry Oakeley, William Rhodehamel, Dr. Thomas
Sheehan, Margaret Smith, Brenda Witherspoon, Sylvia Wood
and staff at the Royal Horticultural Society and the Royal
Botanic Gardens, Kew.

Special thanks to the American Orchid Society for its
invaluable assistance, technical expertise, and access to its
library and awards database.

Photographers
 (Photographers credited may retain copyright (©) to the
listed photographs.)
L = Left, R = Right, C = Center, B = Bottom, T = Top
Robert Aldrich/The Inn at Weston: 162TR; Greg Allikas: 4BL, 6BR, 8T, 12, 15L, 15R, 16BL, 17, 18L, 19T, 19B, 20, 21, 35B, 36C, 43TL, 49, 62TL, 63R, 65BC, 66TLC, 66BLC, 66BL, 67L, 67CR, 69TR, 70C, 75T, 77T, 77C, 84, 85TL, 87TC, 87TR, 88L, 88T, 91BL, 92BR, 93B, 94, 100T, 100L, 103TR, 103CR, 104C, 104TL, 105TL, 105BL, 108TL, 108B, 108R, 109L, 109B, 110T, 110B, 111TC, 111TR, 112, 113BL, 113C, 113BR, 114, 115BR, 116TL, 117T, 117C, 118TL, 118TR, 119BL, 119BR, 119BC, 120TL, 120B, 121C, 121B, 123, 124B, 124T, 125T, 125B, 126, 129, 129BR, 130L, 131TL, 134T, 134BR, 135BR, 136T, 137T, 137BR, 139L, 139C, 143BL, 144T, 145TL, 145TR, 145B, 146TL, 146TR, 146BR, 147T, 147BL, 147BR, 151BL, 152TR, 153TL, 153TR, 153B, 154T, 155BL, 155BR, 155CL, 156T, 157L, 157BL, 157BR, 157TR, 158BL, 158T, 159TL, 159TR, 161BR, 161BL, 162TL, 163BL, 164, 165TL, 166L, 166CR, 167BR, 168B, 169L,169B,170TL, 170TR, 170B, 171L, 171R, 172, 174TR, 176BL, 176TR, 177R, 177B, 178T, 178B, 178C, 179T, 180, 181, 182T, 183L, 185TR,186T, 186B, 187BL, 187BR, 188B, 189TL, 189TR, 189BL, 189BR, 190C, 190BR, 191TL, 191BC, 191BR, 191TR, 193BR, 196L, 197BR, 196B, 198B, 199T, 199C, 200, 202C, 202B, 203TR, 203L, 203B, 204BR, 205T, 205C, 208, 209; Liz Ball/Positive Images: 33, 73; Botonica/GettyImages: 5T; Edwin Boyett/Bio-Photo Services: 168T; Weyland Bussey: 167TL; Linda Baldwin/Chadwick Orchids: 188TR; Barbara J. Coxe: 77B; Stig Dalstrom/Bio-Photo Services: 13BL; Javier Delgado/BloomPhotos: 4T, 4BC, 5LC, 5BC, 6TL, 60; Joseph Dixler/Bio-Photo Services: 211CR, 211BL; Kerry Dressler/Bio-Photo Services: 4R, 5BL, 5BR, 8B, 13TR, 14, 18CL, 20, 21T, 22, 29T, 29B, 31, 36T, 36B, 37TC, 37C, 37B, 39L, 41, 42T, 42B, 43C, 50, 52T, 52B, 54, 58, 68, 74L, 75B, 85TR, 85BL, 86BR, 88BR, 89T, 89BL, 97, 100BR, 101T, 101C, 102, 103BL, 106TR, 107B, 113TL, 115BC, 116TR, 116BR, 117B, 119T, 121T, 127, 128L, 128B, 129TR, 130T, 130B,131B, 132BL, 132TL, 132TR, 132BR, 133T, 134C, 135TC, 135TR, 135BR, 138L, 138R, 139TR, 140C, 141T, 141C, 141B, 142L, 142R, 143TL, 143BR, 146BL, 148L, 148R, 149L, 157C, 163TR, 165BL, 166T, 174TL, 179B, 183T, 184B, 185TL, 193TL, 193C, 193BL, 194, 195T, 195C, 195BR, 198C, 199B, 202TR, 204TL, 206RC, 206B, 207TR, 211TL, 211BR; Charles Marden Fitch: 70B, 92TL, 92BR, 109T; Leon Glicenstein/Bio-Photo Services: 151TR, 152L, 152BC, 154B, 161T, 162BL, 171B, 175CL, 183B, 195BL, 198T, 199B, 206TL, 211TL; John Glover: 144B, 175TR; James Goldner/Bio-Photo Services: 188TL; Alan L. Hoffman/Bio-Photo Services: 201B; Eric Hunt: 165BR, 176BR; Courtesy, Massachusetts Horticultural Society: 10TL, 10TR; Steven McDonald: 79T, 79C, 79B, 81B; Ed Merkle/Bio-Photo Services: 158BR; Courtesy, The Metropolitan Museum of Art: 7R; Martin Motes/Bio-Photo Services: 159B, 204TL; Walter Nagamine: 87B; Henry Oakeley: 149BR; Orchidarium, Inc: 55; James Osen/Bio-Photo Services: 179B; Matt Pedersen/Bio-Photo Services: 155TR, 191TR; Courtesy, T.P. Plimpton: 11T; Positive Images: 73, 99TL; Photofest: 10B; Marv Ragan/Bio-Photo Services: 197TL; Santa Barbara Orchids: 105TR; Woodstream Orchids: 143TR; Pam Spalding/Positive Images: 74R, 99TR; Albert Squillance/Positive Images: 147BC; Steven Struse: 26L, 26C, 26R, 39B, 43B, 45, 48, 51T, 51B, 53, 59, 61BL, 61TR, 62BL, 62BR, 63L, 64, 65T, 65B, 66TL, 66R, 67TRC, 67TR, 67BR, 69TL, 69LC, 69BL, 70TL, 71, 76T, 76B, 78L, 78R, 80TL, 80TR, 81T; Steve Wells/OrchidsOnline: 98, 101B, 101C, 128T, 175BC; judywhite/GardenPhotos: 2-3, 11BL, 16TR, 21B, 23B, 24, 25T, 25B, 27L, 27R, 27BR, 28, 30, 32, 34, 35T, 37, 38, 40, 43TR, 46B, 56T, 56B, 57T, 57B, 61BR, 65TC, 67BR, 72, 74B, 85BR, 86TL, 86BL, 89BR, 90, 91TL, 91R, 93T, 95, 97, 99B, 99TL, 103TL, 103BR, 104BL, 105TR, 105BR, 106BL, 107T, 111BL, 107T, 111LC, 111BL, 118BL, 118BR, 122, 129TL, 131TR, 133B, 136B, 137BL, 143TC, 149TR, 149BC, 150, 151L, 152BR, 156B, 160, 162BR, 163BR, 166BC, 167TR, 167BL, 168L, 169T, 173T, 173B, 174C, 174B, 175BR, 176TL, 177T, 177L, 182L, 182B, 184TL, 184CR, 185BL, 185BR, 187T, 192, 196T, 196CR, 197BL, 197TR, 201T, 202TL, 203C, 204BC, 205B, 206C, 207TL, 207B, 210T, 210B, 211LC; Mark Whitten/Bio-Photo Services: 37T; Courtesy, Yale Medical School Library: 7BL.

On the cover: *Sophrolaeliocattleya* Jewel Box

All of us at Meredith® Books are dedicated to providing
you with the information and ideas you need to enhance
your home and garden. We welcome your comments and
suggestions about this book. Write to us at:
 Meredith Corporation
 Meredith Gardening Books
 1716 Locust St.
 Des Moines, IA 50309–3023

If you would like to purchase any of our gardening, home
improvement, cooking, crafts, or home decorating and
design books, check wherever quality books are sold.
Or visit us at: meredithbooks.com

If you would like more information on other Ortho
products, call 800/225-2883 or visit us at: www.ortho.com